Scholarly Communication in the Next Millennium

Selected Papers from Canada's Policy Conference

Rowland Lorimer, John H. V. Gilbert, and ***Ruth J. Patrick,*** Editors

Canadian Journal of Communication
Volume 22 Issues 3/4 Special Issue

This book is being simultaneously published as a double issue of the *Canadian Journal of Communication* and a monograph. This special edition has been made possible by the many sponsors of the Scholarly Communication in the Next Millennium conference and, in particular, the British Columbia Ministry of Education, Skills and Training. We gratefully acknowledge the assistance provided. The monograph should be cited as:

Lorimer, Rowland, Gilbert, John H. V., & Patrick, Ruth H. (Eds.). (1997). *Scholarly communication in the next millennium: Selected papers from Canada's policy conference*. Vancouver, BC: Canadian Journal of Communication Corporation (distributed by Wilfrid Laurier University Press, Waterloo, ON).

Canadian Cataloguing in Publication Data

Main entry under title:

Scholarly communication in the next millennium

Papers from a conference held in Vancouver, March 5-9, 1997.
ISBN 0-9698983-2-0

1. Scholarly periodicals – Congresses. 2. Electronic publishing – Congresses. 3. Learning and scholarship – Congresses.
I. Lorimer, Rowland, 1944- II. Gilbert, John H. V.
III. Patrick, Ruth J. IV. Canadian Journal of Communication Corporation.

Z286.S37S38 1997 070.5′797′0880901 C97-911012-2

Cover design by Leslie Macredie
adapted from the conference poster design by Gladys We

Printed in Canada

Contents

Papers

Appendices

Scholarly Communication in the Next Millennium: The Policy Agenda and Some Afterthoughts

Rowland Lorimer
Simon Fraser University
John H. V. Gilbert & Ruth J. Patrick
University of British Columbia

Abstract: This paper is a compilation of the principles, policy priorities, and actions recommended for consideration by the participants in the March 1997 Scholarly Communication in the Next Millennium (SCNM) conference. These considerations and recommendations are directed at a wide range of interested parties including universities, research-granting councils, national bodies of universities, librarians and scholars, and governments and their agencies. The paper includes a number of afterthoughts developed by the editors of this selected proceedings.

Résumé: Cet article recense les principes, politiques prioritaires et actions recommandés par les participants à la conférence de mars 1997 sur la Communication savante au prochain millénaire. Ces considérations et recommandations ont pour objectif un large éventail d'acteurs, y compris les universités, les conseils de soutien à la recherche, les organismes nationaux d'universités, de bibliothécaires et de savants, ainsi que les gouvernements et leurs agences. Cet article comprend en outre un nombre de réflections sur la conférence faites par les éditeurs des textes sélectionnés pour ce numéro.

Rowland Lorimer is Editor of the *Canadian Journal of Communication* and a professor of Communication and Director of the Master of Publishing Program at Simon Fraser University, 515 West Hastings Street, Vancouver, BC V6B 5K3. E-mail: Rowland_Lorimer@sfu.ca
John Gilbert is Co-ordinator of Health Sciences and professor of Audiology and Speech Sciences at the University of British Columbia, Vancouver, BC V6T 1Z3. E-mail: johnhvg@unixg.ubc.ca
Ruth Patrick is currently on administrative leave from her position as University Librarian at the University of British Columbia, Vancouver, BC V6T 1Z3. E-mail: rpatrick@unixg.ubc.ca

***Canadian Journal of Communication*, Vol. 22, No. 3/4 (1997) 1-9**

Conference overview

The Scholarly Communication in the Next Millennium (SCNM) conference was held March 5-8, 1997, at Simon Fraser University Harbour Centre in Vancouver, BC. As the program in Appendix 1 of this volume indicates, the conference was composed of two parts—the presentation of papers and participation in workshops designed to bring forward policy considerations. It was attended by approximately 200 people representing all the constituencies concerned with, or directly affected by, scholarly communication.

The SCNM conference was designed with two purposes. The first was to bring forward information descriptive of scholarly communication, with emphasis on scholarly journal publishing. Given that the conference had been conceived in the context of both the scientific, technical, and medical (STM) serials crisis and, to a lesser extent, a concern with the funding of Canadian Humanities and Social Science (HSS) journals, the second purpose was to bring forward policy, principles, and proposals to address pressing issues. Towards that end, the conference ended with four hours of group discussions followed by a plenary. Participants were divided into 12 groups; each group contained representatives from a variety of backgrounds. They were asked to address three fundamental questions as follows:

1. Basic Principles

What basic principles should guide the development of Canada's scholarly communications environment, both electronic and print-on-paper, over the next five to ten years?

2. Policy priorities

What priorities should Canada set in building its scholarly communications environment on these basic principles, through related policy actions and initiatives at the federal, provincial, and local levels?

3. Immediate actions—Local and national

(a) What policy-related actions and initiatives must be developed over the next five years?
(b) What time lines are advisable?
(c) By whom should such actions be effected?

Recommendations of the working groups

The deliberations of the 12 working groups were far-reaching. Insofar as the groups reflected various interests, the points made by each group were not necessarily consistent with each other. There was also overlap in the material brought forward to the final plenary, some of which was eliminated in the summary that follows and some of which was kept to provide a flavour of the different ways in which more than one group articulated much the same point. The submissions made by the groups to the final plenary can be summarized as follows:

Principles

General

Scholarly communication is a process, not a product, and publications are an integral part of that process. Given current economic and technological conditions, we have the opportunity to rethink scholarly communication. Such a rethinking should conceive of research as a network of activities, rather than a linear pipeline.

Scholarly communication is a sequential value-adding process. The various mediated steps in this process are essential to the quality of the process and the outcome.

The primary goal must be to create a sustainable system of scholarly communication serving individuals, organizations, and institutions.

Scholarly communication reflects political, economic, and social values and has a cultural and an ideological dimension.

Equity of access is paramount and diversity must be recognized as an essential feature.

A guiding principle for scholarly communication should be that publicly funded research should be publicly accessible beyond the research community, both to individuals and to non-research-oriented institutions.

Scholarship should be disseminated broadly and in an affordable manner—for scholars, for the public, and for the world community.

Contrary to the apparent assumptions of the Association of Universities and Colleges–Canadian Association of Research Libraries/l'Association des bibliothèques de recherche du Canada (AUCC–CARL/ABRC) final task force report, *The Changing World of Scholarly Communication: Challenges and Choices for Canada* (1996):

- Digitization does not lead to democratization;
- Speedy communication may not be as robust as slower communication;
- Copyright ownership is not necessarily related to price;
- The value of peer review and the editorial process is significant;
- The costs and benefits of electronic communication are not well understood.

The value of peer review and its attendant editorial function is critical to scholarly publishing.

Scholarly communication must be sustainable as a public resource within the existing resource base, but optimized to create maximum benefit.

Non-proprietary, widely accepted technical standards for publication are recommended.

An accessible and affordable system for scholarly publishing is paramount, whether provided by profit or not-for-profit entities.

Three levels of scholarly communication require recognition: an informal level of dialogue and correspondence, a middle level of initial presentation to peers, and a final, value-added level of peer-reviewed material that constitutes the permanent record. New communications technology facilitates communication, especially at the lower levels, but, in itself, does not provide solutions to any current problems.

The foundation of scholarly communications is human resources.

A focus on centres of excellence may undermine the development and dissemination of knowledge.

Individual, national, and international interests must be recognized.

In order to foster co-operative relationships within the scholarly community, all concerned parties, including suppliers and publishers, should be encouraged to participate in the pursuit of solutions for broad, affordable dissemination of scholarly communication.

A meeting similar to that described in Recommendation 3 of the AUCC–CARL/ABRC task force report should be held, but expanded to include Canadian Association of University Teachers (CAUT), Fédération Québécoise des professeures et professeurs d'université (FQPPU), and the research-granting councils.

AUCC, in co-operation with other national bodies, should develop model licences for electronic products.

Scholars

Scholars should affirm quality over quantity as a matter of professional ethics. (In the discussions, much was made of the Harvard model, by which was meant placing a dramatic limitation on the number of articles a scholar can bring forward for consideration for gaining tenure and promotion.)

The awareness and involvement of scholars in addressing critical issues in the scholarly communication process must be addressed.

As a matter of principle, academics should publish in outlets that allow non-exclusive licensing. This principle should be promoted by AUCC, CAUT, and the granting councils.

To encourage non-profit scholarly publishing, academics, especially senior academics, should, as a matter of policy:

- participate in editorial peer-review functions of non-profit publishing outlets over for-profit outlets;
- publish in non-profit outlets when such outlets provide equivalent recognition.

All Canadian academic associations should support not-for-profit scholarly publishing and encourage their members to do so.

Publishers

In general, journals should be run by non-profit entities with the money earned staying within the research/university community.

Reasonable profits should be granted to for-profit publishers in return for service to the community.

The principle "public funds; public good; public access" should be affirmed. That is to say, given that scholarly communication is supported by public funds, it must be organized for the public good, and a paramount element in achieving the public good is maintaining wide public access.

Social profit must be balanced against economic profit.

Librarians

Librarians have a responsibility to make such issues as overpublication, high prices, and restricted access known to the scholarly community and to the general community and then respond to the community as a whole. Librarians should not have to act as watchdogs for the scholarly community as a whole.

Institutions

The publication of articles as a primary means for determining career progress comes at a cost. Such an emphasis should be reviewed, not only for its exclusion of salient elements of scholarly contribution, but also for its unnecessary contribution to excess costs and inefficient information production.

The involvement of senior administration and of the senior professoriate in addressing the issues discussed at this conference is key.

Academic institutions should develop access agreements to the widest range of resources to serve all sectors of the Canadian academic community at the least possible cost. This should be done at the highest level (for example, national, provincial, regional).

Policy priorities

Within scholarly publishing itself, a variety of models must be encouraged. Most importantly, a collaborative infrastructure and a scholar-owned-and-operated, not-for-profit "cottage industry" should be nurtured with sensitivity shown to the information poor within and outside Canada.

There must be strong support for knowledge production and dissemination, especially from federal research funding agencies who should be equally committed to research and communication funding.

The National Library should be supported in its efforts to archive electronic publications.

If information is to be a commodity, librarians must protect the interests of patrons in the name of citizenship rather than as consumers.

The transition to electronic technologies cannot be allowed to decrease access for all or for certain groups.

A sufficient information technology infrastructure must exist for scholars in all fields of inquiry. This infrastructure includes hardware, a wide range of skills, and institutional organizations. Institutional plans to develop that infrastructure should be shared between institutions. Plans should also be thorough, encompassing such obvious considerations as the handling of electronic theses.

The dissemination of government documents in electronic form to all citizens is critical.

Actions

The principle of "publish or perish" as the basis on which promotion and tenure is gained must be challenged and rebuilt. Teaching, as well as broad participation in professional activities, should be recognized.

Universities should be accredited on the basis of quality of publications.

The value of research syntheses should be recognized by federal research funding agencies.

AUCC and CARL should invite participation from the following groups to produce a new document building on *The Changing World of Scholarly Communication* (AUCC–CARL/ABRC, 1996), which would then be followed by educational fora.

- Association of Canadian University Presses
- Canadian Association of University Teachers
- Canadian Association of Learned Journals
- Canadian Federation of Students
- Canadian Alliance of Student Associations
- Humanities and Social Science Federation of Canada.

The AUCC–CARL/ABRC report should also be considered by individual universities.

Improved funding to the research-granting councils for the support of scholarly publishing should be encouraged.

Electronic journals should be peer reviewed and indexed.

A national body should negotiate site licenses for electronic publications.

Support of scholarly publishing should extend to:

- an examination of the continuing need for postal subsidies;
- the removal of sales taxes on books and journals;
- ensuring that charges for communications lines are not levied on the basis of elapsed time.

Financial support for electronic publishing should encourage electronic production in non-proprietary format (that is, Standard Generalized Markup Language [SGML]) and free distribution.

Means of distribution of scholarly publications to poorer countries should be assured.

Intellectual property policy that recognizes the interests of producers, distributors, and users must be developed.

Access to government information through such projects as the Data Liberation Initiative are critical. Joint private sector/public sector projects should generate publicly available information.

Electronic publication should be affirmed and supported.

Widespread and co-ordinated experimentation and innovation with electronic publication should be encouraged and means provided for sharing of results.

Intellectual property policies must be consistent with the new technologies.

Libraries must demand minimally restrictive licences when purchasing electronic products.

Universities should review their scholarly communication policies and shift allocations where appropriate. Universities could be more proactive in setting the agenda for research on scholarly communication and evaluating and encouraging alternative publishing models.

AUCC–CARL/ABRC recommendations 4, 6 through 22 (excluding 19), plus 24 and 26 should be supported. All players should join together to assist in the formatting and dissemination of electronic scholarly information.

A subset of these players should exert their bargaining power to develop a national site-licensing program with international publishers to secure universal, affordable access to electronic journals, databases, and resources.

A different subset of players should discuss guaranteed no-cost bandwidth availability in order to enable electronic scholarly communication to permit institutions to direct resources towards infrastructure investments in workstation technologies and hence to enable access.

Intellectual property legislation and policies should recognize alternative, non-commercial models.

The Canadian Association of Graduate Studies should discuss with graduate students (nationally and locally) the creation of a framework for ownership of student intellectual property.

Various institutions and organizations, especially universities, scholars' associations, and granting councils, should actively discuss and promote the issues raised at the SCNM conference and develop indicators to monitor progress.

Afterthoughts

A number of points were raised in the SCNM conference or seemed implicit in the papers and discussions, yet they are unarticulated in this overview and the following papers. These few points are meant to bring some of those ideas forward.

Scholars must take responsibility for the costs of their publishing activities, including both the number of articles they write and the choice of journals in which they publish. Otherwise, it might seem reasonable for universities to attempt to obtain control over copyright and redesign the STM publication system. An extreme measure would be for universities to try to claim copyright and complete control over the work produced by scholars.

While it is easy to accept the principle of quality over quantity, in practice the application of the principle is rather difficult. In the humanities and social sciences, it is much less common than in the sciences for researchers to slice up research results and present them in a number of journals. More commonly, research is conducted and first reported in article or monograph form. On this basis, scholars may be asked to contribute to anthologies. Scholars often find themselves using data in subsequent publications, adding nuance and interpretation appropriate to the context. Often, no resources other than university-allocated time are provided for contributing to anthologies, hence no new research is undertaken. In such cases, accumulated and ongoing research is interpreted within the framework of the anthology.

While some might claim that such writing clutters the scholarly communication system, because it reports no new research, others might say that such essays are arguably positive insofar as scholars are making basic research available with a context that is likely to be used in classroom teaching. Perhaps a more serious consequence arises when scholars first report their research in anthologies. In this case, often, the research is never properly indexed, article by article. As a result, not only is the state of the field difficult to assess, but critical analysis of existing research cannot be thorough.

It appears that many scientists and, indeed, other scholars, believe that the high cost of access to their research confers a higher status upon them than they might otherwise have and than their colleagues in the humanities and social sciences. This is a groundless vanity for which the public should not pay.

In an attempt to raise awareness, Canadian universities might consider adopting a practice requiring each scholar, in listing his or her article publications, to undertake the following:

- Identify the publisher of each publication.
- Specify whether that publisher is for-profit, a professional association, or a not-for-profit publisher.
- Report, in the case where the scholar has been published by a for-profit publisher, the name of the next most appropriate, not-for-profit or association journal which might have published the article.
- Provide the cost of an annual institutional subscription.

- Specify whether the journal is available in his or her institution.
- Provide the circulation figure of the journal.
- Calculate the number of hours of direct effort spent in gathering new information for preparing the article cited.

For monograph publishing, scholars might be asked to report:

- the name and location of the publisher;
- the price of the monograph and the number of pages;
- the average price of other comparable monographs.

Following the lead of Keith Archer at the University of Calgary, scholars might apprise themselves of the ownership and subscription price of various journals and decline to review articles for certain journals.

It seems apparent that while there is value in the publication process, which is requiring scholars to conduct and report research and to communicate it in a fashion acceptable to other scholars, very little is known about the use of journals. A greater knowledge of journal usage might suggest means for substantially decreasing the drain on the public purse of the very necessary flow of ideas commonly referred to as scholarly communication.

Conclusion

The editors and this journal have moved forward to print and electronic publication with a selected proceedings of *Scholarly Communication in the Next Millennium* for a number of reasons. Like Newby, we take as a given that scholars and universities will move further and further into electronic publishing. We believe that these papers point to many of the different issues that must be considered in that evolution. Action is required at all levels of the system, from individual scholars through individual universities to national policy. Action will also be taken in the private sector by publishers, software developers, and hardware manufacturers. We see this collection, along with the AUCC–CARL/ABRC reports, and indeed other work, as useful for all these actors. Both AUCC and CARL will need to continue to play leading roles in this challenge of transition. However, their efforts will need to be matched by research funding agencies and scholars themselves through both their faculty associations and their journal-related activities.

Reference

AUCC–CARL/ABRC Task Force on Academic Libraries and Scholarly Communication. (1996). *The changing world of scholarly communication: Challenges and choices for Canada*. Ottawa: Author.

Introduction: Scholarly Communication and the STM Serials Pricing Crisis

Rowland Lorimer
Simon Fraser University

Abstract: This paper introduces the scientific, technical, and medical (STM) serials pricing crisis, distinguishing it from a temporary crisis in 1996 in humanities and social science publishing in Canada and from the general constraints operating on scholarly publishing. It then reviews the papers selected for inclusion in this volume.

Résumé: Cet article décrit la crise actuelle dans le prix de journaux scientifiques, techniques, et médicaux (STM), distinguant celle-ci d'une crise temporaire en 1996 dans l'édition canadienne en sciences humaines et sociales, ainsi que des contraintes générales s'imposant sur l'édition savante. Cet article passe ensuite en revue les textes sélectionnés pour ce numéro.

The genesis of scholarly communication in the next millennium

It is a sobering thought to realize that, in the space of 50 years, the late Robert Maxwell built a $3 billion empire on scholarly journals. First, immediately following World War II, he was the sole distributor for Springer Verlag. Following that, he set up Pergamon Press, which he sold, shortly before his death, to Elsevier. True, he also used chicanery: his journals were largely restricted to scientific, technical, and medical (STM) journals, and the *Daily Mirror* contributed some profit once he had acquired it in 1984. But the foundations of the $3 billion or so he paid for Macmillan USA had their roots in scholarly publishing (Bower, 1988).

It might even be said that the extensive literature on scholarly publishing exists essentially as an oppositional literature to the activities of Robert Maxwell. True, the research has not been done to determine whether Maxwell was the lead actor or merely a stage stealer from a small group of powerful

---

Rowland Lorimer is Editor of the *Canadian Journal of Communication* and a professor of Communication and Director of the Master of Publishing Program at Simon Fraser University, 515 West Hastings Street, Vancouver, BC V6B 5K3. E-mail: Rowland_Lorimer@sfu.ca

***Canadian Journal of Communication,* Vol. 22, No. 3/4 (1997) 11-23**

STM publishers, but there is little doubt that his contribution was considerable.

The literature of which I speak is the library literature on the "serials crisis." It deals with an ongoing struggle between STM publishers and university (and other research) librarians. In essence, the struggle is this. Academic and research librarians and librarians of large urban public institutions, who are acting on behalf of researchers and institutions, pay STM publishers enormous amounts to buy back value-added intellectual property that is donated to them by researchers employed with public funds, usually employees of these purchasing institutions. For their trouble, STM publishers make an enormous return on investment (around 25% of gross revenues). These profit levels have been impeding dissemination of knowledge essentially because they represent overcharging. Such overcharging has forced many cancellations of STM journal subscriptions by even the best and most-well-endowed universities.

On the surface of it, STM publishing contrasts dramatically with humanities and social science (HSS) journal and monograph publishing. STM publishing, like legal and reference publishing, is enormously profitable. HSS publishing can and does turn a decent profit for commercial publishers of U.S. and international titles. But in Canada and many other countries outside the U.S. and U.K., HSS publishing is not profitable. Rather, it receives direct public subsidies (in Canada from the Social Science and Humanities Research Council [SSHRC]).

This superficial difference in profitability is apt to lead to the conclusion that STM publishing is healthy, self-sustaining, and indeed powerful—powerful enough to command high prices for its content and keep complaining librarians at bay. In contrast, HSS publishing looks weak, requiring continuous public subsidy. Nothing could be further from the truth. It would be far more accurate to say that STM publishing manages to lever a level of public subsidy sufficient to cover both operations and profits, whereas HSS publishing, at least in Canada, receives sufficient public subsidy only to cover operations.

How can this be so? The answer is not that complex. Public subsidies come in three forms to both types of journals. First, for both STM and HSS publishing, the generation of content is almost completely underwritten by public funds. Professors (and other publicly supported researchers) receive both salaries and grants to conduct research and prepare articles for publication. Second, the major part of the editorial process—the solicitation of papers by the academic editor and review by peers—is undertaken with little or no compensation by the publisher. In other words, the process is undertaken by publicly salaried researchers who take publicly funded time, space, and other resources to perform this professional duty. Third, having received so much, journals ask for and receive more. These additional public funds come in the form of subscription revenue from public institutions, particularly university libraries and government research institutes.

The difference between STM and HSS publishing lies in subscription revenues. STM subscription revenues cover costs and profits, whereas, for Canadian HSS journals, subscription revenues do not even cover operating costs. Why? It would appear that the reason HSS journals undercharge is that historically, the perception has existed in academe that HSS journals are less necessary to the functioning of the humanities and social sciences than are STM journals to the functioning of those disciplines. Therefore, if HSS journals charge their full costs (it is surmised), the price of subscriptions will be too high, leading to cancellations and, for lack of revenue, the HSS journals will cease publication. Whether this is true is both recently untested and, for the moment, moot. The result is that SSHRC is a fourth source of about $3 million in public funding to help Canadian HSS journals balance their books and maintain break-even operations.

What is most interesting is that, based on publishing effort, this HSS regime delivers a far less costly product to the user community than does the STM regime. In other words, after taking into account the extra effort required to deal with presenting scientific, technical, and medical information, it appears that the net return on public expenditures on HSS publishing, including SSHRC subsidies, is far greater than the return on STM publishing. Were STM publishing to be conducted within the same constraints as HSS publishing, considerable public savings would be achieved. Just to drive the point home, by solely using the marketplace to cover publishing costs (over and above content generation and academic editorial and review costs), vast amounts of public funds flow to STM publishers while, by not fully operating within the marketplace, much smaller amounts flow to HSS publishers. (Importance of content should not be taken into account in this equation since the publisher only conveys content, it does not generate content.)

The importance of the above analysis is threefold. First, it points out that that part of the serials crisis that is attributable to publishers overcharging is fairly much confined to STM journals, although, as noted, publishers in other areas are quickly catching on that they, too, can make higher profits. Second, it appears that in the spring of 1996 SSHRC did not understand this situation. This lack of understanding, in combination with loose accounting practices by scholarly associations and inadequate financial analysis and advice to SSHRC, caused SSHRC to withdraw but then reinstate about $1 million in subsidies to over 130 HSS journals (Penrod, 1996). Third, the analysis presented is not the complete story of the serials pricing crisis.

The other major element is this. Following World War II, there was a great expansion of universities in the Western world and, hence, numbers of university faculty. Coincident with that expansion was an increased emphasis, in all disciplines, on the carrying out of research and reporting results. For instance, in the English-speaking world in the social sciences prior to the 1960s, a notable career of teaching and research, especially in Britain, might consist of the publication of a dozen journal articles and culminate in the publication of a single monograph. In contrast, beginning in the 1960s, especially in the U.S., multiple monographs, in addition to copious journal articles and book chapters, increasingly became the norm for productive, yet not outstanding, academics. In science, monographs were less the rage. The value of researchers came to be measured more and more in the number of published articles in refereed journals and a pecking order developed among the various journals in each field. Both tenure and promotion committees and peer evaluators making decisions on research grants looked for a "solid body of work" that could give them the confidence to grant further funding. Not to put too fine a point on it, as everyone's work load increased and specialization became the order of the day, where scientists in a single discipline sometimes had little understanding of the significance of their peers' work, quantification of output in a hierarchical order of peer-reviewed and, therefore, peer-approved journals became an easy way to evaluate a scholar's progress. Yes, it was crude but the prestige of the journals added some refinement. In addition, citation indexes were constructed in an attempt to refine the system further. So scholars developed strategies to get their articles accepted in prestigious journals and adapted the styles to maximize citation of themselves and their colleagues. Publishers took advantage of this overall situation, especially when they were managing prestigious journals. They founded and assumed ownership (not just management responsibility) of new journals in areas where there was an overload of articles. They matched institutional subscription fees of the existing prestigious journals, thereby bestowing them with an instant credibility and equality. And onward went the spiral of production and increased costs.

The system was workable (if costly) and it minimized the need for (and the resulting friction from making) personal qualitative evaluation of one's colleagues. The main disadvantages of this regime were that it was costly and, equally as important, scholars came to be rewarded on the basis of piecework, an exploitative system, the ills of which can be recited by any labour historian. Most interesting in that labour history is the downward slide of product quality.

In short, over and above greedy publishers, the numbers of scholars, the emphasis on research publication, and the lack of incentives anywhere in the university community to reward the refusal to purchase the ever-increasing plethora of publications, created an ever-spiraling upward increase in the number of publications and vastly increased costs to the scholarly community and, hence, to the public. The worst situation, obviously, developed in STM serials, basically because all these forces were combined. This occurred because of the prestige of science, the potential economic reward that can be derived from scientific knowledge, and the fact that, as Copernicus, Newton, Einstein, and Watson and Crick demonstrated, science has the power to turn the world on its ear. But the proliferation of HSS publishing, both in article and monograph form, was not to be ignored.

A Canadian response to the STM journal pricing crisis

In the context of the STM serials pricing crisis (and years of discussion among librarians), the Canadian Association of Research Libraries (CARL) and l'Association des bibliothèques de recherche du Canada (ABRC) put together a collaboration with the Association of Universities and Colleges of Canada (AUCC), the membership of which is university and college presidents, and convened a task force. After the requisite set of meetings, an interim discussion paper was produced, *Towards a New Paradigm for Scholarly Communication* (AUCC–CARL/ABRC, 1995). The discussion paper brought forward a good many issues that had been explored within the library community in the literature surrounding the journals crisis.

While the report was certainly useful, reflective of its full name (the AUCC–CARL/ABRC Task Force on Academic Libraries and Scholarly Communication), it was also quite narrow in conception. Essentially, while opting for a scholar-centred enterprise in an attempt to conceptualize a way of freeing the system from greedy publishers, in fact, the report defined the issues within library and university administrative concerns: for example, levels of spending and locus of control.

This perspective was maintained in the final report, *The Changing World of Scholarly Communication* (AUCC–CARL/ABRC, 1996). A short summary of those points provides a useful context. (See Appendix 2 for the full set of recommendations.) The report began with the notion that technological change is having a major impact on knowledge creation and communication. At the same time, it noted a limited awareness within the scholarly community that scholarly communication is threatened by the volume of material being created, its organization, and its cost.

The awareness of the community to these issues needs to be raised at all levels and amongst all users and participants. Libraries must develop "best practices" for ensuring that they can serve the information needs of their clients, and they need to share these practices. The foundation on which such practices can emerge is a better understanding of usage. Assisted by governments, universities should give high priority to the development of their telecommunications and computing infrastructure, including training, for all scholars and students. To broaden access, libraries should digitize unique collections according to accepted standards and co-ordinate other digitization. Broad community support for appropriately peer-reviewed electronic publishing and support for not-for-profit scholarly publishing should be forthcoming. A central clearing house or registry for electronic publishing projects should be established. The role of copyright should be discussed within the university community and Bill C-32 should be passed with allowance for interlibrary loan and educational and library exceptions on copying. Further legislation on fair dealing should be developed.

Finally, the report suggested that the scholarly community review its tenure and promotion procedures with an eye to emphasizing quality over quantity of publications.

These points are both insightful and valid. However, the difficulty with the interim and final reports is that, while nodding at scholars, it does not adequately address the need to define the necessary elements of an effective system of scholarly communication to serve the interests of scholars and of society. Moreover, in not bringing scholars, academic presses, disciplinary associations, journal editors, students, and others to the table, both the interim and the final report of the task force failed to take into account the established interests and commitments of all parties and to use them as a foundation for developing a framework to rationalize scholarly and especially STM publishing.

For an effective addressing of the issues, the communication needs of the research and education community, and also the communication between that community and the broader community must be reviewed and addressed. All interests must be brought forward: the general social interest, scholars as knowledge producers, scholars and others within and outside the academy as knowledge consumers, students, faculty associations as representatives of the interests of scholars as employees, research- and journal-funding agencies, journal editors, the individual disciplines and areas of study, university and other librarians, university administrators who oversee both research and academic concerns, university presidents, journal owners, journal publishers, journal editors, and technology representatives who have something to contribute to new modes of journal production.

A co-operative effort

It was in this context and as part of my role as director of the Canadian Centre for Studies in Publishing at Simon Fraser University and editor of this journal, that I set out to obtain funds for a conference designed to bring together representatives of all these interests. I informed AUCC and CARL of my intentions and, as a result, University of British Columbia Librarian Ruth Patrick contacted me. Ruth Patrick suggested running a conference hosted jointly by UBC and Simon Fraser University. Such a conference would take advantage of the focus of concern on publishing at Simon Fraser's Canadian Centre for Studies in Publishing. It would also capitalize on a major initiative at UBC involving her and John Gilbert, co-ordinator of Health Sciences, in his role as chair of the Senate Library Committee at UBC. They and others were assessing the information needs of UBC and how to address them using technology and organization. Third, it would bring in a greater range of concerns than existed at Simon Fraser, particularly in the health sciences through John Gilbert. Seeing the wisdom of this approach, we formed a joint local committee and a national committee to hold a major conference, Scholarly Communication in the Next Millennium (SCNM). Lorimer, Patrick, and Gilbert, acting as the executive committee, hired Deborah Kirby as executive director and, with valuable guidance from both the local and national committees, created the conference.

An overview of the selected papers

The importance of these issues both to the scholarly community and the public was underlined by the willingness of a large number of public and private sector sponsors to assist the conference (see Appendix 3 for the list of sponsors) and the presence of both Secretary of State for Science and Technology Jon Gerrard and British Columbia Minister of Education Paul Ramsey.

Usage

In fact, Roberta Lamb's opening paper focuses exactly on the value and dynamics of scholarly publishing in the context of society as a whole. Lamb's research, conducted in California, examines the use made of scholarly publications by various companies and institutions, including the courts. She analyzes how they make use of research published in journals and determine expertise. Her work is representative rather than exhaustive. As most social scientists and humanists know, the mass media are large consumers of research and expertise. Indeed, magazines of commentary feed off research and knowledge generated by universities in the same way that drug companies have an insatiable appetite for scientific journal articles and expert authors.

Two papers carry this usage analysis forward but within the academy. Erwin Warkentin analyzes how scholars within departments of German use traditional and electronic journals, characterizing his colleagues as probably conservative. In performing this analysis, he points to many salient elements affecting the future of electronic journals, some technical, but many not. Ruth Noble and Carol Coughlin provide a parallel analysis carried out across Canada of journal usage of academic chemists. Both indicate a lower level of usage than one might expect, a factor that is significant for two reasons. First, it provides insight into the dynamics of information flows among scholars and the use made of libraries. Second, it is a critical factor for publishers contemplating replacing subscription fees with user fees. The papers also provide insights into the infrastructure required at the user level for going electronic.

Both these papers provide needed information. We have very little analysis of how scholars use journals and, indeed, all information sources. Journal publishers would have us believe that scholars, and especially scientists, as well as professionals, cannot exist without constant reference to journals. Yet it appears that active established researchers make far less use of journals than one might expect, not only in the humanities and social sciences but also the sciences. To some degree, it appears, they rely on graduate students writing papers or younger colleagues to keep them somewhat current with the literature. But it also appears that once they understand an area and have some sense of the orientation and direction of colleagues close to them, through exchange of e-mail, occasional journal checks, conversation within research groups, and so forth, they manage to understand what is going on and what is likely to go on.

What then is the value of journals? Certainly students use them to bring themselves up to speed in an area. Scholars out of the loop of active researchers may use journals more frequently to keep abreast of research (but we really do not know). Conference organizers may search the literature for active researchers, as we did for this conference. And there are users such as the media, companies, and institutions identified by Lamb. There is also the value of the publication process itself. Submitting a paper to a journal for publication and having it accepted confirms one's position as a scholar who can identify a problem and design, conduct, and report the research at a level acceptable to one's peers.

Usage of journals has at least one other dimension, which might be called user friendliness. In the print world, the accessibility of the ideas contained in the text is addressed first by editors. Editors, both academic and professional, ensure that both the writing and the investigative and analytical procedures used are both defensible and comprehensible. To editing is added the dynamics of layout, typography, printing, and binding to ensure the text is easily read and understood, even pleasing in its presentation to the reader. Viewed at another level, publishers address the accessibility of the ideas by presenting the information developed in research in a multitude of market formats. Thus, the *Economist* puts its unique spin on economic research and reflection; newspaper columnists and newsletter publishers present health information; and so forth.

Fytton Rowland and Ian Bell's perspective on the accessibility of ideas in the world of electronic publishing is based on work reported in three studies conducted in the U.K. Rowland and his co-authors draw attention to ergonomic factors in electronic publishing, by which they mean quality and organization of the graphic presentation. They note that such variables and the ability to add value will play an important role in determining how electronic scholarly journals are perceived. The importance of this paper is not only for what it reports. The paper represents the tip of the entire user interface iceberg, which, in the end, involves the full communicational capacity of the medium—sound, image, and text.

The physical-access infrastructure for scholarship

The accessibility of ideas is but one level of overall accessibility. Physical access is another, whether it involves the presence of a print copy of an article in a library identifiable by an end-user; the proper shelving of a volume; appropriate collection building; or the half-life of the medium on which the article is recorded. Two articles in this volume address this issue.

First, Margot Montgomery analyzes the role of the Canada Institute for Scientific and Technical Information (CISTI). CISTI serves the Canadian and, to some extent, the North American scientific community as a central resource for scientific information published anywhere. Montgomery describes CISTI's operations and its philosophy of operation. For Canadian science, CISTI extends this role, reaching back to individual scholars and publishing their research papers. As Aldyth Holmes points out in her paper, CISTI publishes 14 scientific journals covering a variety of fields, two of which are published in electronic form. Since Montgomery's paper was written, CISTI has laid important groundwork for the development of electronic publishing by announcing its willingness to assist Canadian journals to publish in electronic form and even provide space on its server.

While Montgomery's paper addresses the organization of an information institution, Tom Delsey of the National Library of Canada addresses specific developments in the access and archiving function of electronic documents. The key issues brought forward by Delsey deal with legal deposit of electronic publications, the technical infrastructure needed to support the management and long-term preservation of electronic collections, standards for electronic document encoding, proprietary rights to information, and the implications for library services to researchers. Not only does he make apparent the work in progress but also, for scholars, Delsey provides a sense of the taken-for-granted infrastructure already in place for print materials.

Production, finance, and electronic journals

Given the STM serials crisis and the general financial constraints operating on scholarly journals and on scholarly communication as a whole, in our call for papers we were hoping to attract research that would provide some financial and organizational details on the operations of both print and electronic journals. We were not disappointed. Aldyth Holmes, the senior editor of CISTI's 14 print and two parallel electronic journals (officially of the National Research Council of Canada, CISTI's parent organization) provided one such paper. Holmes analyzes the costs of print and electronic journal publication in the sciences, arguing that substantial savings are not to be gained by a switch from print to electronic technologies.

Holmes' discussion is complemented by two papers. First, to replace a paper entitled "Escaping the Giant: A Real Life Story about Becoming a Society Publisher," we were able to obtain a paper presented at the annual meeting of the International Association of Scholarly Publishing in May 1997, in Vancouver. Leaving electronic publishing aside, publishing consultant Walter Ludwig analyzes the added costs and added value of journals administered by large commercial journal publishers. According to his analysis, they do not exist—at least not at an affordable price. On a revenue base of $342,000, using charging levels common to some publishers, a commercially published journal would result in a net cost to a scholarly society of $45,000. Self-published by the society, it could generate a net income of $76,000 after amortization of one-time costs of approximately $25,000. The significant shift in income that Ludwig reports parallels the findings of the above-mentioned paper presented by Rod Parrish at the conference. In the case of Parrish's journal, an increased number of articles and an increased number of articles with the same word count per page were able to be achieved for approximately the same production costs.

A further complement to Holmes' analysis was provided by Michael Jensen. For some time, under Jensen's direction, Johns Hopkins University Press has been carrying out an electronic publishing project called Project Muse. This project provides a package of up to 40 electronically published journals to libraries for a negotiated fee based on a number of factors. As of this writing 216 libraries are involved, 75 of which have subscribed to the complete 40-journal package. As background, Jensen describes the publishing system of the former Soviet Union. It was a system driven by a production mentality independent of the tastes of the market and independent of the ability of the consumer to purchase. When communism collapsed, not only were the vast warehouses of unsellable books exposed, but also, working under the requirement to become profitable, presses found themselves turning to pornography to support their new-found freedom to publish important Western books.

Electronic publishing provides much the same opportunity for producer-driven publishing. It also provides the opportunity for the electronic equivalent both of pornography and vast warehouses of unread material. How to make electronic publishing work for the purposes of scholarly communication is the key. Jensen argues that, at least currently, electronic publishing does not lower costs to any great degree. Further, in an environment where so much is available for free on the Web and so many are able to become Web "publishers," it is difficult to collect needed revenues. Indeed, if collected on a user-pay basis, it is doubtful whether electronic scholarly publishing is feasible at all. Coming from such a prestigious publisher as Johns Hopkins, these are sobering thoughts indeed. They certainly bring into question claims that dramatic savings are possible by moving into publication in electronic form.

Experimentation and reflection

Jonathan Borwein and Richard Smith take the discussion of electronic publishing into the details that have the potential to make or break journals. It is certainly true that electronic technology can provide added value to scholarly communication. Possibilities of video clips, sound, and access to raw data are often mentioned as adding value. E-mail correspondence has already created larger, more dynamic research communities unaffected by geography. However, as Borwein and Smith state explicitly, and as the force of this collection makes clear, a migration from print on paper to electronic publishing implies a good deal more than stopping the presses and placing files on servers. Borwein and Smith examine four dimensions—the technological, commercial, scholarly, and administrative—and conclude that while electronic publishing technology may offer greater control to journals in production and dissemination, in the processing of revenues an increased dependency on other commercial institutions may result, particularly in the processing of payments.

David Beattie and David McCallum examine electronic journal publishing focusing on the efforts of the virtual products division of Industry Canada. Citing their own projects and commissioned studies on electronic publishing, they claim a potential for great savings by moving to centralized electronic journal publishing.

Of scholars and students and scholarly communication

Writing as the chair of the librarian's committee of CAUT, Ken Field provides a wide-ranging paper important for its representation of the issues surrounding electronic publishing and communication from the viewpoint of the scholar. Field's early point, that the emphasis on journal article publication by universities in their evaluations of professors might be reduced, is interesting for its rejection of the notion that scholarship can be equated with numbers of publications. If the professional association representing the professoriate is willing to take such a position, it would seem that the scholarly publishing system is not operating as it should.

Field points to the need for recognition of the full range of scholarly activities—inquiry, teaching, collegial interaction, reviewing, research, and research reporting. He discusses the pre-eminent role of publishing for scholars, the various types of publications that are evolving, and the need for scholars to maintain control over their intellectual property. He also describes national initiatives for technological development and his interpretations of studies on cost savings that electronic publishing can achieve.

The disturbing element associated with Field's paper is the relatively low level of faculty concern with scholarly publishing issues. That lack of concern was manifest at the conference (and the response to the call for papers) in almost complete absence of faculty members *qua* faculty members speaking of their concerns about scholarly publishing and scholarly communication in general or in their particular discipline. To some extent, this lack of interest is difficult to understand. One would think that, if a system of professional communication were under threat, a significant percentage of professionals would be concerned. On the other hand, the area is very charged. Speaking as both a scholar and a journal editor, I am aware that, for many HSS scholars, especially where refusal rates reach 80% (in contrast to refusal rates in the sciences around 20%), submitting articles to journals is something to be endured and avoided if at all possible. Were the journal system to collapse, for many HSS scholars it would be a great relief. It would certainly diminish the publish-or-perish ethic and might lead to more fruitful and more thoughtful collaborations. The paradox is that while "productivity" as measured in numbers of scholarly articles would decrease, and the net cost to society would also decrease, the development and dissemination of useful and insightful knowledge might actually increase.

It is always useful to remember that, assessed at the level of the university or research institution, rather than generating revenue, scholarly productivity costs. Examined beyond the level of the university, after knowledge has fully worked itself through society, knowledge is beyond costing, since it forms the very fabric of society. However, because knowledge-producing nations are rich, rather than poor, one would be hard put to argue that there is an overall net cost to knowledge production.

The second underrepresented group at the conference was students. PhD candidate Richard Nimijean, fresh from his sojourn as senior policy analyst for AUCC responsible for the task force on scholarly communication, and hence a major contributor to the engagement of the task force and its reports, provides the student perspective. The crux of his argument is this: in the face of an oversupply of qualified candidates for the few academic jobs that are now available, the only strategy that makes sense for a young academic is to publish as much and as quickly as possible. To ask young scholars to take any responsibility for an overabundance of articles is to ask that she or he set aside career interests, even the chance at a career, in favour of the general interests of the scholarly community. It is not going to happen.

Scholarship and communicational form

With the context set by electronic publishing activities, Marlene Manoff addresses the rather fundamental McLuhanesque question: How are electronic publishing and retrieval technologies affecting scholarship? Just as the medium of print organizes scholarly inquiry, so, as she points out, technological tools can facilitate certain types of research, whether or not they have great value. Similarly, libraries' decisions to accommodate new technologies can affect scholarship quite significantly, determining what is readily available and what is not. Electronic technology can also affect the creation of scholarly editions and such fundamentals as the creation of canons.

The future according to . . .

The final paper of this collection was written by Gregory Newby who, with Robin Peek (1996), has put together a valuable collection of papers entitled *Scholarly Publishing: The Electronic Frontier*. Newby takes as a given that electronic communications will come to dominate in the scholarly community in the not-too-distant future. He points out how it is already serving scholars interests well, especially for informal communication, but that this may remain quite independent of formal journal and monograph publishing. His paper stimulates consideration of how informal electronic communication may evolve into formal exchanges of a different form than formal journal articles as we know them. Perhaps Newby's most important point is that the capacities of electronic communication are developing quickly and dramatically. Scholarly communication can benefit, provided that an appropriately positive but sceptical attitude is maintained and, largely building on current library structures and services, a proper infrastructure for creation, publication, storage, retrieval, and access is built.

References

AUCC–CARL/ABRC Task Force on Academic Libraries and Scholarly Communication. (1995). *Towards a new paradigm for scholarly communication*. Ottawa: Author.

AUCC–CARL/ABRC Task Force on Academic Libraries and Scholarly Communication. (1996). *The changing world of scholarly communication: Challenges and choices for Canada*. Ottawa: Author.

Bower, Tom. (1988). *Maxwell: The Outsider*. London: Aurum.

Peek, Robin, & Newby, Gregory (Eds.). (1996). *Scholarly publishing: The electronic frontier*. Cambridge, MA: MIT Press.

Penrod, Lynn. (1996, March 28). *Memorandum to grant applicants*. Ottawa: Social Sciences and Humanities Research Council of Canada.

After Scholarship: Making Information Actionable

Roberta Lamb
University of California, Irvine

Abstract: Discussions about scholarly communication and digital library implementations often assume academic contexts of use. However, the information technologies that comprise such systems will also be available to corporate consumers, government organizations, and individuals. In order to make scholarly communication actionable by these non-academics, we need to know how they use current publications in their daily work. This study examines that use, and its findings raise two related issues: that researchers in academia, industry, and government place very different, yet equally legitimate, requirements on a scholarly communication system, and that technological choices about scholarly communication systems may be narrowing around particular forms and formats.

Résumé : En discutant de la communication savante et de la création de bibliothèques digitales, on sous-entend souvent que l'usage qu'on en fera sera principalement académique. Cependant, les technologies d'information que de tels systèmes utilisent seront également disponibles aux hommes et femmes d'affaires, aux employés dans la fonction publique et à d'autres intéressés. Afin que ces non-académiques puissent recourir aisément aux communications savantes, il nous faut savoir comment ils utilisent les publications courantes dans leur travail quotidien. Cette étude examine leur utilisation, et conclut en faisant deux observations reliées : d'une part, les chercheurs en milieux académiques, en affaires et dans la fonction publique ont des exigences très différentes, et pourtant également légitimes, vis-à-vis un système de communication savante; d'autre part, les choix technologiques de systèmes de communication savante sont peut-être en train de se centrer autour de formes et de formats particuliers.

Since delivering this paper, Roberta Lamb has become an assistant professor of Management Information and Decision Systems at Case Western Reserve University, Cleveland, OH 44106-7235. E-mail: rel@po.cwru.edu

***Canadian Journal of Communication,* Vol. 22, No. 3/4 (1997) 25-37**

After scholarship

How shall we conceptualize a new scholarly communication system? New technologies may inspire us to speculate about the benefits of electronically distributed scholarly research. Rapid advancements in fields of knowledge, such as biotechnology, can encourage interdisciplinary collaboration and alliances with commercial firms that expand interests in academic publications. We recognize that these technologies and relationships provide new opportunities for enhancing scholarly communication. However, I believe that a university-centric perspective limits our understanding of the current scholarly communication environment, and it may oversimplify our conceptualizations of any new communications systems that we choose to assemble.

To gain the proper perspective, we need to consider what happens after scholarship. The scholarly research community extends beyond the university into government laboratories, industry consortia, and private research centres. Individual scholars move freely between academia, government, and industry, assuming new roles and acquiring new skills. They rely on publication and personal contacts to disseminate knowledge of their research to other academics and to non-academics throughout this dynamic community.

We tend to gloss over the potentially complicating fact that many of the information technologies we use to assemble our systems—the digital collections, the on-line services, the browsers, and formats—will also be available to corporate consumers, government organizations, and individuals. Instead, our discussions about scholarly communication and digital library implementations often assume that *individuals* perform research within *academic* contexts (National Science Foundation, 1993; Information Infrastructure Task Force, 1994). We may find it easier to think about individuals, working alone or in small groups, rather than in big, messy multinational corporate conglomerates. Some academic documents and data files raise significant interest within small groups with highly particularized information needs. However, people working within larger organizations are more likely to gather research data than the solitary consumer or curious intellectual. Their organizations can take action on information, whereas individuals often lack the resources to do so. We should, therefore, consider how this larger constituency uses scholarly information resources when conceptualizing a new scholarly communication system.

Using scholarly communications

In a recent study, I talked to people in 26 California biotech/pharmaceutical organizations, law firms, and real estate brokerages about how they gather and use information. I examined their needs for scholarly communication, their data-gathering practices, and the interorganizational relationships of their firms (Lamb, 1996). Informants explained how they gather data from a wide array of print and electronic resources and then assemble portions of this data into information packages to meet the communication requirements of their clients, customers, and regulators. These explanations provide clues about how we can avoid assembling a university-centric set of technologies that privilege individual use and scholar-to-scholar communication while ignoring the needs of these other researchers.

This study sheds light on what makes scholarly communication actionable by non-academics. It helps us understand how they use current publications in the organizational context of their daily work. It shows, for example, that within California law firms and biotech companies, relationships with the major institutions of the industry largely determine how much and what kind of data they collect. Firms that interact directly with large regulatory agencies gather more scholarly research data than those that do not. Agencies, such as the U.S. Patent and Trademark Office (PTO) or the Food and Drug Administration (FDA), mandate a docucentric form of communication, and they require delivery of a well-defined information package. Firms in less strongly regulated industries, such as real estate, have also begun to place importance on the information package as a source of legitimacy and as a symbol of professional competency. The sophistication of their packages is increasing, as is the amount of research data those packages contain.

Research and expertise

These information packages contain the expertise of many researchers and scholars. The package signifies that the organization putting it together has a connection to the experts—to people at the leading edge of the field. Interestingly, informants frequently mentioned using scholarly research to identify experts. They want access not only to the research, but also to the people who conduct it. They are not content to merely signal their association with experts. They seek rather to incorporate that expertise into their products and processes. For example, clinical trials groups within biotech firms continually look for research scientists to participate in new drug trials. They rely, as the informant quoted below points out, on scholarly communications to identify the experts who might help evaluate the safety of a new drug or the efficacy of treating a new disease with existing drugs.

> If you're going into new [diseases], you also talk to experts in the area. . . . *You do literature searches to see who's published a lot in certain areas.* You go to the meetings, and you figure out who's doing the research. [BOC1B2]

Company members may gather additional academic research documents if the firm retains the experts. When filing FDA submissions, a company must send profiles (including abstracts or references to research publications) for all physicians and researchers participating in their clinical trials. The company compiles such documentation to show that it has retained the best people in the field, that its teams have followed good clinical practices, that their trial results are reliable, and that the drug is safe. Therefore, demonstrable expertise, in the form of trusted scholarly communications, can be extremely important to a company trying to get FDA approval for the drugs it develops.

Other organizations follow similar practices. Intellectual property lawyers, for example, routinely retain expert witnesses, whether or not they expect to bring the case to trial. But finding an expert willing to provide paid testimony can be too easy. Experts who regularly testify in court can post their availability in various media, including on-line databases. However, a prosecutor who wants to present a convincing argument to a judge and jury will prefer to retain an expert they all believe is motivated to establish the truth rather than to collect a fee. The prosecutor may rely on scholarly publications to identify those experts, and to understand the facts of the case more generally. One paralegal illustrated how academic communications fit into the daily routine of a district attorney's (DA) office. In the interview quoted below, she describes common data-gathering activities by referring to a hypothetical homicide case in which the deceased may have contracted a rare disease called "limbo-limbo."

> A lot of [the data gathering is] just to educate the DA so he could say "Hey, Doc, did you ever hear of limbo-limbo?" and at least know what he's talking about. It doesn't have to be he's an expert in it. He just needs to know what limbo-limbo is, what the symptoms of limbo-limbo show, and why somebody may have had a fatality because of limbo-limbo—I mean, somebody died because of it!—and what the exceptions to limbo-limbo are that we don't have in this case. So, those are the things. Now, if it were that say limbo-limbo needed to be proven that this is the cause of death, or something, perhaps then we would hire *the expert of all experts that have written all the articles* on limbo-limbo. . . . And usually, people that don't want to testify and aren't looking for the bucks to sit on the stand are the ones that you want, that are going to give you an honest opinion. Because if it's not there, they're not going to want to put their reputation on the line. [LOC2A1]

This DA's office, like biotech companies, relies upon academic journals to help retain experts. Through these examples and similar data, this study clearly suggests that one of the most important things that the scholarly communication system currently does for the public is to identify the level of expertise of its scholars and researchers. Journal hierarchies and the peer-review process sustain a trusted, qualified indication of disciplinary expertise that members of other organizations, like lawyers, clinical researchers, and federal regulators, depend upon.

Keeping current

Scientists in commercial research organizations and universities use scholarly journals, in association with other media and personal contacts, to maintain an awareness of what is going on in their field of research. Scientists become members of what Crane (1972) calls invisible colleges to get the inside track on the research breakthroughs of a small group of their colleagues. By extension, commercial research groups, like one in this study, retain or hire university associates to maintain a stable of scientists with complementary or cross-disciplinary expertise. In industry, leading-edge research groups keep themselves current by reading the journals and maintaining close ties with colleagues, but they also track advancements in the field through international patent applications—frequently searching on-line patent indexes and full-text databases.

Keeping current means staying competitive. For commercial enterprises, this includes maintaining an awareness of what is happening in their own or related industries. Scholarly communications serve only part of that need. Such organizations also seek to understand their competitors, potential partners, markets, and customers. Their members try to determine what they must do to remain viable and to assess the chances of other organizations on whom they rely, or with whom they compete, to do the same. They do this in part by compiling profiles, which include a mix of financial, demographic, technical, patent, and academic research data. Profiles, like the one described below, help them evaluate individuals, groups, organizations, and markets.

> Before we start doing business with any company, we always research the company. We will search financially about the company, business strengths, their marketing plans. We'll look at all of the press releases that they've made. We'll look at key players in the company—get bios on those, histories, where they came from, where they studied, who they've done business with in the past. Depending on the type of relationship that we want to develop with this company, we will know as much about them as we do about ourselves. [OOC1A1]

This type of competitive analysis may not interest academic scholars, but their research data helps firms in market economies make strategic evaluations. Analysts integrate scholarly communications into profiles that present a unique organizational perspective on what is currently important in the field, in the industry, or in the larger political and regulatory environment.

Compliance, litigation, and collaboration

Political and regulatory agents play an interesting role by linking commercial organizations to scholarly communications in an important, but perhaps unexpected, way. Much of the data gathering an organization does supports decision-making processes and basic research. But much is also mandated by specific regulations and filing protocols, like the requirements for new drug approvals or patent applications. When firms interact directly with large regulatory agencies to comply with these requirements, they gather more scholarly research data. Agencies such as the PTO or FDA mandate a docucentric form of communication, and they require delivery of a voluminous, well-defined information package. For a pharmaceutical firm wishing to sell drugs in the U.S., regulation entails documentation.

> It's very regulated . . . every single protocol is filed with the FDA. . . . At the end you'd file what's called an NDA, which is a New Drug Application. That NDA contains everything that you've ever done on that particular drug. So it can be 300 volumes of stuff. It goes by truck sometimes to Washington. . . . I mean, it's a very documented industry. [BOC1B2]

The information package for a new drug application contains references to research that supports the filing claims. The submitted dossier must include not only the research that the filing company has done through in-house drug development or clinical trials, but also anything else that has been published about the drug, its compounds, and its medical application. This accumulation of publications is mandated. It shows the regulatory agency what the field knows about this drug, and it builds the case for approval. Organizations comply with this mandate by collecting scholarly research articles, often in a frenzy of last-minute activity.

> Well, anytime that we're getting ready to file an FDA submission, we do massive searches in the literature. And those are very time consuming. And, usually we don't get much warning . . . and they always want the latest data. So it makes sense to wait till the last minute so we can search the information and get the most current stuff. So just before submissions it's crazy for the library, and it's crazy for the regulatory folks as well. [BBA3A1]

If we consider that companies must prepare these packages for every drug in the pipeline, and that a large pharmaceutical firm may have as many as 50 at any one time, and that each one may take 10 or more years (and US$100 million to US$300 million) to develop, we realize that this activity constitutes a significant use of scholarly communications.

Law firms must also conform to very-well-defined information exchange protocols and short time-lines that sometimes require the staff to gather academic publications quickly. When a firm takes a case to court, its team must search the literature and gather everything it needs to make its case on the scheduled appearance date. As the informant quoted below points out, this hurried mode of information retrieval is not unique to litigation cases at the U.S. Supreme Court level—it goes on, more or less, all the time.

> It was the first Supreme Court case, but really we've been just as hard working on other things that haven't gone up to the Supreme Court. It's just how stressed out the attorneys are that makes a difference. And how many times they'll call with yet another thing, because as they're going through their material something else comes up they just can't consolidate. . . . So the air was a little bit more electric around those times. But it's certainly not the only time we've ever [searched the literature like] that. There are a couple of other big things that are boiling over right now. And you know everybody's going nuts. It's just the way things go. [LBA4A1]

These last two examples show that when commercial firms interact directly with large institutions, like the courts or the FDA, they come under a great deal of stress to assimilate huge amounts of information very quickly. They require information-processing support, such as a well-staffed law library or a corporate information centre. If this infrastructure is absent or overloaded with requests, the firm may accomplish its data-gathering tasks by forming a number of well-co-ordinated alliances with outside contractors and information suppliers.

Firms may choose not to interact directly with regulatory bodies and government agencies. A biotech firm, for example, can simply restrict its activities to drug discovery, and let another company take over critical segments of the drug development process. That company would then assume any research-reporting responsibilities associated with mandate compliance. Some informants in my study mentioned following this option during clinical trials.

> In developing drugs, you always have to go into the clinic and test them. So clinical trials are very expensive. That's where we would hand off to somebody else. [BOC4A1]

An organization may also opt to interact directly with the courts and regulators, but to share the data-gathering facilities of other firms rather than develop information infrastructure itself. This arrangement does not shift the data-gathering responsibility, but, as the law firm informant quoted below describes, it does change the nature of data-gathering activities at the firm, making them more collaborative.

> [The legal staff will] go upstairs to the law library there. . . . It's just part of the arrangement we have with them . . . they do allow us to use their LEXIS and NEXIS. So we can go there in their library, and they'll get you set up. [LOC4A1]

The need to comply with regulatory mandates also encourages collaboration. As examples given show, not every firm collects vast quantities of scholarly research data. However, those that regularly gather large volumes of data, and have acquired the information infrastructure to manage that activity, indirectly support the data-gathering needs of other organizations. Small biotech firms often obtain FDA approval for their drugs by partnering with large pharmaceutical companies that can take the drug through documentation-intensive clinical trials. Similarly, law firms that retrieve and assimilate research data for their clients may also make their information resources available to other attorneys on a *quid pro quo* basis. Through these collaborations, commercial firms regularly use scholarly communications to satisfy the information exchange requirements of regulation compliance and litigation.

Displaying competency

The information package that a law firm or biotech/pharmaceutical company puts together can be technically impressive. It looks professional. It contains well-researched data presentations and legal or scientific arguments supported by pages of references and citations. The package builds a reviewer's confidence that the work represented is well done, that the claims the firm makes are true. Firms in strongly regulated industries routinely assemble information packages that display these competencies. But other firms, such as real estate brokerages, have also begun to place importance on the information package as a source of legitimacy and as a symbol of professional competency.

When an individual purchases property, he or she may feel confident in the deal. But an institutional investor must provide data that justifies a purchase to the underwriters or pensioners of a fund. Institutional investors have many investment choices. They can buy properties. They can also purchase stock in publicly traded companies, such as Fortune 100 pharmaceutical firms, or the initial public offerings packaged by securities law firms. Commercial real estate brokers compete with these alternative investments when they deal with institutional investors. These investors can go out and look at a property to satisfy themselves that it is a good buy, but they need information and analysis to take back to their fund members that is comparable to the information packages on other investments in their portfolio. As one information researcher at a California brokerage indicates, the sophistication of real estate investment packages is increasing, as is the amount of research data they contain.

> The packages have to be fancier. They have to have more colour graphics, aerial photographs—more bells and whistles. It takes a lot more to do the same project. In fact, we've really had to gear up and retrain so that we can do really dazzling packages. . . . The guys can't compete with a package that would have been suitable last year or two years or three years ago. [ROC3A1]

Investor group representatives and funding-agency managers need to be able to justify their real estate investment decisions, and they often do this with information packages supplied in part by the broker. The content of the package is important, but so is the form. Professionalism and competence is communicated through the total package.

Scholarly communications have not yet become a routine part of the broker's package, except perhaps for some market-oriented pieces or investment theory publications. However, the academic publication—the scholarly information package—communicates the competency and expertise of its contributors and their community. Scholarly communicators, like commercial real estate brokers, may find it necessary to increase the technical sophistication of their journals to effectively convey the quality and importance of their work to a public that has come to expect highly sophisticated formats.

Gathering documents

The organizations investigated rely on scholarly communications, along with other data resources such as personal contacts or proprietary documents, when locating expertise, keeping current, fulfilling mandates, evaluating options, justifying actions, and displaying competency. Not every firm does this by purchasing and maintaining scholarly journal archives, although some firms do.

Informants reported routinely obtaining scholarly documents by searching on-line databases for citations or abstracts and then going to local university libraries to retrieve and photocopy the full-text articles from expensive journals their firms do not purchase. Private firms rely on university archives for continuous access to scholarly journals. They sometimes make unique arrangements to take advantage of these archives, such as this one between a California biotech firm and a University of California library.

> We have a person down at ——. I don't know if he lives [there] or goes to [UC] or something, who does use that library all the time for us. So we can fax him things and the next day he would get them up to us. [So we basically use the UC library] a lot. [BOC3A1]

Private firms clearly prefer this cost-effective method of obtaining needed documents, and they use it exclusively unless special circumstances warrant a change of tactics, as the librarian at this busy California law firm explains.

> There was such a crunch because there was so much to do that we really couldn't use the physical libraries around us the way we usually do because all of us would have been out all day [photocopying] that stuff and not available to everybody else [in the firm]. So what we did more of was calling outside services to help us retrieve the articles. And it kind of went against the grain because it's so cost effective to be able to go locally and just do the copying yourself. [LBA4A1]

As pointed out earlier, one of the reasons for gathering scholarly research data is to fulfill regulatory submission mandates. An active firm will gather a great deal of scholarly reference material in the process of compiling its submissions. When these data-gathering activities are frequent, a firm may negotiate a flat rate with on-line service providers to access academic publication references, abstracts, full-text or data sets in electronic formats. Electronic formats provide flexible local storage and data manipulation, but firms expressed uncertainty about copyright violation. Firms who take advantage of these technologies to fulfill FDA mandates more efficiently are in an awkward position. They must make and store copies of articles and other publications for submission whenever FDA filings may be required, but they are unsure about when this is a copyright violation. Now that the FDA has begun requesting electronic filings, their uncertainty has increased.

> We are looking at doing [FDA] submissions totally electronically and [the paper] stuff is being scanned in. Now that does raise copyright issues, and I don't know—it's kind of bizarre. I mean you have the government saying, "Well, no that's infringement of copyright. But we'll accept it." [BBA 3A1]

In-situ forms of scholarly communication are complex. The university library plays an economically important dissemination role for the entire community. On-line formats make complying with regulatory requirements easier by allowing for electronic storage, but, at the same time, efficient document-handling practices confound copyright issues. When scholars consider how to make their research accessible to the public, they may not think primarily about biotech companies, law firms, or commercial real estate brokerages, but these are active members of the community that university libraries currently serve. When librarians and publishers grapple with copyright protection issues, they may not be overly worried about multinational pharmaceutical companies or the FDA, but these organizations desperately need electronic copyright issues resolved. They are the public. These are the individuals and organizations that use academic communications after scholarship.

Institutional and technical pressures

The foregoing examples show that the communications systems of academia and industry are intertwined and interdependent—and they are changing. Informants confirm that time constraints and economic considerations provide incentives for adopting new data-gathering practices. They also identify one way in which information technologies can "push" those changes—when, for example, brokers adopt multimedia and information technologies to display professional competency. Some researchers speculate that although "the current [scholarly communication] system . . . is unlikely to change easily or quickly . . . the combined pressures of economics, technological change, and increased demand for plentiful, accurate, and timely information will ultimately overcome this inertia" (AUCC–CARL/ABRC, 1995). This study indicates that institutional pressures also influence data-gathering practices and communication systems. Therefore, I would add that institutional pressures of legitimacy and the associated need to increase the documentation of expertise will strongly shape any scholarly communication system that takes its place.

Summary

Because the research community extends outside academia, we should make an effort to conceptualize scholarly communication as an open process with a heterogeneous field of participants (Kling & Lamb, 1996). Researchers in academia, industry, and government place very different, yet equally legitimate, requirements on scholarly communications. The informants in this study have clearly identified one of these requirements: *the public requires that scholarly communications define the body of current knowledge and identify experts*.

Lawyers, clinical researchers, and federal regulators trust the peer-review system, particularly for scientific journals, to indicate the level of disciplinary expertise of scholars and researchers. Any system that effectively replaces current practices will need to sustain that trust.

By examining how the larger community uses scholarly publications, we can see that journal hierarchies are useful, not only to academics reporting their research and seeking tenure, but also to members of judicial and regulatory organizations. Institutional representatives use scholarly publications to form a documentary basis for the social, judicial, and economic legitimization of their actions and decisions. Any system that effectively replaces current practices will need to preserve or enhance their ability to anchor these legal and commercial interests in legitimate scholarly research.

The informants in this study have also identified one of their expectations about communication systems: *the public expects that the technologies used to deliver scholarly communications will, to some degree, reflect the competency of contributing scholars and the content value of their contributions*. In specific contexts, certain types of information packages and technologies are preferred over others because of their ability to signal professional competence. Real estate brokers, for example, value data that they can easily convert into presentation graphics or audio/video clips. These capabilities may not matter so much to scholars, but scholarly communication systems will also be evaluated by funding agencies, legislators, and committees who use these same external standards to judge the value of the systems they fund and promote.

Policy conclusions

The policy implications of the data I have presented are somewhat counter-intuitive. Although we commonly associate technological change with a wide array of technical choices, public expectation has drastically curtailed those choices. By this I mean that the public, as represented in this study, has adopted electronic forms and integrated desktop formats for managing documents, and they expect scholarly communication systems to follow that lead. Commercial firms and public agencies have systems that they use now—these are ad hoc, but they work—and they define a set of widely adopted preferences. At this point in time, I would say that any new and effective scholarly communication system will need to conform to those preferences.

Public expectations about technology will shape scholarly communications, as will public requirements for certain types of knowledge. Any new scholarly communication system will be effective if it preserves the broader research community's ability to identify experts. It must also sustain or enhance the public's ability to anchor legal, commercial, and social decision-making in legitimate research and academic thought. This can be done in a number of ways, but changes to the system will require changes in social and professional behaviour.

Our set of choices about scholarly communication systems may be narrowing around a few points that make scholarly research publicly available and publicly actionable. These are points of potential reintermediation for academics, publishers, libraries, and public institutions. They involve hard choices and potentially difficult transformations of social and professional behaviour. But some leverage may be obtained by bringing the public into focus more clearly.

In order to make scholarly research actionable within non-academic work contexts and to identify the possibilities for reintermediation, we must consider a broader purview. By understanding the requirements of a more broadly construed research community, I believe we can develop the policies and assemble the technologies that will form the basis of a dynamic, usable scholarly communication system. At the same time, we may come to understand better what makes this effort necessary. We may realize that the impetus for moving toward electronic forms and digital publication comes less from the studied rational deliberation of self-directed scholars than from the legitimation required within non-academic consumer constituencies.

References

AUCC–CARL/ABRC Task Force on Academic Libraries and Scholarly Communication. (1995). *Towards a new paradigm for scholarly communication.* Ottawa: Author. URL: http://www.lib.uwaterloo.ca/documents/scholarly(aucc-carl).html

Crane, D. (1972). *Invisible colleges: Diffusion of knowledge in scientific communities.* Chicago: University of Chicago Press.

Information Infrastructure Task Force. (1994, May). Libraries and the NII. In *Putting the information infrastructure to work* [Microfiche]. Washington, DC: Government Printing Office. URL: http://nii.nist.gov/pubs/sp857/cover.html

Kling, R., & Lamb, R. (1996). Analyzing alternate visions of electronic publishing and digital libraries. In G. B. Newby & R. P. Peek (Eds.), *Scholarly publishing: The electronic frontier* (pp. 19-54). Cambridge, MA: MIT Press.

Lamb, R. (1996). Interorganizational relationships and online information resources. *Proceedings of the 29th annual Hawaii international conference on systems sciences: Vol. 5. Digital documents* (pp. 82-91). Los Alamitos, CA: IEEE Computer Society Press.

National Science Foundation. (1993, September). Research on digital libraries: A joint initiative of the National Science Foundation, Computer and Information Science and Engineering Directorate, Advanced Research Projects Agency Computing Systems Technology Office, National Aeronautics and Space Administration. In *NSF 93-141*. Washington, DC: Author.

Consumer Issues and the Scholarly Journal

Erwin Warkentin
University of Waterloo

Abstract: This paper discusses the new electronic approach to scholarly publishing from the perspective of the consumer. Based on a survey of Germanists in Canada, it suggests that while most scholars are receptive to electronic journals, the majority give them only qualified support. The main stumbling block is the perception that e-journals publish what paper journals won't. At the heart of the problem is the perception that electronic publications do not undergo a rigorous refereeing process. The paper makes recommendations that will enhance the credibility of the electronic medium while it is still in its infancy.

Résumé: Cet article adopte le point de vue du consommateur afin de discuter de la nouvelle approche électronique dans l'édition savante. Se fondant sur un sondage de germanistes au Canada, il suggère que, même si la plupart des savants sont ouverts à l'idée d'un journal électronique, la majorité ne lui donneraient qu'un appui conditionnel. L'obstacle principal, tel que le révèle le sondage, est la perception que les journaux électroniques acceptent ce qu'aucun journal publié ne daignerait accepter. Le sondage révèle en outre que, au coeur du problème, il y a la perception que les publications électroniques ne sont pas soumises à un processus de sélection rigoureux. Cet article conclut avec des recommandations pour augmenter la crédibilité du médium électronique pendant qu'il est encore dans sa petite enfance.

Introduction

Very seldom do scholars stop and consider their journals as consumer products. The fact is that the academic journal is not above the stormy waters of a market-driven economy. A journal survives by providing a product that is used by a group of consumers who in turn value the product enough to support

Erwin Warkentin is an assistant professor of German in the Department of Germanic and Slavic Languages and Literatures at the University of Waterloo, Waterloo, ON N2L 3G1. E-mail: ewarkent@uwaterloo.ca

***Canadian Journal of Communication,* Vol. 22, No. 3/4 (1997) 39-47**

the journal in a compensatory fashion. This is true whether the journal is produced by a scholarly society on a non-profit basis or by a for-profit private concern. Support for the journal must be demonstrated, otherwise it will not continue to be produced.

The following paper provides a cross-section of opinion regarding the desirability and implementation of electronic journals within German Studies in Canada. (German Studies in this case does not refer to a specific niche, but includes all aspects of German language, literature, and cultural studies.)

In comparison with other disciplines, "Germanistik" is very conservative and traditional in nature. The pool of possible respondents used in this study is perhaps more resistant to change than one might find in many other disciplines. While Germanists have proven themselves very innovative in the area of language teaching, the matter of how research is disseminated still remains firmly entrenched in the paper culture. It is with this attitude in mind that one must understand the results of this survey.

The survey results

Of the 128 who were sent questionnaires, 26% responded. Only one response was removed from the pool. It read: "I guess an electronic questionnaire is what counts as research in the electronic age." This response could easily serve as a summation of how many—actually about 58% of Germanists who responded to this survey—feel about using electronic journals in their professional lives. However, no other put it quite so eloquently or, perhaps better, said it in such a typically Teutonic manner.

Age differences

The other respondents did, however, provide interesting and at times lengthy feedback on their concerns in dealing with this newest way of accessing and communicating knowledge. In fact, upon analysis, some of the results were surprising. For example, they showed that those who are most sceptical about e-journals are not necessarily older colleagues—those with more than 20 years in the profession—but rather those with between 11 and 20 years. This was unexpected, but it provides important information when one considers who needs to be convinced of the necessity of moving scholarly communication into the electronic age. Those who had just begun their careers and those still in graduate programs showed little reservation towards electronic journals. Those in the latter years of their careers approached the electronic journal as a novelty or plaything. Those in the middle years of their career seemed to think the e-journal was simply another imposition.

Subscription frequency and use

Statistics concerning subscription frequency and journal use are also revealing. On average, Canadian Germanists subscribe to 4.1 paper journals each. However, they claim to read or use 5.2 journals on a regular basis. The statistics for electronic journals are considerably lower, with a subscription rate of 0.7. This figure is somewhat skewed in that many subscribe to no e-journals at all, while those who do seldom subscribe to only one. In fact, according to this survey 63% of Germanists in Canada do not subscribe to any e-journals. It must also be noted that the number of electronic journals used versus subscription frequency is consistent with those for paper journals. Only 0.8 electronic journals were used per respondent compared with the 0.7 subscription rate.

Reading habits

The statistics concerning the reading habits of Germanists in this study also reveal unexpected results. Respondents tended to subscribe to the journals they use. Only 20% of the journal material they employ in research and teaching is found in their university libraries; the rest they have in their offices—Germanists tend to have their own copies of the tools of their trade. While one of the most important functions of a university library is to collect the journals necessary for research conducted at that university, the survey results indicate this is not the case for Germanists.

A number of factors might explain this. Because of the relative size of German departments in Canadian universities, their journals budgets are smaller than other disciplines, even though a comparable amount of material is published. Therefore it has been necessary for Germanists to rely on their own resources for access to journals, which has not been the case with many other larger disciplines.

Research support

The small number of journals specific to Germanistik held by university libraries in Canada limits the research that can be conducted. This problem could be alleviated by the economies afforded by the electronic format. A solid core of Germanistik e-journal users already exists in Canada—over one third of the respondents to this survey, in any case. Unfortunately, unless the presentation and delivery of electronic journals change, this number is not likely to grow.

Affordability

The cost of subscribing to Germanistik-related journals is also significant. The great majority of journals are produced by societies that rely on volunteerism to make their products affordable. While a scientific or medical journal might cost thousands of dollars per subscription, this is not the case in Germanistik. For example, membership in the Canadian Association of University Teachers of German costs $50. With the membership comes a subscription to *Seminar*, a journal that is consistently ranked in the top journals supported by the Social Science and Humanities Research Council (SSHRC).

Resistance

For this reason, one can also understand why there might be some resistance to electronic journals. One of the main reasons for considering electronic publishing is cost. In the case of Germanistik, and one might easily generalize in this case to include all of the humanities, savings are not significant, and the initial outlay of capital for the conversion to an electronic format would take too long to recover.

Augmenting paper journals with electronic versions

An analysis of the journal-reading patterns of Germanists, regardless of what they might think of electronic journals, is, however, a compelling argument for augmenting the current paper journals with electronic versions. When asked about their reading habits, 89% of respondents said that they skimmed the contents of journals and read an article if it seemed of interest. The remaining 11% skimmed the contents, read the articles that seemed of interest, and then proceeded to read all of the book reviews. In essence, the journal served the function of a scholarly index and in many respects was used in the same way that one might use a search engine on the World Wide Web. While one cannot make an economic argument for electronic journals in Germanistik, one can certainly argue the efficiency of the electronic medium over paper.

Prestige of electronic journals

In addition to collecting data on how Germanists use, or do not use, the scholarly journal, information on how they regard the position of the electronic journal within their scholarly community was recorded. While only 36% of Germanists subscribed to or used electronic journals, 58% said they would be willing to submit an article to such a journal. (In reaching this figure, I disqualified those who responded in a non-committal way.) While the users of e-journals are not yet the majority, it would appear that the majority are willing to give qualified support to the idea of "electronic" scholarship.

This addresses an issue that is seldom broached in the context of scholarly journals and their function within the academic community. One of the main purposes of academic publishing as extrapolated from the responses to this survey is not so much the issues that are dealt with in a given article, but the value publication has in building an impressive CV for the purposes of tenure and promotion. Resistance to electronic publishing might stem from the fact that research findings will be exposed to a wider audience, providing potential for greater scrutiny and attack. In addition, the searchability of the World Wide Web means more difficulty in recycling old articles and receiving academic credit twice for the same work.

Respondents' concerns

In addition to specific questions, respondents were given the opportunity to comment on the answers they gave. Seventy-two percent of those who said that they would accept information that came from an electronic source also stated that they had some reservations.

Verification

Twenty-seven percent of the respondents said that they were unsure how to verify cited information. Their primary concern was how to find information cited by someone else—a concern that results from the lack of standardization in electronic journals. When dealing with a paper journal, a citation will take the reader to within a paragraph or two of where the reference can be found. While one could counter-argue that the search functions available today make it easier to verify information obtained from an electronic source, a large number of colleagues view this as too much work.

Another 45% would only accept the citation if they knew that a peer-review process was in place to ensure the reliability of the information being used. While certainly some electronic sources are almost beyond reproach, the proliferation of electronic sources may have the effect of calling even the most reputable electronic journals into question.

Changing URLs

Another concern raised by 21% of the respondents was that the virtual journal was simply too "virtual." For many, the journal—electronic or otherwise—does not exist until it is printed on paper. A connected problem is that the e-journal seems to move around too much. A change in an URL constitutes, as far as many readers are concerned, a physical move, which undermines the journal's credibility. If one is never sure that the address cited this week will allow a subsequent reader to access the same information next week, then there is reason to be suspicious of the citation in the first place. Germanists surveyed in this study will not cite or accept information they cannot verify easily. While this point might be turned aside by the confident computer user, the unsure user will most likely remain sceptical of information that does not appear to have any permanence, or that has, at the very least, a short shelf life.

Reliability

The gravest concern respondents had about electronic journals was the reliability of information. When allowed to comment freely on the concept of the electronic journal, 68% mentioned this issue. Some representative comments follow:

- "Is the material authentic, reliable, and quotable?"
- "[Electronic journals] are not recognized yet institutionally. They have an extreme virtual existence."
- "[They are] not refereed, [are held in] low esteem, [and] lack durability."
- "[They have] very uneven credibility."
- "Consumers are very wary about quality. What will my peers think? Print journals still have more prestige."
- "[There] is no control of quality. Too many articles [that have been] rejected elsewhere appear in e-journals."

Whether these comments are fact or fiction is unimportant. Journals sell perceived prestige and perceived esteem. Respondents associated little prestige or esteem with the material that is available electronically. Of greater concern is that the above comments are not from those who do not accept e-journals as legitimate, but from those who are willing to give the electronic medium a chance. In fact, the majority of the above comments were taken from respondents who embrace electronic journals as a useful tool. It is clear that something must be done to bolster the image of the e-journal before it can be accepted on par with paper-based journals.

Graduate students' perspective

A further question to be considered when looking at the scholarly journal and its role in academic life is how it is viewed by graduate students. Whereas academics with tenured or tenure-track positions look at the scholarly journal primarily as a means of building careers and reputations, graduate students use it to acquire careers in the first place. Initially, it was thought that graduate students' usage patterns would vary from those of their mentors, but the results indicated this is only true to an extent. Graduate students, while subscribing to less than one journal each on average, are the big users of the libraries—they access and read a far greater number of journals than their teachers. They are in the business of acquiring a reliable repertoire of sources for their dissertations and their hoped-for careers. For them, the major problem is the sheer volume of material that they need to digest.

However, in this survey, students were the smallest group of e-journal users. Despite the fact that they all have computer accounts and are familiar with the computer, the Internet, and the World Wide Web, they are concerned that citing an electronic source will put the quality of their dissertations in question. They are unwilling to gamble their careers on the possibility that someone on their dissertation committee will not like citations of electronic sources. This problem will only be resolved when electronic journals are more widely accepted.

Future considerations

The survey results lead to the following conclusions, some of which are already part of the electronic scholarly journal debate.

Electronic journals in smaller disciplines

Libraries, to the extent that they collect periodicals for the smaller disciplines, do not provide sufficient journal material to support effective research in these disciplines. (Many professors already collect this material on their own.) Germanists, and in this case all academics, spend a great deal of time skimming journals looking for sources of information, spending hours doing what a computer could do with far greater accuracy in seconds. These two issues can be addressed by making the move to digitized journals. This is not to say that every back issue needs to be in an electronic format, just those that are recognized within disciplines as being the most important.

Scholars' responsibility

Scholars will need to take greater responsibility for communicating the results of their research. Perhaps the humanities serves as a model. Right now, in the production of paper-based or electronic journals the author must do a great deal of the work in document preparation to create camera-ready copy. Coupled with electronic publishing, the university community has an economical means of producing journals. The document can be posted directly to a WWW site at little additional cost. An article appearing in a paper journal incurs the added cost of printing and distribution. Electronic publishing allows the producers of scholarship to retain ownership of that which they have created. If the electronic alternative is not taken, journals will continue to concern themselves more with the corporate bottom line than scholarly excellence and academic concerns.

The perception of instability

Electronic journals appear to move around too much and give the impression of being too unstable. This must be remedied. We will need to insist that electronic journals' URLs do not change or give the appearance of changing. This is something that can be achieved if users insist that the operators of our networks not constantly change addresses.

Standardized formats

A major impediment to the acceptance of the e-journal is lack of a standardized format. One would certainly not want to argue against healthy diversity, but, if too much diversity continues in the formatting of electronic journals, then the greater academic community will not accept this new medium, despite the efficiencies it offers. A national committee should be struck to develop a set of formatting guidelines for electronic journals. In doing so, Canadian universities could take the lead internationally in the development of the electronic journal as a reliable means of exchanging knowledge.

Credibility

Electronic journals have not yet established credibility within the scholarly community because they lack much of what lends prestige to a journal. The most important is the appearance of a reliable system of checks, which ensures the information's reliability. The information must not only be reliable but it must also appear to be reliable. Anyone with a rudimentary knowledge of hypertext markup language (HTML) and a little bit of money can post an "article" on the World Wide Web. While it may be easy to determine the reliability of material that appears on a Web site upon reading it, it takes too much time to separate all of the grain from the chaff given the proliferation of information that appears on the Web. This results in legitimate scholarly work being lost in the noise of cybertrash. As long as it remains an impediment to the broad acceptance of the electronic medium as a reliable means of publishing research, electronic journals will need to promote how they ensure the reliability of the research they publish.

Safeguards to ensure the scholarly value of an electronic journal are one thing, academics' belief that a rigorous refereeing process is in place is quite another. The fact is that the majority of Germanists in the survey (68%) believe that the scholarship published in today's electronic journals is second rate or even third rate, undergoing little or questionable peer review. To gain credibility in the scholarly community, electronic journals need to demonstrate their value as scholarly tools.

This should be approached in two ways. Existing journals should be encouraged to produce electronic versions of their current offerings and eventually their back issues as well. Financial and technical incentives should be offered that will enable these journals to make the transition to the electronic format. In the long term, a saving should be realized. While e-journals that are offshoots of prestigious paper journals will have little trouble making the transition to the electronic format, a greater difficulty will be encountered by those that do not have a prestigious paper-based parallel. As soon as possible, these journals need to establish credibility and demonstrate that they will not simply publish other journals' rejects.

A voluntary accreditation system should be introduced for electronic journals. This system would be comprised of a committee that investigates individual publishing practices. It would ensure the reliability of the research that is published. Such a committee would not dictate the content of a given journal, but it would grant accreditation on the basis of the journal's refereeing process, accessibility, and format.

The accreditation committee should also audit the accredited journals on an annual basis to ensure the continued quality of the journal. In this way, scholars would be more likely to support and use electronic journals, because they could rely on a minimum standard based on its accreditation.

Conclusion

There is no question that the scholarly journal will undergo a great deal of change over the coming years. It might be in order to rethink what the scholarly journal really is. The results of the survey are conclusive on this point—scholarly journals are little more than databases. Journal users treat them in exactly the same way that one might treat any database—with a concern for reliability, value, and consistency.

Information-Seeking Practices of Canadian Academic Chemists: A Study of Information Needs and Use of Resources in Chemistry

Ruth L. Noble & Carol Coughlin
Concordia University

Abstract: This paper presents selected results from a survey of Canadian academic chemists carried out in March 1996. These focus on the chemists' use of the journal literature and aspects of their experience with new information technologies. A discussion of these issues as they relate to libraries and scholarly communication is included.

Résumé: Cet article présente un choix de résultats obtenus lors d'un sondage effectué auprès de chimistes de certaines universités canadiennes au mois de mars 1996. Ces résultats portent sur l'utilisation des périodiques et des nouvelles technologies de l'information. L'article inclut aussi une discussion de ces sujets dans le contexte des bibliothèques universitaires et de la communication savante.

The study was carried out to investigate patterns of research and information-seeking practices of chemists in Canadian universities. The purpose was to obtain a better understanding of academic chemists' information needs, preferences, and practices; their experiences with new information technologies; and their perceptions of the university libraries' capacity to meet these information needs. There were no hypotheses being tested; the study was intended to produce a portrait of the survey population at that given time. It was hoped that this would then be useful when information issues concerning chemists were undergoing consideration.

Ruth L. Noble and Carol Coughlin are associate librarians at Webster Library, Concordia University, 1455 de Maisonneuve West, Montreal, QC H3G 1M8. E-mail: noblerl@vax2.concordia.ca and cbc@alcor.concordia.ca

Canadian Journal of Communication, Vol. 22, No. 3/4 (1997) 49-60

A number of factors had suggested this study would be a timely undertaking. The first was the rapidly expanding volume of the chemical literature. *Chemical Abstracts*, which began in 1907 with abstracts of a modest 11,847 publications, has now reached over 16 million records (Chemical Abstracts Service, Columbus, OH, personal communication, February 27, 1997). Looking at this as a present rate of 13,000 journal articles and other documents per week, it is clear that current awareness would be a challenge for chemists, particularly those doing considerable research. The second factor was the cost associated with obtaining this literature. The cost of journals in the sciences and their continuing escalation has been well documented. Journals in chemistry have been top of the average price list for many years. The 1992 study prepared for the Andrew W. Mellon Foundation gives an historical development picture of the ongoing serials cost situation (Cummings, Witte, Bowen, Lazarus, & Ekman, 1992). A good summary of the history of scientific journals and related issues appears in Schaffner (1994). Thirdly, libraries have generally seen their budgets for collections unable to keep up with inflation and publishers' subscription price increases. The result of this situation has been the inability of university libraries to maintain the collections of journals that have traditionally supported work of their chemistry faculties. Finally, there was the proliferation of electronically based information resources and growth of the Internet, which were radically changing the information environment.

Literature review

A review of the literature found little that specifically looked at Canadian chemists and their information practices. In 1975, Katherine Packer's dissertation presented results of a survey of faculty in departments of chemistry and chemical engineering at Canadian universities. Her study was designed to investigate how scientists maintain current awareness in their fields of specialization and to discover the relative importance of their various means of communication, both formal and informal. A study by Schuegraf, Keliher, & van Bommel in 1992 looked at personal journal subscriptions of science faculty at a small undergraduate university, St. Francis Xavier University, and overlap with the library collections, among other factors. Recent works originating in Australia, Britain, and the United States, have examined use of the literature and information technology by scientists, particularly or including chemists. These include articles by Adams & Bonk (1995), Charton (1992), Heller (1994), Llull (1991), Meadows & Buckle (1992), Pötzscher & Wilson (1990), Rice & Tarin (1993), Schauder (1994), and Williams (1993). Jan Olsen's book (1994) reports on in-depth interviews with 16 chemists, as well as other scholars. From the British Library, of particular interest are the report by Philip & Cunningham (1995) and a 1993 Royal Society report which examined in detail the scientific, technical, and medical information system in the United Kingdom. Our study has adapted elements from many of the above to create a survey instrument from which data collected could be compared with certain earlier results. Many works on electronic journals appeared after this survey, and will be significant as electronic chemistry literature develops; these include the report on the CORE project (Stewart, 1996) and an extensive study by Harter & Kim (1996).

Survey population

Because the pressures of information gathering were likely to be heaviest upon academic chemists expected to do the most research, faculty in departments with graduate programs were the target population. University calendar lists of faculty in departments of chemistry and of chemistry and biochemistry that had doctoral programs were used to identify names of faculty and the number of faculty in the departments. Emeritus professors and certain names clearly associated with technical support or other adjunct positions were excluded.

The departments were placed into three categories based on number of faculty—small being less than 25; medium-sized, 25 to 35; and large being over 35 members. Twelve departments from nine provinces were then selected to achieve a geographical balance. The number of faculty in each category of faculty size was comparable. Biochemists in separate departments of biochemistry or within other departments like medicine were not surveyed. Chemical engineers were also excluded.

Survey methodology

Questionnaires were sent to individual faculty in each of the departments selected to be surveyed. The questionnaire was accompanied by a letter explaining the purpose of the survey, as well as a return envelope. Space for written comments was included on the questionnaire. Further detail about the methodology and survey instrument can be obtained from the authors.

Responses and the respondents

Of 355 questionnaires sent, 131 usable returns represented a 37% return rate. This is 19% of the number of faculty in departments which met our original criteria.

The 131 respondents represent the primary sub-fields of chemistry, and included 11 analytical, 26 inorganic, 38 organic, and 35 physical chemists as well as 18 biochemists. Two respondents gave their fields as education, and one did not identify a specialty. By faculty rank, just over 50% were full professors, 28% were associate professors, and 15% assistant professors; 6% held other ranks. By age groupings, 53% were over 50 years of age, 23% each in the 40-to-49 and 30-to-39 age groups. Only one respondent was under 30.

Nearly 70% supervised graduate students at master's or doctoral level or both. More than one half the respondents spent greater than 45% of their time doing research, with half of this group (one quarter of respondents) estimating that research took over 60% of their time. Two thirds of respondents had done research in collaboration with faculty at other Canadian or international universities during the past three years. In the same time span, just under one half of respondents had done some amount of research on contract with industry or external organizations.

The use of journals

How important are journals to these academic chemists? Browsing print journals in their specialty was ranked highest (85% agreement) of all activities that the chemists relied upon to keep up to date with the literature in their fields of interest. When asked how often they find important articles by browsing recent journal issues, 78% replied either "very often" or "quite often." The importance of browsing journals has been well documented in investigations of the information-seeking habits of scientists for many years. Don Schauder (1994, p. 84) summarizes a number of studies attesting to the prevalence and value of browsing to academics.

Asked to indicate the number of journals significantly related to their current primary research fields, 40% stated "more than 10" and 43% "between 6 and 9." Of the 131 respondents, 98 have personal subscriptions to journals; most of these have 3 or fewer subscriptions, 23 have between 4 and 6, while 4 chemists stated they get more than 6 journals. Charton (1992, p. 201) found that chemists pay for books and journal subscriptions to support their research "both from their own funds and with whatever grant and departmental money they have available." The chemists interviewed by Olsen (1994, p.16) subscribed to an average of five journals each.

How do libraries fit into the journal picture? The chemists were asked approximately how many journals they would "try not to miss" scanning regularly in university library collections. Responses ranged from "none" (6%) to "more than 10" (21%); 38% replied 6 to 9, and 1 to 5 journals was the response of 34%. To compare, a British study gives the average number of journals that 97 chemists (90 academics) try not to miss as 11.72 (Williams, 1993). Many of the Canadian chemists said that most of the journals they themselves subscribe to are also available in their university's library, although 13 chemists replied that few or none of their subscriptions were. Asked to rate their university's performance in subscribing to the journals they need, 45% rated this "acceptable," 30% "good," and 20% "poor." A similar distribution of opinion was found in an international survey of 582 academics in Australia, the U.K., and the U.S. who were asked to rate their university's journal provision performance (Schauder, 1994, p. 90).

Current awareness strategies

Is information overload a reality for academic chemists? Respondents were asked to express a level of agreement or disagreement with the statement: "It is virtually impossible to keep up with the literature." Only 9% strongly disagreed. Those who agreed (41) or strongly agreed (41) were 63% of the survey group, or 82 of 131 respondents. It is interesting to compare with the early-1970s' survey of Canadian chemists and chemical engineers, where only 34 of 135 said they had difficulty keeping up to date, and only 4 of these acknowledged "great difficulty" in doing so (Packer, 1975, p. 56).

Reconciling the traditional behaviour of browsing with the volume of published material, chemists have developed the following strategies in their information gathering: Replying to questions on using the literature to keep up to date, 80% agreed that they tend to skim rather than read literature; 78% agreed that they have little time to read non-central articles; 77% agreed that they read more abstracts than complete papers. Generally the chemists considered the abstract to be either somewhat or very reliable as an indicator of the interest an article will hold for them. Almost 60% of those surveyed agreed that for current awareness they rely considerably on Tables of Contents (TOCs) from print or electronic sources. However, in a related question intended to corroborate opinions on TOCs, 46% agreed that Tables of Contents alone are not very useful. Clearly, sources that provide abstracts are considered more valuable. Organic chemists in particular commented that current awareness is strongly dependent upon being able to actually skim journals and see the graphic content because of the importance of chemical structures. Chemists interviewed by Olsen (1994, p. 33) strongly pointed out the need to have such graphics in any electronic journal.

Some electronic information resources were being used as current-awareness providers. Of our 131 respondents, 23 received updating services in CD-ROM format and 15 received journals on CD-ROM; however, only six chemists had journals electronically delivered. There were, in fact, not many electronic journals in chemistry at the time of the survey, although some full-text versions of print journals were available. This is illustrated by the relatively small number of articles from e-journals indexed by *Chemical Abstracts*. Editor David Weisgerber (1996) has pointed out that only 210 electronic papers from 14 on-line journals and 45 papers from two on-line conferences have made the cut since April 1995.

The "invisible college" and informal communication are still important to the chemists surveyed. In keeping current, 44% of the chemists relied considerably on colleagues and external collaborators; 33% indicated they kept up better by attending conferences than by reading. Thus, personal contacts rather than the literature alone are significant to many of these chemists. Electronic mail has greatly facilitated communication among networks of contacts in the research communities. Although 10% of respondents said they rarely or never used e-mail, 83% used it daily. Only 27% of respondents regularly accessed electronic bulletin boards or listservs. Pre-prints and pre-publication works by other researchers were important and relied upon by 20% of those surveyed.

Familiarity with electronic equipment and resources

Among the chemists surveyed, 99% had computers, 89% had access to communication software, and 87% were connected to the campus network, although it is not clear whether this network access was direct or by dial-in. Some replied specifically that they lacked ethernet connection. Fax was accessible to 97%, mostly at departmental offices. CD-ROM-equipped computers were available to 64% of the chemists. Asked to rate their knowledge of electronic information technology, 57% said it was "moderate," and 55% gave the same moderate ranking to their knowledge of how to access relevant electronic resources.

How have the chemists learned about computers and information technology? Primarily they are self-taught (78%), but they have also learned from colleagues (70%). In some instances (37%) there has been a "computer expert" on the department staff, with this response perhaps including fellow faculty as well as individuals hired to give computer support in departments or labs. Some 22% indicated they have received some information via the library, but only 17% have received help from computing services departments at their universities. Many respondents indicated that they learned from their students.

What electronic information resources were the chemists using? Some 40% used the campus on-line catalogue at least weekly; for others, use was monthly, rarely, or never. Databases and indexes available on the campus network or catalogue were used by 60%, while only 25% regularly used databases on CD-ROM in the library. (The resources actually available will of course vary from institution to institution.) Index and abstract databases from commercial systems were used by 43%, with 77% indicating they had database literature searches done at varying frequencies during a year. A considerable number of chemists considered their knowledge on how to use the Internet and World Wide Web moderate to good, 41% and 37% respectively. Their familiarity with specialized software for information retrieval within the chemistry field was rated "moderate" by 32%, with 56% rating themselves "poor" in this area.

Obstacles to using electronic information technology

Chemists were asked to check one or more obstacles they believed hindered them in their use of electronic information technologies. Results are presented in Table 1.

Table 1
Obstacles to Using Electronic Information Technologies

	Percentage of respondents
Lack time to explore technologies	73%
Lack operating funds	38%
Lack training in how to access electronic resources	35%
Lack information on available databases/resources	24%
Lack hardware	15%
Lack software	15%
Lack interest or need	11%

Fifteen of the 131 chemists reported that they lacked interest or need to use these technologies. One said, "I like to browse print on paper" (and added in parentheses, "old man!"); another commented, "I like to read, I resist the 'electronic world,' I recognize that it is the way of the future but. . . ." It would seem that, having established patterns that worked for you in the past, motivation to change is not automatic. Why attempt unproven practices for literature searching, particularly if the tools needed are regarded as less than straightforward in their functions—and less than user friendly, as some comments expressed.

Neither lack of hardware nor of software was viewed as a major obstacle to exploring new technologies, but lack of information on what resources were available, as well as lack of training in how to access these resources, were felt to be greater impediments. The most frequently noted obstacle was lack of time to explore the technologies. The multiple responsibilities of chemists in academia make this understandable.

To illustrate with the chemists' own words:

- "The biggest problem is TIME. Given the time, the facilities are available and simply require training. My graduate students have these skills, and I rely on them for information and/or help."
- "I would be thrilled to have greater access to on-line search/retrieval programs and journals, but know little about this area. . . . It's frustrating knowing that these new technologies exist but that I just don't know how to access them."
- "Finding the *time* to keep current, whether this refers to the literature or the technology to access it, is my biggest difficulty."
- "The software is not yet sufficiently "user friendly" and takes too much of my time."

The problems created by lack of operating funds can perhaps best be summed up by the following statement from an assistant professor of organic chemistry, in the under-40 age group, who spends over 60% of his or her time in research:

> [The] biggest problem is COST. We get less [financial] support from our administration each year. This means fewer journals each year. But less support also means the cost of on-line or CD-ROM access is more and more passed on to individual researchers. But . . . NSERC [National Sciences and Engineering Research Council of Canada] grants are smaller each year too, and chemicals cost more each year, so I don't have any money to buy access to the on-line journals, etc., which are supposed to replace the "expensive" bound journals. Result: my information-gathering ability gets less each year. [And in capital letters, the following:] LIBRARY ACCESS IS VITAL INFRASTRUCTURE!

The library as infrastructure

From the library perspective, the question is: How well can academic libraries provide this infrastructure? There is less money in the system for research, for universities, and for libraries. Driven by cost and technology factors, libraries are trying to deal with the rapid transition into the electronic information age. Our ability to maintain our contribution to the continuum that is the chemists' scholarly communication process seems threatened.

Our portrait of 131 academic chemists one year ago shows them to be versatile in their information gathering. Journals are still the main vehicle for their formal communication and it is essential that researchers know what has just been published in them in order to keep up with their fields. If present pricing and budget trends continue, libraries will have to continue to cancel journals and the opportunities for browsing print will become rarer. But before we are too quick to say that there are other obvious alternatives for current awareness, we should reflect that there is more to traditional browsing of journal issues than the comfortable feel of paper and convenient portability. Jan Olsen's 1994 study on electronic journal literature included in-depth interviews with a group of chemists. A significant conclusion is that:

> [Their] actual purposes in interacting with the literature are learning, creative thinking, and analytical thinking. . . . Functions such as selecting articles or browsing the latest literature appear to be tasks which a computer can be programmed to perform well, but in practice the computer performs them *quickly*, but *not* well. (p. 71)

Academic chemists already use electronically based information resources and continue to adapt their information-seeking habits. What they miss in this transition from print to electronic browsing is the likelihood of unexpectedly encountering something exciting in the literature strictly through serendipity.

Chemists see journal collections shrinking, but, not unreasonably, expect their libraries to continue as the main provider of information resources. They also recognize that more of these resources likely are going to be electronic.

They will be more willing to make the transition to electronic resources if they get adequate content and coverage of the literature as well as convenience of access. Already, a range of electronic products, systems, and delivery mechanisms exist that can serve chemists. For librarians, this raises several questions: How can libraries make the best choices? What resources can we afford to provide, particularly if the user group is relatively small? Can we find advantages by contracting through local or national consortia?

Another issue for academic libraries is our mixed user population and the need to provide for students who use the collections. Their journal usage and requirements do not necessarily parallel or coincide with faculty research interests. Libraries have to strive to maintain core journals regardless of format in order to serve this group as well. If we decide to provide electronic access to resources that students will need to use, off-site access is almost essential if we want to maximize our investment. Universities then need to have adequately networked systems to provide this access to their student population. Harter & Kim (1996, p. 453) conclude that since many users will not have the necessary hardware and software to utilize e-journals on their own computers, academic libraries will need to provide appropriate equipment and software for users to access e-journals and to print and manipulate related files. Are there then any cost savings to be realized by abandoning print journals in favour of electronic?

The chemists see the costs of obtaining information being passed on to them. They may subscribe to some journals, but most are out of reach because of price. On-line databases, particularly those from Chemical Abstracts Service, have always provided the best comprehensive coverage of the latest chemical literature, as well as the most precision for specialized topics; for these, there are searching charges. Chemists must now get more articles from outside their own libraries as local collections are cut back. Our survey showed that very few chemists ordered documents from commercial services, but used the library to obtain them. Since chemists usually pay at least part of the cost for each article, these costs for document delivery add up. What part of these costs can and should libraries absorb, given their own financial constraints and responsibilities to other services and users?

One of the chemists commented, "I prefer to get my information free over the Internet." Another stated, "Inexpensive electronic media (literature searches, on-line journals) are very useful." Electronic journals and databases can reach scholars' desktops, and indications are that they will be used, if their costs are not prohibitive. There are assumptions that electronic publications will be (or should be) cheaper than any print equivalent, but to date these expectations have not proven realistic. Publishers of scholarly journals point to the printing and distribution costs as only a small part of the final cost of production. In the electronic sector, publishers have the potential to widen their user base by offering affordable products, both to the scholar and to the institutions. The pricing models for electronic subscriptions alone and for combined print with electronic access are still "under construction." This complicates library decisions because we are less able to predict what next year will bring. One model, that of charging an additional fee to the print subscription cost for "value-added" access to the electronic version, seems to many librarians as extractive, and a policy to be resisted.

Bridging the transitional challenges

From the data and chemists' comments, there appear to be three major areas where changes and improvements will assist in enhancing their adoption of, and adaptation to, an increasingly larger electronic realm.

Operating fund support

Libraries and universities have an obligation to support their academic programs and research. However, reality for these institutions often means a precarious balancing act of attempting to confront shrinking institutional budgets, maintain serials collections as prices constantly rise, providing more services in electronic formats, and moving to a greater reliance on document delivery services. As a result, some of the information acquisition costs are being shifted onto the shoulders of the users.

Research funding agencies must recognize that the costs of acquiring information are rising and researchers may require increased support when local institutions cannot meet their needs. Concurrently, researchers must anticipate their information acquisition requirements and incorporate these costs in applications for grants.

Technology support

The basic hardware infrastructure has to be in place to enable connectivity for the individual researcher. Campuses and libraries need to be networked to a currently acceptable standard, which will permit high-speed transmission of text and data. Additionally, the on-site hardware and software must be capable of receiving electronic journals and databases with images and specialized data.

Training support

Linked to the technology support is, of course, the ongoing need for training to enable individuals to use equipment and hardware at levels appropriate to their needs. Training, whether institutionally supported by programs and services offered by computing services, the library, or elsewhere, remains important to a percentage of faculty for development of their information technology skills.

Libraries have traditionally provided training and instruction in the use of their resources and will continue in this role. Now, however, given the widespread non-standardization of interfaces, publishers and producers cannot assume that librarians have the time or staff to act as on-site experts or product promoters on their behalf. Publishers and producers need to supply clear information about their electronic products that is geared towards new users, detailing what they need to have and how to go about using a particular resource. "User friendly" should really be the operative term for all products, including those in information technology. And the less training involved the better, because time is the least available commodity in the chemist's repertoire.

We may not be able to provide time—the essential ingredient which these chemists lack—but adequate hardware, software, networked connections to electronic resources, and training to use them should be within our collective capacity to arrange. It is certain that, to achieve conditions that encourage scholarly communication in an electronic age, we must have ongoing and constant technical support by all of the agencies that form part of the chain. It will be then that the initiatives of the individual participants can flourish.

References

Adams, Judith A., & Bonk, Sharon C. (1995, March). Electronic information technologies and resources: Use by university faculty and faculty preferences for related library services. *College & Research Libraries*, *56*, 119-131.

Charton, Barbara. (1992). Chemsits' [*sic*] use of libraries. *Journal of Chemical Information & Computer Sciences*, *32*(3), 199-203.

Cummings, Anthony M., Witte, Marcia L., Bowen, William G., Lazarus, Laura O., & Ekman, Richard H. (1992). *University libraries and scholarly communication: A study prepared for the Andrew W. Mellon Foundation*. Washington, DC: Association of Research Libraries.

Harter, Stephen P., & Kim, Hak Joon. (1996, September). Accessing electronic journals and other e-publications. *College & Research Libraries*, *57*, 440-456.

Heller, Stephen R. (1994). Gazing into the future of chemical information activities. In H. Collier (Ed.), *Further advances in chemical information* (pp. 16-34). Proceedings of the Montreux International Chemical Information Conference, Annecy, France, October 18-20, 1993 (Special Publication 142). Cambridge, UK: Royal Society of Chemistry.

Llull, Harry. (1991). Meeting the academic and research information needs of scientists and engineers in the university environment. In Cynthia Steinke (Ed.), *Information seeking and communicating behavior of scientists and engineers* (pp. 83-90). New York: Haworth Press.

Meadows, A. J., & Buckle, P. (1992, September). Changing communication activities in the British scientific community. *Journal of Documentation*, *48*, 276-290.

Olsen, Jan. (1994). *Electronic journal literature: Implications for scholars*. Westport: Mecklermedia.

Packer, Katherine Helen. (1975). *Methods used by chemists and chemical engineers in Canadian universities to maintain current awareness with special reference to the use of SDI systems*. Unpublished doctoral dissertation, University of Maryland.

Philip, G., with the assistance of Cunningham, F. P. (1995). *Availability and use of automated chemical information systems by academic chemists in the United Kingdom* (Report No. 6184). [London]: British Library Research & Development Department.

Pötzscher, Gunter, & Wilson, A. J. C. (1990). User needs in chemical information. *Journal of Chemical Information & Computer Sciences*, *30*(2), 169-173.

Rice, Ronald E., & Tarin, Patricia. (1993, October). Staying informed: Scientific communication and use of information sources within disciplines. *Proceedings of the 56th American Society for Information Science Annual Meeting* (pp. 160-164). Medford, NJ: Learned Information.

Royal Society. (1993). *The scientific, technical, and medical information system in the UK* (British Library Research & Development Department Report No. 6123). [London]: Royal Society, The British Library, and The Association of Learned and Professional Society Publishers.

Schaffner, Ann C. (1994, December). The future of scientific journals: Lessons from the past. *Information Technology and Libraries*, *3*(4), 239-247.

Schauder, Don. (1994). Electronic publishing of professional articles: Attitudes of academics and implications for the scholarly communication industry. *Journal of the American Society for Information Science*, *45*(2), 73-100.

Schuegraf, Ernst J., Keliher, Liam T., & van Bommel, Martin F. (1992). An analysis of personal journal subscriptions of university faculty. Part I. Science. *Journal of the American Society for Information Science*, *43*(1), 28-33.

Stewart, Linda. (1996, July). User acceptance of electronic journals: Interviews with chemists at Cornell University. *College & Research Libraries*, *57*, 339-349.

Weisgerber, David W. (1996, December 9). Few electronic papers make the grade at Chemical Abstracts [Interview]. *Chemical & Engineering News*, *74*, 32.

Williams, Ivor A. (1993, April). How chemists use the literature. *Learned Publishing*, *6*, 7-14.

Human and Economic Factors Affecting the Acceptance of Electronic Journals by Readers

Fytton Rowland, Ian Bell, & Catherine Falconer
Loughborough University, UK

Abstract: Human factors that influence the acceptability of electronic journals to users include the interface, the hypertext structure, the searching and browsing functionalities, and the speed of the network response. Economic factors that influence the progress of electronic journals include not only the level of prices charged, but also the pricing structures adopted. Three recent studies of the acceptance of electronic journals by users and other published work are considered. It is concluded that the continued provision of high-quality scholarly publications to readers in the electronic era will require that publishers provide the needed design quality at prices that are significantly lower than those charged today for printed journals.

Résumé : Parmi les influences humaines sur le degré d'acceptabilité de journaux électroniques pour les lecteurs, il y a l'interface, la structure hypertextuelle, la facilité de faire des recherches et d'explorer, et le temps de réponse d'un réseau. Parmi les influences économiques, il y a non seulement le montant chargé pour un journal électronique, mais aussi les structures de prix adoptées. Nous considérons trois études récentes sur l'acceptabilité de journaux électroniques pour les usagers et ces travaux et d'autres études publiées. Nous concluons que les éditeurs de journaux électroniques devront fournir une mise en page comparable à celles de journaux publiés, mais ce à un prix bien plus bas, s'ils veulent continuer à produire des publications savantes de haute qualité pour leurs lecteurs à l'ère électronique.

Fytton Rowland is a lecturer in the Department of Information and Library Studies, Loughborough University, Loughborough, Leicestershire, UK LE11 3TU. E-mail: J.F.Rowland@lboro.ac.uk
Ian Bell is Senior Information Executive at the British Tourist Authority, Thames Tower, Black's Road, Hammersmith, London, UK W6 9EL. E-mail: ibell@mail.bta.org.uk
Catherine Falconer is an assistant librarian at Brooklands College of Further and Higher Education, Heath Road, Weybridge, Surrey, UK KT13 8TT. E-mail: ga23@dial.pipex.com

***Canadian Journal of Communication*, Vol. 22, No. 3/4 (1997) 61-75**

Introduction

Electronic publication of scholarly research findings has been the subject of a great deal of study, development, and comment over the last few years (Rowland, 1995). Much of this work has been technical and has concerned the provision of workable and trouble-free channels for the dissemination of information in electronic form. There has also been much comment, a large proportion of it taking place through electronic discussion lists and newsgroups, about the attitude of scholars to electronic publication. Most of this comment has, however, been concerned with the scholar as author and in particular has dealt with the acceptability of electronic publications for the purpose of measurement of scholarly output in considerations of job appointments, tenure, promotion, and research funding. Relatively few workers have considered the response of information users to electronic publications; this is unsurprising, because until recently the number of scholarly publications available in electronic form was small, and therefore there was necessarily little usage to observe.

This situation is now changing rapidly. The number of genuinely scholarly electronic periodicals has been charted regularly by such observers as Bailey (1997) and Okerson (1996), and, while still small compared with the total number of printed scholarly journals, the number of titles available free of charge over the Internet is now substantial. Harter & Kim (1996), however, have noted that the average size of these periodicals (in terms of number of articles published per annum) is small. Thus, if one measures publication by number of articles rather than number of periodicals, the electronic proportion becomes smaller.

The major breakthrough, however, has come with the decisions by most major publishers of established printed scholarly journals to make their titles available in parallel electronic and printed forms. Some publishers started their programs of conversion in 1995, more in 1996, and yet more in 1997. In the scientific, technical, and medical (STM) field, Hitchcock, Carr, & Hall (1996) looked at the situation at the close of 1995 and aptly subtitled their report *The Calm before the Storm*. The ready availability of hundreds of titles in electronic form, including many that are core journals of their respective scholarly disciplines, means that one can now mount realistic user studies of electronic scholarly journals.

Early electronic journal studies, such as the work of Senders (1977) and the BLEND and Quartet studies (Shackel, 1991; Tuck, McKnight, Hayet, & Archer, 1990), foundered largely on the inadequacy of the technical infrastructure available. Too few potential users had easy access to terminals; available networks were inadequate in capacity and quality of transmission; there was too much incompatibility between different software packages. Today, these constraints have been largely overcome, at least in the developed world.

Although much debate continues on electronic publishing discussion lists and newsgroups about detailed technical matters, problems on the technical side of electronic publishing may be regarded as soluble where they are not already solved.

Effective availability of electronic journals to users, especially to students and other users in universities, will therefore now depend on non-technical factors: principally the ergonomic acceptability of the interface provided and the economic availability of the journals to these users at an affordable price. These two types of factor are the subject of this paper.

Human factors: User studies of electronic journals

Several research studies on electronic journals have been undertaken at Loughborough University. Three—ELVYN, InfoTrain, and Café Jus—were funded by the British Library Research and Development Department (BLR&DD) (now renamed the British Library Research and Innovation Centre) (Meadows, Rowland, & Yates-Mercer, 1997; Rowland, McKnight, & Meadows, 1995; Woodward, McKnight, Meadows, Pritchett, & Rowland, 1997a, 1997b). Another two were the topics of masters' dissertations (Bell, 1996; Falconer, 1995). Two further BLR&DD-funded studies, one at Loughborough University concerning information-seeking behaviour of biological scientists (Rolinson, Meadows, & Smith, 1995) and one at the University of Sheffield (Wood, Ford, Miller, Sobczyk, & Duffin, 1996), which looked *inter alia* at the electronic information-seeking activities of academics at that university, are also examined.

ELVYN

The ELVYN (Electronic Versions: Why Not?) study (Rowland et al., 1995) focused on the electronic version of a single newly established journal from an established scientific publisher (Institute of Physics Publishing [IoPP]) entitled *Modelling and Simulation in Materials Science and Engineering* (*MSMSE*). IoPP wished to test a model that included electronic delivery of files to each individual institution. The journal was mounted on local machines at each participating university, for delivery over their own campus network. Part of the study involved testing usage of the electronic version of *MSMSE* with groups of materials-science students in each of the participating universities.

One important conclusion from the ELVYN study was that trained information specialists, when contemplating information retrieval, tend to think of a search mode for accessing information—that is, that the user arrives at the system with a particular information need and requires documents that provide the information. Academics and researchers, on the other hand, tend to assume a browsing mode—they look quickly through the latest issues of journals, trying to spot interesting articles. Interfaces have to allow for both modes of retrieval.

In ELVYN we interviewed potential users before the electronic journal system was designed, in order to provide facilities that the users wanted. However, even when a major effort had been made to provide the functions that materials scientists said that they wanted, it was difficult to recruit users for the experimental journal. Although the journal was newly launched in printed form, users with a research interest in its subject field had been sought. The conclusion that we drew from this was that to make it worthwhile for users to learn to use an electronic journals system, there needed to be a critical mass of journals available. They did not see the point in climbing the learning curve to use one journal.

ELVYN used several different methods to distribute the data at different universities. The most commonly used was a World Wide Web (WWW) interface, with the papers tagged in hypertext markup language (HTML) that was algorithmically derived from the publisher's standard generalized markup language (SGML) coding. At that time, HTML could not handle special characters (the Greek alphabet and mathematical symbols), so these items had to be converted algorithmically into small in-line graphics. Downloading and display of these graphics slowed down considerably the delivery of files to the user. Furthermore, the early version of HTML in use at that time did not allow very ready provision of tables. The figures in the papers had to be displayed by another viewer program (External Viewer, xv), which had to be launched each time a user wished to view a graphic. All of these problems have, of course, to varying degrees since been solved. But the difficulty encountered in ELVYN in providing the service required by materials scientists did emphasize that scientific users require a solution to the problems of graphics, tables, and special characters before an electronic journal is regarded as satisfactory.

Another university was using a WAIS server at the time. Users could search the full texts but not display their hits; they had to request a printout from the university computer centre. Not surprisingly, at this location "Lack of figures, tables, and equations" was listed as the chief disadvantage, but "Fast searching" as the chief advantage.

InfoTrain

The InfoTrain (Training Electronic Journal) project (Meadows et al., 1997) created an electronic journal jointly between three universities (two in the U.K. and one in Australia), specifically for the purpose of teaching information-science students how to create, how to use, and how to assist clients to use electronic journals. This study was predicated on the assumption that one could not modify or alter the structure of a real electronic journal available on the World Wide Web, but a journal created specifically for teaching purposes could be modified by students themselves in the cause of active learning. Though this was not explicitly a user study, the initial responses of information students to design features of the InfoTrain journal, and the suggestions for improvement that they have made, provided useful data about human factors affecting the acceptability of electronic journals to real users.

One part of the course work undertaken by Loughborough undergraduate information studies students using the InfoTrain electronic journal involved a comparative evaluation of several electronic journals from a design point of view. They were asked to compare the designs used at the other two participating universities (the City University in London and the University of South Australia) with "real" electronic journals, one free and one commercial. Favourable and adverse comments were equal in number for the commercial journal, but were about 2:1 adverse to favourable for the other InfoTrain versions and for the free electronic journal. This latter ratio suggests that the application of professional design skills to an electronic journal does have some beneficial effects. Among the adverse comments were such things as: "Unable to see document as a whole," "Unable to change onscreen text size," "Hard to distinguish detail," which referred to the full-text display, "Problems accessing tables and figures," "Problems locating articles," and "Help function is of little use," which referred to difficulties in hypertext navigation.

Café Jus

Café Jus (Commercial and Free Electronic Journals User Study) is the most recent of these projects (Woodward et al., 1997a, 1997b). It took advantage of the much greater number of electronic journals available over the WWW in 1996 than before and investigated the usage of many different electronic journals, both commercial and free, by academic staff and postgraduate students in numerous departments at Loughborough University. Again its purpose was to cast light on those human factors that might limit or encourage the rapid acceptance of electronic journals by users. Important to this study, as to the earlier ELVYN study, was the fact that the users concerned were not necessarily enthusiasts for, or especially knowledgeable about, electronic journals or indeed information technology itself. They could be regarded as a cross-section of normal, average users of academic information—albeit located in a university where administrators at the highest levels hold considerable enthusiasm for information technology (IT), networking, and the Internet.

Groups of postgraduate students from six departments spread across engineering, science, and social science disciplines were shown how to access electronic journals, of which over 300 were provided by the university library at the time. They were asked to perform searches on one or more journals with subject coverage that was of real interest to them and then fill in a questionnaire giving their views of the journals (similar to the one used with undergraduates in the InfoTrain study). The most common difficulty was slow access time, especially for commercial publishers' sites that carry a large number of titles. Publishers need to recognize that if access via the Internet is to become a major feature of their product lines, they will need to invest in adequate hardware, software, and network links to provide reasonable speed of access to many users simultaneously. Recent anecdotal evidence, quoted in the general press in the U.K., suggests that Elsevier, at least, has appreciated this point. When launching their ScienceDirect service, which will include all Elsevier's titles and will be at least 10 times larger than any of the other publishers' services currently running, Elsevier admitted that this service when fully operational will be the largest installation linked to the Internet anywhere.

To reach an individual journal article from first logging on to the publisher's home page often involves passing through many navigational screens, and when access is slow this can be very frustrating. Again, as in ELVYN, there seems to be a lack of recognition that users wish to browse as well as search. In some cases, pretty appearance, dictated perhaps by the publisher's marketing department, seems to have taken precedence over efficiency of hypertext navigation (for example, by it not being obvious which colour of text is used for hotspots for hypertext links).

Most of the commercial journals, but few of the free ones, use page-integrity viewers such as Adobe Acrobat or RealPage. These require the users to have a copy of the viewer on their own machine; this is free of charge, but does have to be downloaded from a WWW site and does take up space on the user's machine. Students use open-access laboratories, where there is clearly competition for space on the machines with other more versatile programs such as statistics packages, spreadsheets, and graphics software. Publishers favour these viewers because, while permitting full-text searching, they preserve the design and appearance of the printed page. For users, however, this is not necessarily advantageous. Most machines now have Netscape (if not always the latest version), and so journals presented in HTML format can be read without the need for further software. Furthermore, the different shape of a printed page (vertical format) and the computer screen (horizontal) means that printed page designs, especially two- or three-column layouts, are unpleasant to read on the screen if page integrity is preserved. Many of the adverse comments in the questionnaire survey referred to the failings of Acrobat; its icons are not intuitive, for example, so it was not obvious to students that they could zoom to make the text larger and more legible. The attachment of publishers to page integrity may be misplaced, and may show a lack of appreciation that design criteria for an electronic publication are different from those of a printed one. The importance of really effective and intuitive hypertext link structures needs to be stressed. In this connection the Open Journal project, at Southampton University in the U.K., needs to be mentioned (Hitchcock, 1996). It seeks to provide software that facilitates the provision of the hypertext link structure separately from the information content.

Despite these criticisms, two thirds of the students found the electronic journals easier to access than the print versions. About the same proportion found the print version easier to use. This apparent contradiction is rationalized by suggesting that the hypertext navigational characteristics of electronic journals are appreciated as an aid to searching and browsing, but that once one has arrived at the full text that is wanted, it is more pleasant to read it in the print version.

Users in industry

One of us (Ian Bell) undertook research for a master's dissertation in a major pharmaceutical company, investigating attitudes to and usage of electronic journals by both information staff and laboratory research staff there (Bell, 1996; Bell & Rowland, 1997). This followed up an earlier comparative study (Rolinson et al., 1995) when the usage of IT generally was observed at the same company and compared with usage in other biological research establishments and biological departments in universities in the U.K. This study had demonstrated a considerably greater usage of electronic information sources in the industrial situation than in the academic world or government research laboratories, but was undertaken before many primary research journals were available in electronic form.

Bell used questionnaire surveys with two groups in the company: information services staff and laboratory research workers. He also interviewed managers in both types of department (information and research). The most striking findings were that the research staff were not only better informed about electronic journals and keener to use them than the information services staff assumed, but the researchers were also better informed about electronic journals than information services staff. This was a surprising finding, given that the information services department at the company in question has a high reputation in the U.K. information world. This finding contrasted sharply with the findings of our various user studies at Loughborough University.

In the pharmaceutical industry, it seems, the end users are now ready to use electronic information resources. However, they also had a lot more respect for electronic versions of established printed journals than they did for new electronic-only ones. This was because the recognized quality of the leading journals was of paramount importance. One research worker said, "Greater convenience is not sufficient justification for threatening the quality of our research enterprise." There was agreement among both information and research staff that both categories of worker needed training about electronic journals—and we in the universities would agree that we have a similar need. Research staff also appreciated the "gatekeeper" role of information staff: the work of evaluating, sorting, and sifting the mass of available information on behalf of the research staff remains a task for information professionals.

Finally, there remained concern about how electronic journal publications will be paid for. Again, industry and academia share this concern, which leads on to the other major topic of this paper: the economics of electronic scholarly journals.

Economic factors

There has been a great deal of controversy about the appropriate level of pricing for scholarly information. Publishers and subscription agents contend that, if electronic journals are to provide a high level of quality, in all senses of that word, then costs cannot be much lower than at present. Even if printing ceases altogether, only the costs of paper stock, print machining, and distribution will be saved, and those costs typically make up less than one-quarter of the price of a scholarly journal. Indeed, publishers maintain that as long as dual publication (electronic and print) continues, their costs will actually be higher than before. Meanwhile, some academics and academic librarians, especially in North America, believe that by adopting a zero-budgeting approach they could devise workable publishing mechanisms using the Internet that need cost no more than 25% to 30% of traditional journal prices (E-journal costs, 1995). Whatever the truth of the matter, there is certainly discontent that publishers make substantial profits out of research results that are provided to them by the academic community free of charge.

These matters will be decided by pragmatic rather than moral arguments. The major groups of customers for scholarly information are found in universities—academics, research staff, and students. Outside North America, personal purchases of scholarly journals out of one's private finances are few. Most scholars and students depend on their university to provide them with information, either by "holdings"—actual ownership of books, journals, and CD-ROMs by the university library—or by "access"—provision of information services to networked PCs on academics' desks, regardless of where the information may actually be held. The existence of e-mail discussion groups, newsgroups, gophers, and especially the World Wide Web has led to academics and students becoming used to the idea of free information; indeed, academics find that many students now look first at the WWW for all information and have to be reminded of the need to look in printed sources and other electronic sources as well.

For several years now, academic libraries in most developed countries have found their resources under considerable strain. This is due to a number of factors, among them the widespread election of governments committed to lower taxation and lower public expenditure, and the growth of student numbers leading to a greater emphasis on the university library as an undergraduate teaching resource rather than a research resource. In developing countries, of course, resources for university libraries have always been inadequate. Journal subscription prices regularly rise by percentages much greater than the general rate of price inflation. There are a number of reasons for this: journals may publish more pages, leading to higher prices even if the price per page remains the same; new journals are launched, leading to an increase in the cost of maintaining a comprehensive collection in a given subject field; currency exchange rate fluctuations can lead to sharp increases on imported journals; but, above all, there is a vicious spiral whereby as prices rise, sales fall. Fixed costs then have to be spread among fewer sales, leading to further price increases, further falls in circulation, and so on. Whatever the reason, libraries see their costs increasing out of reach of their budgets. Rightly or wrongly, they see electronic publication as a potential solution to this problem.

As noted earlier, most of the free Internet journals are quite small (Harter & Kim, 1996). By contrast, many traditional journals are very large; for example, the *Journal of Biological Chemistry*, published by the American Society for Biochemistry and Molecular Biology and available on-line since April 1995, publishes over 30,000 pages per annum. The even larger *Biochimica et Biophysica Acta* is published by Elsevier and will presumably become available in electronic form during 1997 as part of Elsevier's ScienceDirect program to make all of its journals available on the Internet. To publish this number of pages the journals' staffs must have processed an even larger number, since some papers will have been rejected, and these too generate work. It has therefore been argued elsewhere (Rowland, 1996) that the sheer size of such operations necessitates the employment of full-time administrative staff of a reasonable quality, regardless of the medium employed for distribution. Thus, provided that some fundamental pattern of publication not unlike the present one persists, journals are likely to continue to be sold at substantial prices, though not necessarily as high as at present.

There are, however, other possible patterns. It has been suggested many times—going right back to Bernal (1939)—that primary dissemination of research results might be achieved by some form of central repository system. This idea was revived in the U.K. more recently by Swinnerton-Dyer (1992), the mathematician who at one time headed the Universities Funding Council. Computer and telecommunications technologies have made this idea more feasible than it was in Bernal's day, when the repository would have had to operate in a manual way. Bernal and Swinnerton-Dyer's ideas assume, of course, that the fundamental purpose of publication is to provide ongoing availability of tested, quality-controlled information. At the other end of the spectrum, one finds the Internet libertarians, who regard any form of refereeing or quality control an affront to free speech and a form of Establishment censorship. They would see free discussion over the Internet as the major form of communication among scholars and believe that the only reason for a refereeing system in the past was the expense of paper publication: material needed to be assessed prior to publication as one could not afford to print everything. Now, one can put everything up on the WWW and allow all scholars—not just a couple of referees—to judge its worth. To this argument, one may respond that there is another scarce resource, the scholar's time. No one has the time to read everything that is written in their subject area, the good, the indifferent, and the crackpot. Referees do us a service by filtering out work that is not worth others wasting their time on. They also often make useful suggestions for the improvement of those articles that are published.

Another widely advanced suggestion is that the university where research originated should publish it, rather than transferring copyright to a publisher who then makes money from it. Each university would have a WWW site containing quality-controlled work produced by its own academics and students, and WWW search engines would enable all other workers elsewhere to access relevant material. A variant on this idea, which would preserve the useful concept of journals specialized by subject, would be for each university to publish a limited number of journals electronically and for universities to agree amongst themselves as to who would cover which subjects. Gail McMillan (1994) sees this as moving from a position where each university library provides many journals for (relatively) few people—the community of that one university—to one where it provides a few journals for an enormous number of people—essentially the whole world. These models are attractive, and there is no superficially obvious reason why they could not work, but anecdotal evidence suggests that internal university politics might be a major obstacle to their effective and impartial operation. One also quails at the thought of the complex multilateral, indeed multinational, negotiations between universities that would be needed to set up the McMillan model.

Despite all these alternative suggestions, it seems unlikely that existing publishers will quietly retire from the field of scholarly journal publishing. For-profit companies will continue to seek a financial return on their properties, and established journals of repute are very valuable properties. Not-for-profit publishers such as university presses and learned societies, on the other hand, see themselves as retaining a role in the control of scholarly quality through their publishing operations. Though both types of publisher will no doubt wish to remain in this field, they will only do so if they can provide a service to scholarly communities at a price those communities can afford. At present they seem intent on charging prices for electronic journals that are the same as, or higher than, those of their printed journals. There is little general difference between the for-profit and not-for-profit sectors in this respect; however, certain not-for-profit publishers, such as the Johns Hopkins University Press with its Project Muse (Johns Hopkins, 1997) and the Association for Computing Machinery (Denning, 1996), seem to be displaying a more flexible, less finance-oriented approach than some others. But the American Society for Biochemistry and Molecular Biology, which has done an excellent job on the design side with the electronic version of the *Journal of Biological Chemistry*, has sadly used the occasion to bring in a general price increase.

There has also been considerable debate about pricing structures for electronic publication, in contrast to the question of the absolute level of prices. The available options were usefully summarized by Tom Graham, then university librarian at the University of York in the U.K. and recently moved to the University of Newcastle upon Tyne (Graham, 1996). These ranged from national site licence agreements—as being experimented with at present in U.K. higher education (Bekhradnia, 1995)—through institutional site licences, to personal subscriptions with alternatives of pay-per-access or pay-per-delivery for occasional users, to grants for publication (the electronic version of page charges). The central problem for publishers is to ensure that the first-copy costs are covered from the various sources of income. The universities' ideal is that on payment of a known annual sum (preferably smaller than that now paid for the printed version) all *bona fide* users on their campus—staff and students—can have unlimited access to each journal from their own desks or from open-access student PC laboratories. Access from machines in halls of residence would also be permitted, but problems arise with off-campus students, staff working from home, and especially distance learners and part-time students studying for only a few hours per week. Where and how does one draw the line between users who are paid for by a campus licence and those who are accessing the journal from home and might reasonably be expected to pay either a personal subscription or on a pay-as-you-go basis? Efforts have been made by CD-ROM publishers and some producers of computer-assisted learning (CAL) materials to limit the number of simultaneous accesses to their products on the campus: thus the licence might allow only 10 simultaneous connections to a networked CD-ROM, say. This might be workable for journals held in electronic form locally (analogous to a networked CD-ROM), and perhaps might work for files held remotely if the publisher had suitable software to identify the origin of the search, though caching and mirroring will certainly render such an approach more difficult.

Given the shortage of funds for university libraries this is not a tenable position. New technology must be used to provide improved value for money and improved access for users. If existing publishers refuse to provide this, they can only expect the pressures for them to be bypassed will increase and, in that case, other players will undoubtedly arise to fill the need.

Conclusions

On the basis of work undertaken at Loughborough (Bell & Rowland, 1997; Meadows et al., 1997; Rowland et al., 1995; Woodward et al., 1997a, 1997b) and other studies recorded in the published literature and summarized in Peek & Newby (1996), one arrives at the conclusion that the days when the growth of usage of electronic journals was limited by technical shortcomings of hardware, software, and networks are over. This view is subject to the caveat that it is largely applicable only to the developed world. Even there, there are often problems of inadequate capacity of the information superhighway, which at times seems to approach gridlock. Users in Europe are well aware of the need to do their netsurfing in the morning, when it is the middle of the night in North America! In our studies, users on the whole were fairly tolerant of the slow delivery of information. Thus, despite these frustrations, the infrastructure is now largely adequate, and computer and networking specialists continue to make steady improvements.

The factors limiting the acceptance and use of electronic journals by academics, researchers, and graduate students now are twofold: human and economic.

Electronic journals need to be designed for the computer screen, even though at the end of the search the user may wish to print out copies of a proportion of articles. In particular, the "navigational" screens—the ones that the user has to go through en route to the actual articles of interest—must be designed with particular care, as must the structure of hypertext links within and between articles, and the search engines provided should operate in a reasonably intuitive manner. Given that the network is often congested and slow, publishers must try to keep to a minimum the number of different screens the user needs to go through to get from the home page to an actual full-text article of interest. Change for its own sake should be avoided. Users find it hard enough to keep up with work in their own discipline; they should not be expected to try to keep up to date in the disciplines of electronic publishing and computer networking as well. Nor should publishers assume that everyone has the latest versions of all hardware and software; in universities, at least, they certainly do not.

Commercial publishers in general believe that "page integrity"—the preservation in the electronic version of the layout of the pages from the printed version—is of importance, and many therefore use systems such as Adobe Acrobat and RealPage to achieve this. It is not clear that users take the same view. Pages in a portrait (vertical) format do not fit well on the computer screen in landscape (horizontal) format, especially when a two- or three-column layout is used in the print version. Furthermore the capacity of the screen is smaller if the text is going to be presented at a size that is comfortable for users of all ages to read. Free electronic journals have no equivalent printed version, and so "pages" are irrelevant and their editors have not in general tried to make their journals resemble a printed publication in appearance. There is by now a substantial number of people with expertise in WWW design and where this expertise has been used in the design of electronic journals, there have sometimes been very satisfactory results.

The preference of established publishers for page integrity, and especially their liking for Adobe Acrobat, may be due more to economic than to ergonomic factors. If the publication is prepared for printing by using PostScript, the conversion to publication distribution file (PDF) format used by Acrobat is relatively straightforward and inexpensive. Conversion to HTML, on the other hand, is more costly unless the publishers use an SGML system for internal handling of their files. Thus it may be that the attraction to publishers of page integrity systems may not be, as they claim, a matter of user preference for page integrity, but more a matter of economy for the publisher.

The question of economy for the publishers, however, is of some interest to the user. If journals—printed or electronic—are beyond the means of the users or of their library to buy, then it becomes a matter of little interest how well designed they might be. Publishers clearly have been investing considerably in their electronic products and reasonably expect to find a return on their investments eventually. Much of this need for investment is clearly a consequence of the sheer size of major journals, as Elsevier has clearly recognized (and some academics have not). However, as commercial undertakings they also recognize the concept of charging what the market will bear; and there is mounting evidence that they have in some cases gone beyond that point already. Those British publishers who are collaborating in the Higher Education Funding Councils' (HEFC) National Site Licence Initiative (Bekhradnia, 1995) may well have a more realistic approach than some others. If publishers do not moderate their financial demands, they may find that the universities—which, as well as being major customers for the journals, also provide much of the content free of royalty—may decide to refuse to assign copyright to commercial publishers.

References

Bailey, C. W. (1997). *Scholarly electronic publishing bibliography* (5th ed.). URL: http://info.lib.uh.edu/sepb/sepb.html

Bekhradnia, B. (1995). Pilot national site licence initiative for academic journals. *Serials*, *8*(4), 247-250.

Bell, I. D. (1996). *Issues surrounding electronic journals and their implementation within Glaxo Wellcome Research & Development*. Unpublished master's dissertation, Loughborough University, Loughborough, UK.

Bell, I., & Rowland, F. (1997). E-Journals in an industrial environment. *Serials*, *10*(1), 58-64.

Bernal, J. D. (1939). *The social function of science*. London: Routledge.

Denning, P. (1996, September). Electronic publishing plan a must. *Computing Research News*. URL: http://www.acm.org/pubs/JournalsEnd.html

E-journal costs. (1995, June). Thread on the hyperjournal-forum. URL: gopher://nisp.ncl.ac.uk:70/0R168907-171823-/lists-f-j/hyperjournal-forum/archives/1995-06andlate

Falconer, Catherine. (1995). *Publishers' opinions on the future of the academic electronic journal*. Unpublished master's dissertation, Loughborough University, Loughborough, UK.

Graham, T. W. (1996, March 27). *Electronic journals: Pricing models*. Message sent to lis-elib electronic discussion list. E-mail: lis-elib@mailbase.ac.uk

Harter, S. P., & Kim, H. J. (1996, May). *Electronic journals and scholarly communication: A citation and reference study*. Paper presented at the American Society for Information Science (ASIS) Midyear Meeting, San Diego, CA. URL: http://ezinfo.ucs.indiana.edu/~harter/harter-asis96midtxt.htm

Hitchcock, S. (1996). Open journals. *Ariadne*, *5*, 9. URL: http://www.ariadne.ac.uk/issue5/open/

Hitchcock, S., Carr, L., & Hall, W. (1996, January). *A survey of STM online journals 1990-95: The calm before the storm*. URL: http://journals.ecs.soton.ac.uk/survey/survey.html

Johns Hopkins University Press. (1997). *Project Muse online journals*. URL: http://muse.jhu.edu/pricing.html

McMillan, Gail. (1994, July 27). The VT [Virginia Tech] model. Message posted to the VPIEJ-L discussion list.

Meadows, J., Rowland, F., & Yates-Mercer, P. (1997). An online electronic journal for teaching purposes. *ALT-J, Association for Learning Technology Journal*, *5*(1), 13-18.

Okerson, A. (Ed.). (1996). *Directory of electronic journals, newsletters and academic discussion lists* (6th ed.). Washington, DC: Association of Research Libraries. URL: http://www.gold.ac.uk/history/hyperjournal/arl.htm

Peek, R. P., & Newby, G. B. (Eds.). (1996). *Scholarly publishing: The electronic frontier*. Cambridge, MA: MIT Press.

Rolinson, J., Meadows, J., & Smith, H. (1995). Use of information technology by biological researchers. *Journal of Information Science*, *21*(2), 133-139.

Rowland, F. (1995). Recent and current electronic journal projects. In F. Rowland, C. McKnight, & J. Meadows (Eds.), *Project ELVYN: An experiment in electronic journal delivery: Facts, figures and findings* (pp. 15-36). London: Bowker Saur.

Rowland, F. (1996). The need for management of electronic journals. In R. P. Peek & G. B. Newby (Eds.), *Scholarly publishing: The electronic frontier* (pp. 243-250). Cambridge, MA: MIT Press.

Rowland, F., McKnight, C., & Meadows, J. (Eds.). (1995). *Project ELVYN: An experiment in electronic journal delivery: Facts, figures and findings*. London: Bowker Saur.

Senders, J. W. (1977). An online scientific journal. *Information Scientist*, *11*(1), 3-9.

Shackel, B. (1991). *BLEND-9: Overview and appraisal* (Research Paper No. 82). London: British Library Research and Development Department.

Swinnerton-Dyer, Sir H. P. F. (1992). A system of electronic journals for the United Kingdom. *Serials*, *5*(3), 33-35.

Tuck, B., McKnight, C., Hayet, M., & Archer, D. (1990). *Project Quartet* (LIR Report No. 76). London: British Library Research and Development Department.

Wood, F. E., Ford, N., Miller, D., Sobczyk, G., & Duffin, R. (1996). Information skills, searching behaviour and cognitive styles for student centred learning: A computer assisted learning approach. *Journal of Information Science*, *22*(2), 79-96.

Woodward, H., McKnight, C., Meadows, J., Pritchett, C., & Rowland, F. (1997a). Electronic journals: Myths and realities. *Library Management*, *18*(3), 155-162.

Woodward, H., McKnight, C., Meadows, J., Pritchett, C., & Rowland, F. (1997b). Use of electronic journals by academic staff and postgraduate students in an information-literate university. In J. Zeeman & R. A. C. Bruyns (Eds.). *New Book Economy: Proceedings of the 5th International BOBCATSSS Symposium, Budapest, Hungary* (pp. 274-281). Amsterdam: Hogeschool van Amsterdam.

Providing Links Among Government, Academia, and Industry: The Role of CISTI in Scholarly Communication

Margot J. Montgomery
National Research Council of Canada

Abstract: Canada's success as a modern, knowledge-based economy depends on a strong national information infrastructure that is responsive to the needs of the country's innovation system for industrial development. The Canada Institute for Scientific and Technical Information (CISTI) at the National Research Council (NRC) is uniquely positioned to meet the needs of Canadian researchers and contribute to the Canadian innovation system by providing Canadian access to worldwide scholarly scientific, technical, and medical (STM) information and by leading in the development of the national information infrastructure linking Canadian industry, academia, and government. The emerging world of electronic information is transforming scholarly communication and changing the roles of researchers, users, publishers, and librarians. Increased collaboration will be critical to maintaining a robust national information infrastructure.

Résumé: Le succès d'une économie canadienne axée sur le savoir dépend d'une solide infrastructure d'information nationale pouvant satisfaire aux besoins de développement industriel éprouvés dans le système d'innovation du pays. L'Institut canadien de l'information scientifique et technique (ICIST) est en position idéale pour répondre aux besoins des chercheurs canadiens et pour contribuer au système d'innovation national en donnant accès pour les Canadiens à l'information scientifique, technique, et médicale du monde entier et en orchestrant le développement d'une infrastructure nationale d'information qui relierait entre eux l'industrie, l'université, et le gouvernement. Le monde de l'information électronique en émergence est en train de transformer la communication savante ainsi que le rôle de chercheurs, usagers, éditeurs, et bibliothé-

---

Margot J. Montgomery is Director General of the Canada Institute for Scientific and Technical Information at the National Research Council, M-55, Montreal Road, Ottawa, ON K1A 0S2. E-mail: margot.montgomery@nrc.ca

***Canadian Journal of Communication*, Vol. 22, No. 3/4 (1997) 77-88**

caires. Une collaboration accrue entre ceux-ci sera essentielle pour maintenir une infrastructure d'information nationale robuste.

Introduction

Canada is building an information-based society characterized by an economy guided by a corpus of knowledge (Information Highway Advisory Council, 1996). To facilitate entrepreneurial innovation, the country needs a national information infrastructure to support the competitiveness of research and development (R&D) performers. The timely use of relevant, validated, scientific, technical, and medical (STM) information by these performers helps the development of new and improved products, processes, or services. This infrastructure defines the modern knowledge-based economy.

The present national information infrastructure must adapt to the global nature of the information society, emerging international markets, and new information technologies such as the World Wide Web. This paper will consider STM information, its impact on innovation by R&D performers, and the changing national information infrastructure in Canada.

Innovation is a term broadly conceived to mean the development of new products, services, or processes that can be successfully introduced into the marketplace. Industrial innovation is a turbulent and iterative process with numerous interactions among players leading to the incremental improvements that constitute innovation. Innovation can be introduced anywhere in the R&D technology production spectrum, revisiting points in the spectrum as need arises (National Research Council of Canada, 1994). Both new knowledge and the diffusion of know-how are critical to industrial innovation. These depend on the amount and quality of R&D performed, the effectiveness of diffusion, and the application of new technology.

The National Research Council of Canada (NRC) and other public bodies help create and sustain the environment that nurtures our innovators by associating knowledge with applications and by building links among players. As Canada's foremost R&D agency, NRC aims to be a leader in the development of an innovative, knowledge-based economy through science and technology.

The Canadian innovation system

Canada's innovation system has many interacting players (Figure 1). At the centre of the system are individual firms acquiring and applying new knowledge and willing to bear the risks of innovation. Canadian industry is the prime vehicle for transforming innovative ideas, products, and processes into jobs, exports, and economic growth. Knowledge generators and knowledge facilitators fill complementary roles and share the information infrastructure. In quantitative terms, the knowledge generators in Canada's innovation system include: 4,485 industrial firms performing R&D, 35 research-intensive universities with their hundreds of laboratories, more than 140 federal and about 90 provincial research institutions, 14 national centres of excellence (NCEs), research consortia, and numerous teaching hospitals.

Figure 1
The Canadian Innovation System

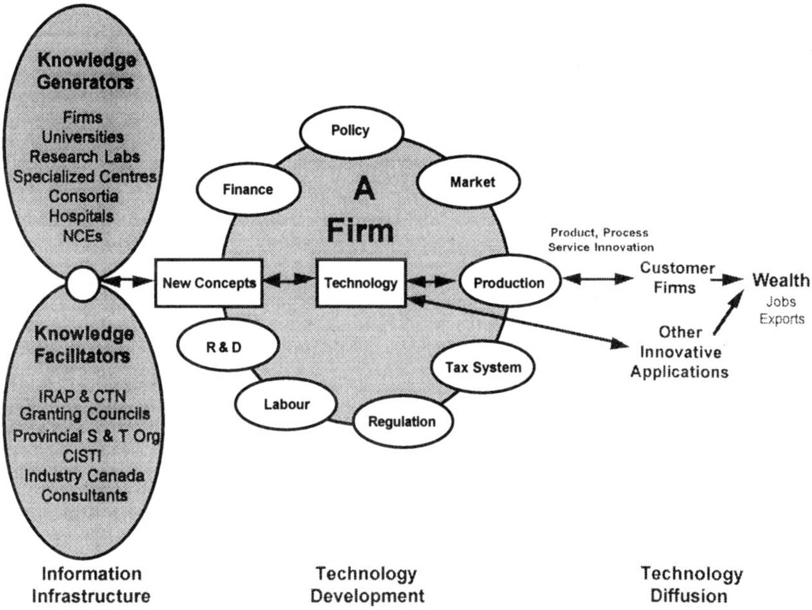

The knowledge facilitators comprise: national programs for knowledge transfer, such as NRC's Industrial Research Assistance Program (IRAP) and the Canadian Technology Network (CTN), Industry Canada, the national granting councils, various national and regional science and technology organizations, NRC's Canada Institute for Scientific and Technical Information (CISTI), and the many firms providing both expertise and products such as patents, technology training, and engineering consulting.

The purpose of scholarly communication is to build the foundation for generating new knowledge. Scholarly communication can therefore be viewed as a subsystem of the larger innovation system. Increased co-operation, joint ventures, and sharing of infrastructure among the players in the scholarly communication system will improve the effectiveness of the national innovation system and deliver enhanced economic benefits.

The national information infrastructure

Canada's information infrastructure is shared by university, government, and industrial sectors and encourages exchange and collaboration among academic and government information producers, publishers, commercial information brokers, trade and professional groups (including scholarly and learned societies), researchers, libraries, and information technology developers. This infrastructure consists of the information itself, the dissemination systems and networks for using it, and the people and organizations who create it, add value to it, use it, and make it available. A distinction can be made between codified or published information versus tacit or contextual information, which carries the "spin" that can render codified information especially relevant.

CISTI's role within this complex information infrastructure is to provide Canadians with timely access to worldwide STM information and to lead in developing and adapting the national information infrastructure in response to the needs of STM information users and producers. As a hybrid organization, CISTI fills, on the one hand, a public policy role in developing the information systems linking Canadian industry, academia, and government, and, on the other hand, operates publishing and document delivery services as not-for-profit business lines based on Canadian strengths in electronic connectivity, research, and information resources.

Information creation, organization, dissemination, and archiving are integral to effective scholarly communication. Each contributes to the innovative process in a system of scholarly communication. In the mid-1990s we find ourselves in a transition from paper-based information systems to electronic systems, and this transition will continue for the foreseeable future as the pace of change accelerates towards fully electronic information systems. During this transition to a fully electronic information world, the roles of researchers, users, publishers, and librarians will evolve and continue to change (Montgomery, 1993). The players in the scholarly communication system (Figure 2) can be considered to fall into the following categories:

- **researchers** or scholars, who are both the authors (knowledge generators) and users,
- **publishers**, who manage the knowledge-validation process, adding editorial value and distributing knowledge, and
- **librarians**, who supply knowledge and filter, organize, and archive information for retrieval on behalf of users.

The scientific article and the journals in which it first appeared have their origins in the seventeenth century. With the refinement of the Gutenberg printing press, publishing gradually evolved into our present-day system. The role of information intermediaries remains significant, owing to the volume of publications and the escalating costs of information, especially in STM publishing (Carrigan, 1995). Intermediaries organize, retrieve, and archive information for scholars. Although works of scholarship produced in and through the electronic media will change to exploit new technologies, information systems in the electronic world will, more than ever, require information intermediaries to add the value of filtering, organizing, and preserving.

Figure 2
Scholarly Communication Roles

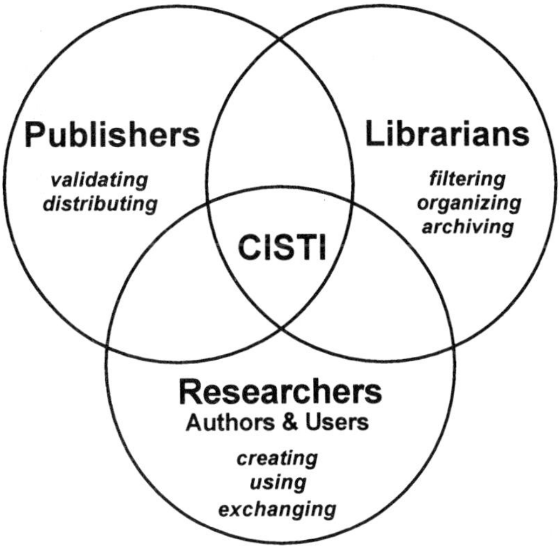

The knowledge-validation or peer-review process is widely acknowledged to make a critical contribution to the scholarly process (Bishop, 1984). It is also inherently conservative and may slow the development of knowledge. Peer commentary has been proposed as an alternative (Harnad, 1996) that complements the existing peer-review system. Refereed journals are widely recognized as adding value through validation, readability, and searchability.

Secondary publishing or indexing and library cataloguing and reference services add value by organizing and retrieving information for the user. Preservation is a key role that traditionally has been carried out by libraries to ensure the availability of scholarly resources over time, regardless of format. With the proliferation of electronic media, preservation of electronic resources will include migration from one platform to another. Information producers, intermediaries, and users will have to collaborate to ensure that today's electronic resources are available tomorrow.

Communication among researchers may take the form of correspondence (fax, post, and e-mail), mediated exchanges (journals and books, conferences), or information technology systems (the World Wide Web, bulletin boards, listservs, discussion lists) (Covi, 1996). Improving information access and distribution can improve scholarly communication. University and government systems for reward and recognition, such as research funding and researcher career promotion, rely on the traditional and formal means for communicating research results. However, informal information exchange, particularly where contextual or tacit information enriches the validated or codified information, leads to equally or more effective innovation and related economic benefits. Organizations such as NRC are beginning to adapt their recognition systems to reward technology transfer and industry collaboration.

Models of scholarly communication

The following four models (Figure 3) of scholarly communication are proposed, which deliberately emphasize differences to illustrate the impact of electronic information technologies. These differences focus on role changes among players, which may bring related shifts in costs.

Scholar-sustained model

In this model, direct scholar-to-scholar communication takes place informally within the research community. This model parallels the "invisible colleges" or social circles of powerful peers that exist within academia (Crane, 1972). These networks of scholars-in-the-know tend toward exclusivity, presenting barriers to access for those outside the relatively closed knowledge system. The scholar-sustained model is driven by the information producer who may not be motivated to add value to the information. Industry players risk being denied access to useful new knowledge relevant to innovation except through people networks and collaborative research projects. As electronic technologies evolve, scholars take on the functions and attendant costs for information organization, retrieval, and preservation—that is now handled by librarians—and validation and dissemination, now the purview of publishers.

Network-driven model

This is a disintermediation model and a variation on the scholar-sustained model. In such a system, there are no libraries, no publishers, no intermediaries. Instead, information passes from the researcher straight into information systems or networks. The particular challenges of disintermediation are the need for common formats and standards for access, presentation, organization, retrieval, and preservation. Users risk being overwhelmed by the volume of information in an unfiltered system. Storage of the information may be sporadic and non-standard, and therefore not reliable as a foundation on which to build further knowledge. Industrial innovators are forced to develop these skills themselves or pay others to retrieve information from vast and unorganized sources such as the World Wide Web.

Figure 3
Models of Scholarly Communications

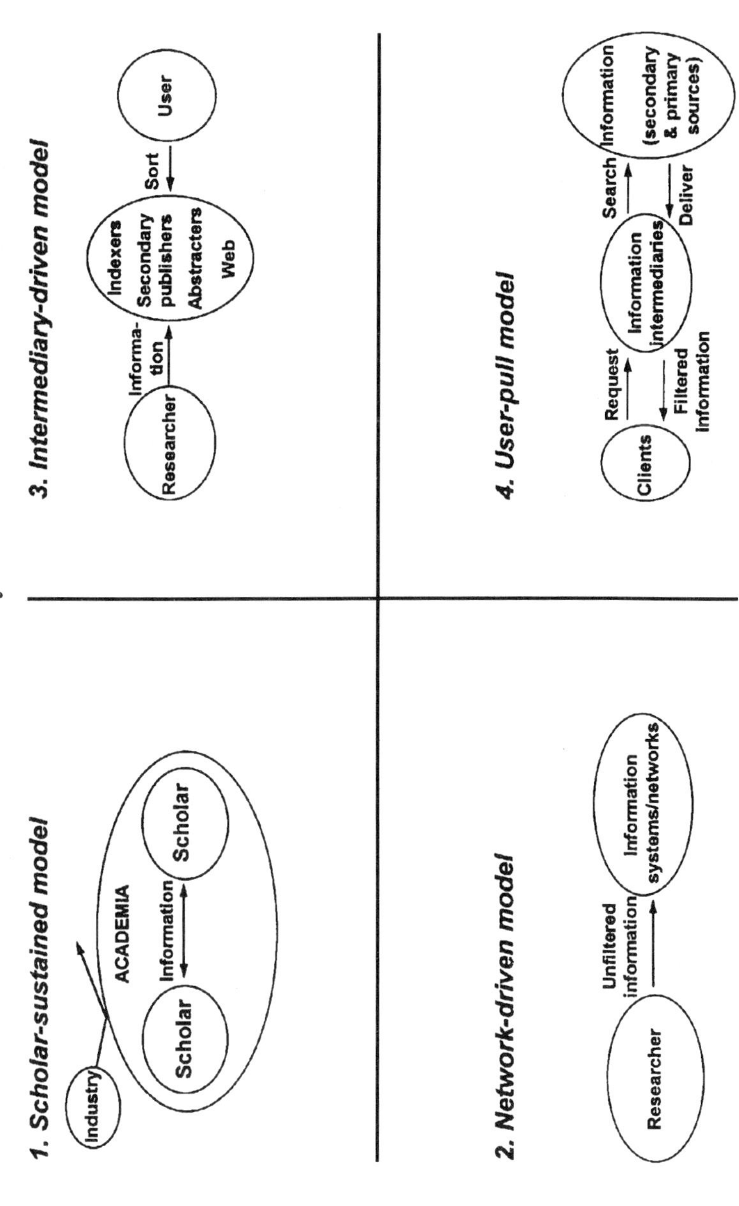

Intermediary-driven model

Secondary publishers, abstracters, indexers, and, for the Web, producers who assemble resources and navigate to other relevant sites are the lead players in the intermediary-driven model. There are no primary publishers except institutional and government self-publishers. Researchers make information available to others who gather, organize, and store it. Researchers, or their funding sponsors, must assume responsibility for submitting the information. In this model, the validation and peer-review functions of primary publishers are lost or replaced by "pointers" or citation bibliometrics. Again, the need for common formats and standards present a major challenge. At the other end of the system, users have to sort through all the possible locations for relevant material. Needless to say, the market for electronic finding tools builds. In combination with the scholar-sustained model, insider groups thrive.

User-pull model

In this model, clients initiate the knowledge-exchange process with an information request and seek the support of information intermediaries who search for the information in secondary and primary sources. Once located, information is delivered to the client, either fully or partially filtered for quality, possibly with customized packaging, and according to personalized interest profiles. This is a service model carrying implications for costs to cover the role of the information intermediary and risks related to the availability of information professionals and the market viability for customized information products.

CISTI's role

CISTI's role is to provide Canadian access to worldwide STM information and to lead nationally in developing the information infrastructure underpinning a knowledge-based economy. Since its founding in 1924, CISTI has evolved from its early role as the library of NRC, to a National Science Library (1957), to its present focus on collaborating with Canadian research institutions to serve researchers and Canadian-based industry in seeking national economic advantage. The Canadian research community remains both an important client group and a key partner for CISTI. CISTI is Canada's largest scientific publisher and also operates a world-class document delivery service. These principal business lines are supported by academic, industrial, and government clients in Canada and internationally.

The document delivery service provides copies and loans of documents from CISTI's collection, typically about 2,500 copies daily, increasingly via electronic ordering and delivery means. Through government allocation, the people of Canada own the most extensive and complete STM collection of journals, technical reports, conference proceedings, and books on the North

American continent. This is a critical national resource, whose exploitation depends on an effective and innovative information infrastructure within CISTI, based on the core competence of skilled information specialists, networks, computers, and applications. Through recent collaborative agreements with consortia of Canadian university and government research libraries, CISTI offers guaranteed affordable access to STM information, while sharing risks in information technology development.

NRC Research Press publishes 14 refereed scientific journals and a number of books and scholarly conference proceedings with the invaluable aid of many of Canada's and the world's scientists as editors and reviewers. Since 1929, when NRC began publishing the *Canadian Journal of Research*, close collaboration between government and academic researchers has been the foundation of this successful publishing endeavor.

Within NRC, CISTI contributes information-management expertise and systems. Examples include developing the NRC Intranet; hosting and advising on external Web sites for research programs and institutes; developing standards for the electronic information network at the core of the people-oriented Canadian Technology Network for small and medium-sized enterprises (SMEs); and co-ordinating a corporate expertise database to facilitate internal collaboration. Along with NRC's IRAP, whose role is to foster innovation, technology awareness, and technology foresight in SMEs, CISTI constitutes a key element of NRC's outreach activity and distributed innovation service to Canadian industry.

Information trends

The information environment is changing rapidly and profoundly. The past decade has seen the proliferation of new information technologies, a multitude of information channels, and the use of multimedia formats. Increasingly, firms and governments depend on information in order to make effective and timely decisions. Consequently, information providers must contend with a competitive, dynamic, and challenging world.

A number of specific trends affect CISTI's future:

1. Clients expect direct information access, leading to new roles for information intermediaries, producers, and users.
2. To help advance innovation, clients need business, interdisciplinary, and time-limited information, in addition to traditional STM sources.
3. The media for information capture, transfer, and analysis are currently unstable and rapidly evolving.
4. Escalating costs of information force information gatekeepers in business, government, and academia to seek new solutions for acquiring just-in-time STM information.

As the library and information service provider for 2,000 NRC researchers across Canada, CISTI is developing and applying virtual library technologies to provide desktop electronic information access and delivery. Using internal clients as a testbed for developing new processes and products, CISTI is integrating its diverse services and giving researchers choices that take account of different technological, disciplinary, and social imperatives specific to research communities and their communication systems.

Cost containment is another priority as a response to client concern about managing rapid change in the information world in a fiscally constrained public R&D sector. CISTI's local presence within NRC research labs across Canada, coupled with national and international STM links, positions it to meet the needs of Canadian communities and to contribute effectively to the Canadian innovation system. This contribution can be made directly to STM information users and producers or through partners such as university libraries, scientific societies, trade associations, the information industry, and individual scholars and their sponsors.

Automated systems and networks underpin all CISTI products and services. As a result, CISTI and NRC plan to invest in technologies to support a virtual national science library that is integrated with electronic publishing technologies. This project recognizes the ubiquity of computers and network access at the desktop, the emergence and presence of the Internet as the conduit for access to worldwide information, and the rapid progress in the development of tools for authoring, publishing, storing, and disseminating information. CISTI's Strategic Plan to 2001 (CISTI, 1996) calls for the Institute to contribute to technological competitiveness and innovation in information products and processes for Canadian R&D performers. Specifically, CISTI aims to apply electronic publishing technologies to improve the speed of information dissemination, to reduce the time required to deliver information directly to researchers' desktops, and to offer researchers more powerful information management and analysis tools, based on the Internet.

Conclusions

Canada's success as a modern knowledge-based economy depends on a strong national information infrastructure that is responsive to the needs of the country's innovation system. Innovation in firms is key to competitiveness and national economic benefits. The innovation system, and, within it, scholarly communication, are enhanced by Canadian researchers having access to worldwide STM information sources via a flexible information infrastructure. CISTI plays a lead role in adapting and evolving the national information infrastructure. In the future, increased collaboration among government, university, information industry, and research organizations in Canada will be critical to maintaining a robust and sustainable national information infrastructure.

References

Bishop, Claude T. (1984). The review process. In *How to edit a scientific journal* (pp. 43-52). Philadelphia: ISI Press.

Canada Institute for Scientific and Technical Information (CISTI). (1996). *CISTI Strategic Plan 1996-2001*. Ottawa: National Research Council of Canada.

Carrigan, Dennis P. (1995, April). From just-in-case to just-in-time: Limits to the Alternative Library Service Model. *Journal of Scholarly Publishing*, *26*(3), 173-182.

Covi, Lisa. (1996, April). The scholarly communication and information technology (SCIT) project: How academic researchers use digital libraries for scholarly communication. In *Proceedings of a symposium on researchers' uses of electronic resources* (pp. 1-11). Chicago: Center for Research Libraries.

Crane, Diana. (1972). *Invisible colleges: Diffusion of knowledge in scientific communities*. Chicago: University of Chicago Press.

Harnad, Stevan. (1996). Implementing peer review on the net: Scientific quality control in scholarly electronic journals. In R. P. Peek & G. B. Newby (Eds.), *Scholarly publishing: The electronic frontier* (pp. 103-118). Cambridge: MIT Press.

Information Highway Advisory Council Secretariat. (1996). *Building the information society: Moving Canada into the 21st century*. Ottawa: Industry Canada.

Montgomery, Margot J. (1993). Document supply in a changing world. *Interlending and Document Supply*, *21*(4), 24-29.

National Research Council of Canada. (1994). *National systems of innovation: A research paper on innovation and innovation systems in Canada*. Ottawa: Author.

Additional readings

Association of Research Libraries. (1996). *New collaborative strategies for promoting non-profit scholarly publishing in the networked environment*. Washington, DC: Association of Research Libraries.

Braman, Sandra. (1995). Scholarly publishing in the information economy. In A. Okerson (Ed.), *Scholarly publishing on the electronic networks: Filling the pipeline and paying the piper—Proceedings of the Fourth Symposium, November 5-7, 1994* (pp. 39-49). Washington, DC: Association of Research Libraries.

Butler, H. Julene. (1995, July). Where does scholarly electronic publishing get you? *Journal of Scholarly Publishing*, *26*, 234-246.

Chodorow, Stanley. (1996). The medieval future of intellectual culture: Scholars and librarians in the age of the electron. *ARL: A Bimonthly Newsletter of Research Library Issues and Actions*, p. 189.

Ginsparg, Paul. (1996, February). Winners and losers in the global research village. In D. Shaw & H. Moore (Eds.), *Electronic publishing in science: Proceedings of the Joint ICSU Press/UNESCO Expert Conference* (pp. 83-88). Paris, France: ICSU Press/UNESCO Export Conference.

Godin, Benoît. (1996). Research and the practice of publication in industries. *Research Policy Research*, *25*, 587-606.

Halpenny, Frances G. (1993). Responsibilities of scholarly publishers. *Journal of Scholarly Publishing*, *24*(4), 223-231.

Lyrette, Jacques. (1997). The Canadian Innovation System. *Technological entrepreneurship and engineering in Canada: A report of the Canadian Academy of Engineering* (pp. 69-91). Montreal: Publications Transcontinentales.

McFetridge, Donald G. (1993). The Canadian system of industrial innovation. In R. R. Nelson (Ed.), *National innovation systems: A comparative analysis* (pp. 299-323). New York: Oxford.

The National Library's Role in Facilitating Scholarly Communications

Tom Delsey
National Library of Canada

Abstract: This paper reviews the role the National Library of Canada plays in supporting effective and efficient access both to current research findings and the scholarly archive of Canadian publications. The impact of electronic dissemination of scholarly information is examined in the context of collections development, services to scholars and researchers, and co-operative initiatives. The paper focuses on emerging issues surrounding electronic publications relating to legal deposit, preservation, standards for encoding, proprietary rights to information, and research services. It also explores the potential for enhancements to the National Library's Canadian Theses Program in the context of an electronic environment.

Résumé : Cet article examine le rôle que joue la Bibliothèque nationale du Canada à assurer un accès rapide et efficace aux résultats de recherche courants et aux archives de publications savantes canadiennes. Il examine en outre l'impact de la dissémination électronique de l'information savante sur le développement des collections, les services offerts aux savants et aux chercheurs, et les initiatives coopératives. L'article met l'accent sur les questions émergentes portant sur les publications électroniques, y compris le dépôt légal, la conservation, les normes de codage, les droits de propriété à l'information, et les services de recherche. L'article explore aussi les améliorations possible au Programme des thèses canadiennes de la Bibliothèque nationale dans un environnement électronique.

From whatever perspective we view scholarly communications, we would all agree that the enterprise as a whole depends heavily on the strength of the individual components of the communications infrastructure, both formal and informal, and the ease with which those components can be called into play to

Tom Delsey is Director-General, Corporate Policy and Communications, at the National Library of Canada, 395 Wellington, Ottawa, ON K1A 0N4. E-mail: tom.delsey@nlc-bnc.ca

***Canadian Journal of Communication*, Vol. 22, No. 3/4 (1997) 89-104**

support effective and efficient access, not only to current research findings, but also to what we might call the scholarly archive. In part, the enterprise depends on an informal infrastructure that operates at the level of individual initiative and interpersonal communication. But to a large extent, it depends on a formal infrastructure that functions at an institutional, corporate, and network level, making use of the resources of universities, libraries, publishers, the information technology industry, and telecommunications carriers and relying on their collaborative, as well as individual, efforts.

Among the many institutional players that are part of the Canadian infrastructure supporting scholarly communications, the National Library is a relative newcomer. It was established less than 50 years ago, after many years of lobbying by academics and librarians from across Canada. Ultimately, it was the Massey Commission Report (Royal Commission, 1951) that served as the catalyst for drafting the legislation that established the National Library. The Commission underscored the need for a national institution that would provide more effective access to the whole range of publications produced in this country and ensure the preservation of that material for future generations of scholars and researchers.

The *National Library Act* (*Revised Statutes of Canada*, 1952) provided the legislative framework needed to achieve those goals. The federal government has provided the resources to support the institution. Through co-operation with other libraries, with universities and colleges, with publishers, and with the information technology industry, the National Library has been successful in putting in place a number of programs that make it easier for scholars and researchers to know what has been published in their field within Canada. The Library also helps ensure that they have at their disposal a comprehensive resource encompassing both current and retrospective Canadian publications.

Today the National Library, like virtually all institutions that form part of the infrastructure supporting scholarly communications, is faced with adapting and re-aligning its programs and services to the new realities of a digital environment, to the emergence of new technologies for the communication and dissemination of information, and to new relationships between players in the information marketplace. The changes taking place throughout the information environment bring with them a wide range of issues that have to be addressed—issues that may be technical, legal, or economic in nature. Change also brings with it opportunities for innovation and for new alliances with other players in the infrastructure that will enable the Library to serve scholars and researchers more effectively.

This paper provides a brief overview of three National Library programs that function as important components of the current infrastructure supporting scholarly communications in Canada. It also highlights some of the major issues the Library has to address in adapting those programs to a digital/

networked environment and the opportunities that the new environment presents to us. Finally, it identifies, from the Library's perspective, a number of strategic priorities for future development that will require collaborative effort with other players in the infrastructure.

Components of the current infrastructure

The Canadiana collection

Over a period of 40-some years, the National Library has assembled a collection of published materials that includes almost 10 million pieces of Canadiana. The scope of coverage for the collection includes not only works published in Canada, but also works by Canadians and works dealing with Canadian topics published abroad. The collection contains materials in a broad range of formats: books, periodicals, newspapers, printed music, sound recordings, microforms, audio-visual materials, and electronic publications. It is the most comprehensive library collection of Canadiana held anywhere in the country, serving both as an archive of Canadian publishing and as a national resource supporting research in all fields of relevance to Canada's development as a nation—historical, political, social, economic, and cultural.

The National Library acquires a significant amount of the material in its collection through purchase; exchanges with other institutions; arrangements with federal, provincial, and municipal governments; and private donation. But the chief means of acquiring Canadian materials is a system of legal deposit under which publishers in Canada are required to send the National Library copies of all their newly released publications. By statute, the copies must be deposited at the publisher's own expense and within one week of the date of publication. It is largely through legal deposit that the Library is able to maintain the comprehensive scope of its collection of Canadian publications.

The national bibliography

Since 1950, the Canadiana materials acquired for the National Library's collection (and even some that the Library has not managed to obtain) have been catalogued and listed in the national bibliography. Today those records form the core of a database that is accessible on-line to users right across Canada. The database contains well over a million Canadiana records and is the authoritative source for bibliographic information on materials published in Canada as well as on Canadiana published abroad. Records for current materials are used to generate print, microfiche, and electronic products. These records help Canadian publishers promote their new publications, enable libraries to add copies of Canadiana materials to their collections without having the expense of cataloguing the items on their own, and assist scholars and researchers in finding out what has been published in Canada on topics of interest to them. The Canadiana database serves both as a comprehensive register of Canadian publications, and as a key tool to support multifaceted bibliographic access to the content of those publications.

The Canadian Theses Program

In the 30-some years since it was first established, the Canadian Theses Program has created an archive of more than 150,000 masters and doctoral theses submitted to degree-granting institutions in Canada. Currently, with 51 universities and colleges participating in the program, more than 10,000 theses are microfilmed each year. Bibliographic records and abstracts for each thesis are published by UMI in *Dissertation Abstracts International* (1989) and *Masters Abstracts International* (1986), and the records can be accessed through the National Library's on-line database as well. The program serves not only as a means of ensuring that Canadian theses are preserved on microfilm produced to meet stringent archival standards, but also as a vehicle for making the results of research conducted in Canadian universities and colleges better known—not just within Canada, but worldwide. Access to Canadian theses is further enhanced through the publication-on-demand component of the program that is provided through arrangements with Micromedia and UMI.

Issues, challenges, and opportunities

Legal deposit

Most of the legal deposit systems operating today were first established at a time when print was the exclusive, or at least predominant, medium of publication. In some countries, in fact, it was the printer, not the publisher, who was obligated by statute to deposit copies with the national library. It has only been in the past several years that a number of countries have undertaken to revise their legal deposit legislation to make it more inclusive. In several countries new legislation is still pending, and the current statutes still cover nothing more than printed materials. (For a survey of the current status of legal deposit legislation in some 15 countries in Europe, North America, and the Pacific, see Hoare, 1996.)

In order for legal deposit systems to serve as effective instruments for safeguarding a nation's published heritage, it is essential that they keep pace with changes occurring within what might be broadly defined as the publishing industry. But because most systems of deposit were originally developed within the context of a print-dominated industry, it has not always been a simple matter for national libraries to respond quickly to emerging forms of non-print publication. Legislation often needs to be revised, publishers need to be made aware of their obligation to deposit new forms of publication, new procedures for handling acquisitions need to be developed, specialized storage requirements for new media have to be met, and issues relating to access have to be addressed. With the development of new digital and optical media, the emergence of electronic publishing, and the explosive growth of the Internet and the World Wide Web as vehicles for publication, national libraries are faced with what is undoubtedly the biggest challenge they have had to face so far in adapting their systems of legal deposit to current-day realities.

Application of legal deposit statutes to electronic publications

In Canada, the first provisions for legal deposit as such were put in place under the *National Library Act* (*Revised Statues of Canada*, 1952, chapter 31, section 11). Unlike many of its European antecedents, from the outset the Canadian statute was intended to be comprehensive in scope. Although the Act uses the term *book* to indicate what it is that publishers are required to deposit, the Act has always had an interpretive clause that defines the term book to encompass "library matter of every kind, nature, and description" (chapter 31, section 2). The scope of the statute was made more explicit through an amendment in 1969, adding that "book" was to be interpreted to include "any document, paper, record, tape or other thing published by a publisher, on or in which information is written, recorded, stored, or reproduced" (*Revised Statues of Canada*, 1969, chapter 47, section 2).

Implementation of the statutory provisions for legal deposit in Canada has evolved over the years as new forms of publishing have emerged. Between 1953 and 1969, the legal deposit provisions of the Act were, in fact, exercised to acquire printed materials only—books, pamphlets, annuals, and periodicals. In 1969, the legal deposit requirement began to be applied to sound recordings. Three years later, the application was extended to educational kits. In 1988, the National Library began applying legal deposit requirements to microform publications, and, in 1993, to published videos and CD-ROMs.

From a legal point of view, the transition in application of the legal deposit requirement from printed materials to sound recordings, kits, videos, and even CD-ROMs has been relatively straightforward. In each instance, the scope of the term "book," as defined in the *National Library Act* was deemed sufficiently broad to encompass the new medium of production. Similarly, the mode of dissemination was in each instance sufficiently analogous to that used in the publication of printed materials that it was deemed to fall within what the Act defined as "published in Canada," that is, "released in Canada for public distribution or sale" (*Revised Statutes of Canada,* 1952, chapter 31, section 2).

For electronic publications produced in forms such as tape, diskette, CD-ROM, and CD-I and distributed as individual copies, there has been virtually no question that the requirements of the legal deposit provisions apply. However, for electronic documents that are made public only by means of access to communications networks such as the Internet, the question of applicability of the legal deposit provisions of the Act is not quite so clear-cut. What is at issue is not whether such documents would qualify as books under the definition provided in the Act, but whether or not they have been "published." The National Library is currently trying to establish, in consultation with lawyers in the Department of Justice, whether the definition of the term "published in Canada" (that is, "released in Canada for public distribution or sale") is sufficiently broad to cover public on-line dissemination as a form of publishing. As yet we have no definitive answer as to whether the current wording of the Act is sufficient, or whether we would require an amendment to ensure the applicability of legal deposit to on-line electronic publications.

Copyright and access issues

Assuming for the moment that the publisher's legal obligation to deposit a copy of an electronic document disseminated on-line is in fact confirmed, a number of other questions relating to the National Library's right to provide access to those documents are equally significant.

With other forms of publication—whether they be books, periodicals, sound recordings, or videos—access to copies obtained through legal deposit is linked more or less directly to the availability of the physical object. Normally, the deposited copy of the publication is made available to a researcher for consultation on site or through interlibrary loan. In depositing the copy with the Library, the publisher transfers ownership of the copy, and the Library has the right to lend that copy just as it would have the right to lend a copy that it had purchased. However, ownership of the intellectual property represented in the deposit copy is retained by the copyright owner, and the National Library must respect the copyright owner's rights just as any library is obliged to respect copyright in a copy that is purchased. Thus, if a researcher requests the Library to reproduce material in the Library's collection that is protected by copyright, the Library must ensure that the amount of material reproduced and the purposes for which it is to be used are consistent with the uses permitted by copyright law or by any licence the Library may have with the copyright owner or with a collective representing the copyright owner.

With electronic publications, the line between providing access to the physical object and permitted uses of the intellectual property represented in that object is much less clear-cut. Even with an electronic publication issued on diskette or CD-ROM, questions regarding permitted use arise the moment the transaction between the Library and the researcher goes beyond the simple lending of the physical object. If, in response to user needs, the Library loads the publication on to an individual workstation or on to a local area network (LAN) server, there is a form of reproduction involved that is inherent in the way the technology processes the digitally encoded content of the publication.

With on-line publications, providing access to the user is impossible without involving, in a strictly technical sense, reproduction.

The argument has been made by some copyright owners that all forms of reproduction, even those that are incidental or transient in nature and are simply a function of digital technology, are potentially infringements of copyright. They maintain that the owner of copyright in the work has the exclusive right to authorize such acts of reproduction. That interpretation has, of course, been challenged by the users of copyrighted works. They maintain that to include all such transactions under the rubric of the reproduction right is tantamount to giving the copyright owner the exclusive right to authorize the "reading" of a work. The issues around the interpretation and extent of the reproduction right and its implications in a digital environment are of significant current concern in Canada, the United States, and other countries throughout the world. The issues were debated at the recent World Intellectual Property Organization (WIPO) diplomatic conference in Geneva as part of the deliberations over a proposed article in a new copyright treaty aimed at clarifying the extent of the reproduction right in the Berne Convention, but no resolution was reached in that forum.

With the issue of access to electronic publications unresolved in terms of copyright law, a parallel debate has emerged specifically in relation to publications deposited with national libraries under the statutory provisions of legal deposit. On the one side, publishers maintain that access in a digital environment is qualitatively different from access in the analog print environment, providing as it does a significantly greater opportunity for exploitation of a work and the potential for undermining the commercial interests of the copyright owner. They argue, therefore, that the *modus vivendi* that has been accepted with respect to the use of deposit copies of printed publications cannot be used as a model for the use of deposit copies of electronic publications. Librarians, on the other hand, argue that exceptions provided for in the Berne Convention should apply to digital formats just as they apply to print. They contend that copyright should not limit the user's right to browse or read a work, or to make "fair use" of a work for purposes of research or private study; nor should it prevent a library from lending a work for legitimate purposes, regardless of the format of the publication.

The debate was escalated somewhat in April of last year, when the International Publishers' Association (IPA) passed a resolution urging its members to ensure that systems of legal deposit permit access to deposited publications free of charge only at single sites in the national library's own reading rooms, and that any further use of their deposited publications be permitted only on terms agreed to by the publisher (International Publishers' Association, 1996). In May, the International Federation of Library Associations (IFLA) issued a position paper on copyright in the electronic environment, asserting the right of the library user to read, listen to, view, or browse copyrighted works in a digital format without incurring a charge or seeking permission, and to copy a reasonable portion of a digital work for personal or educational use. The position paper also asserted the right of libraries to lend works in a digital format for legitimate purposes and to make a temporary digital copy of a work for purposes of electronic document delivery (International Federation of Library Associations and Institutions, 1996).

Current initiatives

While the debate continues on a philosophical level, and the legal questions remain unresolved, a few national libraries have begun to experiment with the practicalities of implementing deposit procedures for electronic publications. The National Library of Canada notified publishers that they would have to deposit all new CD-ROMs published on or after January 1993. The procedures that were established parallel those for conventional print and recorded materials, and publishers have co-operated fully. The Library of Congress initiated deposit procedures for CD-ROMs in 1994, but has taken the precaution of restricting access to the deposited materials according to the terms of agreements signed with the publishers. Some of the agreements limit access to single, stand-alone workstations; others permit networked access within Library of Congress buildings. If there is no signed agreement with the publisher, researchers are not permitted access to the CD-ROM. The Bibliothèque nationale in France also initiated deposit requirements for CD-ROMs in 1994 under newly revised legislation. Copies of CD-ROMs have been deposited, and policies have been established on access (restricting access to stand-alone workstations within the library and prohibiting downloading), but researchers will not actually have access to the materials until new facilities at Tolbiac are fully operational. The Nasjonalbiblioteket in Norway has also initiated the deposit of CD-ROMs under legislation that was revised in 1990, but researchers are not allowed access, pending the issue of regulations under Norway's new copyright act. (For additional information on these and other similar initiatives, see Hoare, 1996, and Anglo Nordic Seminar on Legal Deposit, 1995.)

Only two initiatives to date have addressed the deposit of on-line electronic publications, one at the Koninklijke Bibliotheek in the Netherlands and the other at the National Library of Canada. Both are being conducted as pilot projects, and in neither case is the national library actually exercising the statutory provisions of legal deposit.

The Netherlands, in fact, has no legal deposit legislation. For the past 20 years, the Koninklijke Bibliotheek has operated a voluntary system of deposit that has become effectively comprehensive through negotiation with Dutch publishers. In 1993, the library initiated planning to extend existing voluntary arrangements to electronic publications. In 1995, the technical platform was put in place to support a pilot project, and by the end of the year the library had negotiated the deposit of some 50 electronic journals and 100 other electronic publications. The project is focused primarily on the technical aspects of acquiring, cataloguing, and storing electronic documents. Researchers can access material on a very restrictive basis. (For additional information on this project, see Feijen, 1996.)

In 1994, the National Library of Canada also began a pilot project for the deposit of on-line electronic publications, using hands-on experience to examine issues related to acquisitions, cataloguing, file management, and preservation. By October 1995, a collection of 25 electronic journals had been assembled as part of the pilot project, and the project team had developed some 30 recommendations on both policy and technical matters. (For additional information on the project, see National Library of Canada, 1995.) With the completion of the initial pilot phase of the project, the National Library has continued to develop its electronic collection and has now mounted on its server more than 200 electronic journals and other on-line publications. The deposit of these publications is continuing on a voluntary basis, with priority given to electronic publications that are not available in any other format, particularly publications issued by the federal government. The publishers transmit their publications and updates to the National Library by e-mail or file transfer protocol (FTP), or, in some cases, permit the National Library to "mirror" the publication. As all of the publications acquired to date have been free, publishers have expressed relatively little concern about the National Library providing public access to the documents.

Long-term access and preservation

The legal issues related to proprietary interests and copyright are less problematic when viewed in the context of preservation. Publishers generally have little difficulty acknowledging the role that national libraries play in preserving the country's published output. To the extent that the preservation role can be separated from issues related to public access, they are generally supportive of national library efforts to create an archive of the country's published heritage, regardless of whether the publications are in conventional print or recorded formats or in electronic form. Even on copyright issues, publishers have indicated a willingness to permit certain exceptions in legislation that would enable a library to reproduce a rare, fragile, or damaged out-of-print work in its collection in order to preserve its content. They have also shown some willingness to make accommodation in the law for the migration of a work from a technically obsolete format to one that can be used with currently available technology. The debate surrounding the reproduction right and its implications for access is thus somewhat attenuated when put in the context of long-term preservation.

The technical challenge of preserving electronic publications is another matter. The first source of difficulty is the nature of the storage medium. With all its shortcomings, paper (at least alkaline paper) is the most stable medium available to us for the preservation of documentary materials. Rag papers have lasted hundreds of years. Paper manufactured today to standards approved for permanence can also be expected to last 400 years or more. By comparison, the magnetic media used for storing electronic data are much more fragile and susceptible to deterioration over a relatively short time frame. The newer optical media are largely unproven, and unlikely to remain intact anywhere near as long as permanent paper or archival-quality microfilm, 10 to 15 years on average. Therefore, if documents in electronic form are to be preserved over the long term, continuous migration from one store (or information carrier) to another on a relatively short cycle will be a prerequisite. Unless the costs of electronic storage media decline significantly, and the life expectancy of the media increases substantially, the cost of migrating electronic documents for preservation purposes may prove to be prohibitive, even for institutions with a preservation mandate such as national libraries.

Even more problematic is the issue of intelligibility of electronic documents over the long term. Because the intelligibility of digitally encoded documents is inextricably linked to coding schema, applications software, and even operating systems and peripherals, technological development and change in any of those areas can effectively render a document obsolete. Maintaining a museum of outmoded hardware and software is not an option national libraries can contemplate as a means of ensuring the preservation of the intelligibility of the content of electronic documents.

Bibliographic access

The emergence of electronic publishing poses challenges for bibliographic control and access that in many ways parallel the challenges of adapting legal deposit systems to the new modes of publishing. Most national bibliographies, like most systems of legal deposit, were initiated at a time when print was the predominant, if not exclusive, medium of publication. As a result, the scope of coverage for national bibliographies has tended to be centred largely on the print media, and several have retained that orientation even though the volume of non-print publishing has increased substantially over time. Similarly, the cataloguing conventions used to describe publications listed in the national bibliography are strongly rooted in practices developed originally for the description of print materials. Although they have been adapted over time to accommodate the description of non-print materials, the fit has not always been as comfortable as one might wish.

The value of a national bibliography, like that of a national system of legal deposit, is linked in a very direct way to its comprehensiveness. To maintain its value both as a register and as a bibliographic access tool, the national bibliography must ensure that its scope of coverage is continuously broadened to include emerging forms of publication. With new forms of publication, new mechanisms often have to be put in place to capture the data that is needed to create the bibliographic record. Cataloguing rules and conventions have to be adapted to accommodate the characteristics of the new media and new modes of dissemination. And the interfaces between the national bibliography per se and related systems of bibliographic control and access need to be re-aligned and re-tuned.

Registration of electronic publications

Canadiana (1953), Canada's national bibliography, has served as a comprehensive register of newly published Canadian materials since its inception in 1950. Although for the first 20 years it listed only print publications, its coverage has been extended over time, more or less in sync with the extension of legal deposit, to include published sound recordings, microforms, audiovisual, multimedia, video, and electronic materials. Within the last year, records have been added for the on-line journals and other on-line publications acquired during and subsequent to the National Library's electronic publications pilot project.

However, comprehensive registration of Canadian on-line publications can only be achieved if the National Library has a systematic means of identifying all new publications. Clearly, legal deposit of on-line publications offers the potential of providing that means once the legal issues have been settled and the deposit mechanisms are in place. In the interim, the National Library can be alerted to the existence of a new Canadian on-line publication by alternative means.

As the Canadian agency for the International Standard Serials Numbering (ISSN) system, the National Library receives requests from serials publishers who want ISSNs assigned to their new publications. As part of the assignment process, the National Library obtains the necessary bibliographic data from the publisher and creates a record to be reported to the international register of serials. The same data forms the core of the record for that serial to be included in the national bibliography. With the recent extension of the ISSN program to include electronic serials, this system serves at least in part as an alternative registration mechanism. Unlike the legal deposit system, however, the ISSN system is entirely voluntary. Registration is normally initiated only at the publisher's request.

The National Library also acts as one of the two Canadian agencies responsible for assigning ISBNs under the International Standard Book Numbering system. The Bibliothèque nationale du Québec assigns blocks of ISBNs to French-language publishers primarily in Quebec, and the National Library handles assignments primarily for English-language publishers. The ISBN system operates differently than the ISSN system, however, in that normally the publisher is assigned a block of ISBNs rather than a single number for a particular publication, and the assigning agency does not register bibliographic data. Another difference is that decisions have not yet been made at the international level as to whether and how ISBNs should be assigned to electronic publications. At this juncture, therefore, use of the ISBN system as an alternative mechanism for alerting the National Library to the existence of a new on-line publication is not really feasible.

Apart from requests for ISSNs coming in from publishers of new on-line journals, the only means the National Library has of tracking new on-line publications is through monitoring the communication networks—surfing the Internet, making use of various resource discovery tools, monitoring newsgroups, and even tracking the print media for announcements of new on-line publications. That activity is rather labour-intensive and somewhat serendipitous at best.

Capturing metadata

From a cataloguer's perspective, electronic publications have at least one advantage over conventional print publications. Potentially, a substantial portion of the data required to compile a bibliographic record for the publication can be captured and incorporated into the bibliographic record with minimal effort. Given that the bibliographic record is being created on-line, that certain key elements of the description are normally to be transcribed as they appear in the publication itself, and that it is possible to develop applications that would transfer the digitally encoded data in the publication directly to the digitally encoded bibliographic record, considerable potential exists for minimizing the effort involved in the more mechanical aspects of the cataloguer's task. The potential for reducing the time and level of effort required to compile the bibliographic record is of real interest to the National Library, especially since the resources available for the bibliographic activity are being strained by budget cuts and down-sizing.

To capitalize on the potential savings, however, a certain degree of standardization is needed in the way metadata (data about data) is structured and encoded in a publication. Work in this area is under way on several fronts in both North America and Europe. The Text Encoding Initiative (TEI), the development of the Dublin Core Metadata Element Set, and the Development of a European Service for Information on Research and Education (DESIRE) project in Europe are among the key initiatives aimed at bringing a greater level of standardization to the encoding of metadata within on-line publications. There has also been some work done in mapping the proposed metadata structures to the Machine-Readable Cataloguing (MARC) format that is the library standard for recording bibliographic data within a machine-readable catalogue record. However, these initiatives are still in a relatively early stage of development and a considerable amount of further work will be required to standardize the encoding of metadata and to promote widespread implementation of the standards. (For a bibliography and directory of reports on current metada initiatives, see the IFLANet Web site [URL: http://www.nlc-bnc.ca/ifla/II/metadata.htm].) Without a well-defined and reasonably stable standard that is widely used across various sectors of the on-line publishing industry, it will be next to impossible to develop the applications software that would be needed to support the seamless transfer of metadata embedded in on-line publications to the bibliographic records that form the national registry.

If efforts to standardize the metadata embedded in on-line publications are successful, the time and effort that agencies like the National Library currently expend on some of the more mechanical aspects of data capture for bibliographic records can be redirected to the more important value-added aspects of record creation. Cataloguers creating records for the national bibliography add real value through the establishment of uniform headings for the names of authors, the creation of the network of "see" references that assist users in finding works by those authors, the development of thesauri of subject terms, the analysis of document content, and the assignment of appropriate subject terms and classification indices. If more of the data needed to identify and describe the publication simply as a publication can be ported into the record with minimal effort, then that much more effort can be spent on creating data that will assist the user in situating that publication in the context of other related publications, of other works by the same author, and of other works in the same subject area.

Interfacing with indexing services and resource discovery tools

In their original form, national bibliographies functioned as more or less discrete tools. They would be placed on library shelves next to other bibliographies and printed catalogues to be searched *seriatim* as sources of data to be used in the library's own catalogue, as tools for verifying data on publications requested by users, or to assist the user in conducting bibliographic searches for material on particular topics of interest. With the proliferation of on-line bibliographic databases, the records created for the national bibliography are now part and parcel of a larger, multifunctional data resource. Within the National Library's AMICUS database, the records created for the national bibliography occupy space with records created by the Library of Congress, records created on-line by federal departments and agencies such as the Canada Institute for Scientific and Technical Information (CISTI), and records created by academic, public, and special libraries right across Canada that have been used to report holdings to the national union catalogue. In addition, the interconnection of bibliographic databases through the Internet and the development of standardized search protocols have served to virtualize the bibliographic data resource, effectively bringing into one shared space catalogue data created by libraries, data created by abstracting and indexing services, and a whole new range of resource discovery tools created to help users navigate the Internet and the World Wide Web.

Assisting the user in conducting searches that cross from one bibliographic data resource to another has been part of the rationale for integrating bibliographic control activities such as the assignment of ISBNs and ISSNs with the creation of the national bibliographic record. Even before the on-line database became the primary tool for conducting bibliographic searches, it was recognized that single-key, unique identifiers such as the ISBN and ISSN could serve as very useful devices to help bridge the different bibliographic conventions used in different sectors of the information industry. They provide a key link between publishers' databases, abstracting and indexing databases, and library catalogues. It is important to ensure that those same systems are adapted where possible to accommodate electronic publications, and that new systems are devised to accommodate new types of information objects that cannot be accommodated by the existing systems.

Canadian Theses Program

When the Canadian Theses Program was initiated in 1965, only four universities participated. Within a relatively short period of time, the number of participating universities grew substantially. Today, 51 universities and colleges take part in the program. With 10,000 theses being microfilmed each year, the program is estimated to cover about 85% of all theses currently accepted for degrees in Canada at both the masters and doctoral level. Maintaining, and if possible enhancing, that level of comprehensiveness is a key program objective.

Up until now, all theses covered by the program have been submitted in a paper format. The manuscripts and accompanying documentation are sent directly by the participating universities and colleges to the National Library's agent, Micromedia, and filmed to archival standards. Preservation copies of the microfilm are stored in vaults at the National Library, and service copies are produced both for the National Library and for the originating university or college. Micromedia operates a publication-on-demand service, responding to orders from within Canada. Orders from outside Canada are filled through arrangements with UMI.

The widespread current use of document processing software to create thesis manuscripts has prompted university administrators and librarians to consider the potential for integrating electronic theses into the systems that serve to facilitate access to theses, both at the local campus level and more widely at the national and international level. Several Canadian universities have begun to experiment with the practical implications of accepting theses in a digital format and making them available in that form through their libraries. The Electronic Theses Project Team at the University of Waterloo has recently undertaken a survey to determine how other universities are dealing with policy and procedural issues, intellectual property issues, and technical matters related to access, distribution, storage, and preservation of electronic theses. (For details on the questionnaire, see the University of Waterloo Electronic Theses Project Team, EDT Questionnaire [URL: http://library.uwaterloo.ca/~uw-etpt/survey.html].) In the U.S., a number of universities participate in the Electronic Thesis and Dissertation Project, which is aimed at exploiting digital technology to make the production, collection, and storage of theses more efficient and to enhance user access to graduate research results. (For additional information on the project, see the Electronic Thesis and Dissertation Project Web site [URL: http://etd.vt.edu/universities/description.html].) UMI has also recently expanded its program to encompass digital dissertations. (For a description of the service, see the ProQuest Digital Dissertations pilot site [URL: http://www.lib.umi.com/solutions/22.1.1.html].) The partners in the Canadian Theses Program—the universities and colleges, the National Library, Micromedia, and UMI—have also informally begun to assess the potential for the integration of electronic theses into the program.

As with other electronic documents, however, the real challenge will be in finding ways to ensure the preservation of electronic theses and to guarantee the intelligibility of their content over the long term. Until the viability of long-term archiving of digital theses can be assured, it will be essential to maintain the archival microfilming component of the program.

Strategic priorities

From the National Library's perspective, three key issues among those outlined above are of strategic priority and require collaborative effort among the various stakeholders in the scholarly communications enterprise.

First is the need to address the issues relating to public access to electronic publications acquired by the National Library through legal deposit. Inasmuch as the copyright issues around digital materials are not likely to be resolved in the near future, especially given the recent pace of copyright revisions in Canada, it is critically important that publishers, scholars, and the National Library work together to establish mutually agreed guidelines governing access to electronic publications deposited with the National Library.

Second is the need to develop and implement standards for recording metadata in electronic publications that will facilitate new modes of access to those documents and more efficient means of porting data from the documents themselves to the bibliographic databases that serve as key research support tools.

Third is the need for collaboration between Canadian universities, the National Library, and service providers to develop document standards for theses in digital formats and to expedite the integration of digital theses into the Canadian Theses Program.

References

Anglo-Nordic Seminar on Legal Deposit. (1995). *Legal deposit with special reference to the archiving of electronic materials: Proceedings of a seminar organized by NORDINFO and the British Library Research and Development Department.* Esbo, Finland: NORDINFO.

Canadiana. (1953). Ottawa: National Library of Canada.

Dissertation Abstracts International. C. Worldwide. (1989). Ann Arbor, MI: UMI.

Feijen, Martin. (1996). DDEP: The Dutch Depository of Electronic Publications. In Peter Hoare, *Legal deposit of non-print material: An international overview* (pp. 103-114). London: British Library Research and Development Department.

Hoare, Peter. (1996). *Legal deposit of non-print material: An international overview.* London: British Library Research and Development Department.

International Federation of Library Associations and Institutions. (1996). *Position paper on copyright in the electronic environment* [Press release]. URL: http://www.nlc-bnc.ca/ifla/V/press/pr961002.html

International Publishers' Association. (1996). Resolution passed at the 25th IPA Congress, Barcelona, April 22-26, 1996.

Masters Abstracts International. (1986). Ann Arbor, MI: UMI.

National Library of Canada. (1995). *Electronic publications pilot project (EPPP): Final report.* Ottawa: Author. URL: http://www.nlc-bnc.ca/e-coll-e/edown.htm

Revised Statues of Canada (Chapter 31). (1952). Ottawa: Queen's Printer.

Revised Statues of Canada (Chapter 47). (1969). Ottawa: Queen's Printer.

Royal Commission on national development in the arts, letters, and sciences. (1951). *Report*. Ottawa: King's Printer.

Electronic Publishing in Science: Reality Check

Aldyth Holmes
National Research Council of Canada

Abstract: The role of the primary publisher in the changing context of today's scholarly communication is explored in the face of the electronic publishing debate. NRC Research Press's experience provides practical data by examining the costs of implementing electronic versions of *Canadian Journal of Fisheries and Aquatic Sciences* and the *Canadian Journal of Physiology and Pharmacology*. Data on early patterns of use, some associated outcomes, and a comparison of information from other scholarly publishers are presented. It is concluded that electronic journals are not significantly less expensive to produce than paper publications. The relative merits of various methods for recovering costs in an electronic environment are compared in order to identify and address specific problems.

Résumé: Nous explorons le rôle de l'éditeur dans le contexte changeant de la communication savante aujourd'hui en nous penchant sur les débats entourant l'édition électronique. L'expérience des Presses scientifiques du CNRC nous a permis d'obtenir des données sur les coûts de publier deux de ses revues savantes sous forme électronique, soit le *Journal canadien des sciences halieutiques et aquatiques* et la *Revue canadienne de physiologie et pharmacologie.* Nous discutons des données sur l'usage que les premiers lecteurs ont fait de ces revues ainsi que de résultats connexes, et nous comparons l'expérience des Presses scientifiques à celles d'autres éditeurs de publications savantes. Nous concluons que les journaux savants électroniques ne sont pas tellement moins chers à produire que les publications traditionnelles. Nous comparons différentes méthodes de récupérer les dépenses pour les revues électronique afin d'identifier et d'aborder certains problèmes.

Aldyth Holmes is Director of NRC Research Press at the Canada Institute for Scientific and Technical Information at the National Research Council, M-55, Montreal Road, Ottawa, ON K1A 0R6. E-mail: aldyth.holmes@nrc.ca

***Canadian Journal of Communication,* Vol. 22, No. 3/4 (1997) 105-116**

Introduction: The role of the publisher

Publishing has always played a key role in scientific, technical, and medical (STM) scholarly communication. It performs the social function of conferring what Professor Lederburg called "dignity" on the work (Lederburg, 1996). This dignity is conferred by the imprimatur of the editors and gives the author prestige that assists in attracting students, grants, and promotions. Underlying this prestige is the practical validation or filtering function carried out by the editors, supported by the reviewers, who screen the material, excluding inaccurate or incomplete information. Publication organizes material to help accessibility, grouping articles in related areas in particular publications and providing abstracts, keywords, and indexes. It provides the raw material for archives so that information 50 or 100 years old can still be located and retrieved. Some of these functions are delegated by the primary publisher to secondary publishers and librarians, but they are still integral parts of the scholarly communication process. The publication format, paper or electronic, does not change the need for the services that the publishers and librarians provide, but rather changes the way in which dissemination of the information is undertaken. The conclusion is that as long as scholars need a social structure that validates their work so that it will be funded, and a practical structure for locating and retrieving useful information, the activities now carried out by the publisher will be required, so there is a need for an economic structure to support this process.

As computer networks have matured and global telecommunications have become an affordable reality, a debate has raged over the future of paper as the medium for scholarly communication. We should first acknowledge the fact that the process of publishing is not necessarily central to STM communication. The sharing of esoteric information among experts in a particular field is occurring at conferences and in informal exchanges through electronic mail. Those who are actively engaged in scholarship in a specific field have their "invisible colleges" with whom they regularly share information. This research information will then become the subject of a formal paper and published so that it is available to those outside the "in-crowd." The publishing process makes information available in a form that has been validated; the rough edges that were the subject of debate in the invisible college are smoothed out and the material is organized into a clearly recognizable and retrievable format that can be stored for the students of today and the scholars of tomorrow, with the author's name clearly attached to the work.

Will this change in a world of electronic publishing? The paper journal has been with us for a long time; the Royal Society published its first transactions in 1665. Standards have evolved for the scientific paper; it represents an efficient and concise way of communicating the results of research. However, the electronic format presents new opportunities. Scholars are exploring the potential of the new medium, and we are at the beginning of an age of transition, but the same imperatives of accuracy and accessibility will apply. While the scholars have always been accountable for the accuracy of the scholarship, it is the publishers and librarians who have made it accessible. Can or will this model continue in the electronic world? The librarians have been supported financially by the scholars' institutions or the state. The publishers have found various models. The not-for-profit publishers rely on financial support from the members of their societies or on government funding, plus cost recovery from the scholars or their institutions via page charges and subscriptions. The commercial publishers pay scholars to support the publication process and are also able to get volunteer labour to support the peer-review process. As scholars begin to insist on compensation for the time they spend as editors and reviewers, the costs of the product will increase. As costs go up, subscription prices rise, libraries cancel subscriptions, and unit costs are forced up even further. Can electronic publishing break this vicious circle?

NRC Research Press

To understand the background to the economics of scholarly publishing, one must first examine the use of the material being published. It is difficult for a publisher to assess the usage of journals published in paper; copyright revenue, the only direct measure, represents a mere 0.2% or less of the revenue stream, as most copying is done claiming fair dealing/fair use exemptions. Librarians make studies of usage to justify cancellations. Citation data are extremely limited in that they show nothing about the use of the information by the non-publishing community—for example, the student or industrial development scientist—or about the incidence of "read but not cited." The publisher is responsible only for delivering the journal to the individual or institution, so the only data available are about the subscribers. The following information about the *Canadian Journal of Fisheries and Aquatic Sciences* (*CJFAS*), one of the top three in its field, is typical of the information a publisher has on usage. This journal is now available in both paper and electronic formats. It is individuals who cite material from journals, but, as in the case of *CJFAS*, it is primarily institutions who subscribe to them. Figure 1 shows the international scope of the journal's purchasers and the split between institutional and personal subscribers.

Information on the electronic version of the journal after a year of availability takes a different form. We can see which articles are being accessed, and we can analyze the source of the enquiry to a limited extent. The high number of unresolved Internet provider (IP) addresses (that cannot be traced to a source) makes this information of minimal usefulness beyond the fact that the journal is indeed reaching readers around the world in its electronic format. Of the addresses that could be resolved, in one month 27% of the hits came from outside North America, 31% from the U.S.A., and 42% from Canada. None of this information addresses the question of who is actually reading the journal.

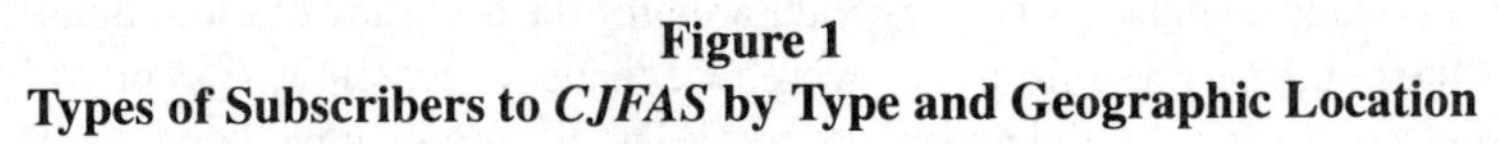

Figure 1
Types of Subscribers to *CJFAS* by Type and Geographic Location

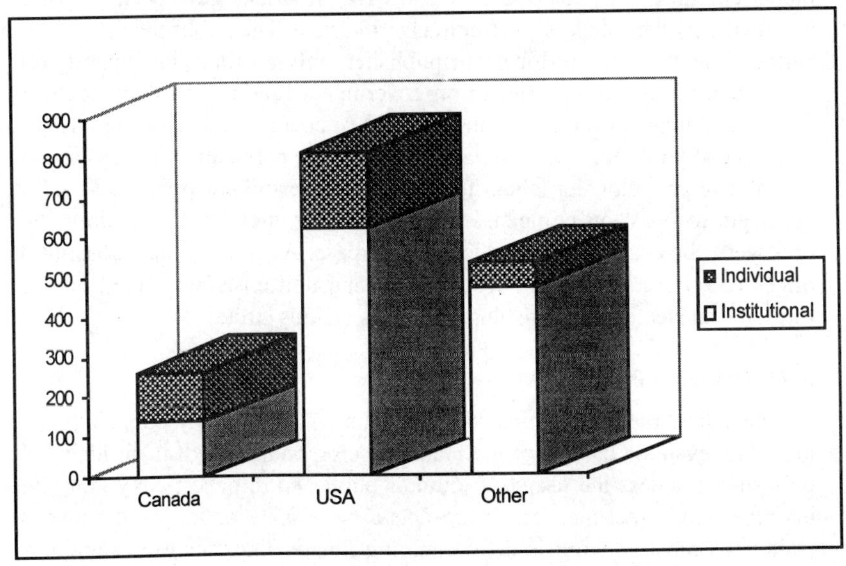

But, for the first time, we have a means of observing which papers are being accessed. This is a change from determining which journals get most citations. Information on citation of individual articles in paper journals is available, at considerable expense, but this is not a measure of the true use of the article or the interest it generated. In the electronic world we have a means of measuring these. Figure 2 shows the number of times each paper was accessed in its second month of release. (The second month was chosen in order to eliminate differences in loading dates.) This access relates to the (fixed) portable document format (PDF) file and, unlike the tables of contents, should not include Web crawlers or maintenance access. The x axis shows the range of hits or accesses during the month and the y axis the number of papers that fall into each access level. Over the eight months covered, a typical paper was accessed 10 to 20 times in its second month of publication.

It is possible for the publisher, when gathering the above information, to identify the papers being accessed. This information is routinely passed to the journal editor to assist in editorial decisions about areas of current interest where papers should be encouraged. The one paper that registered over 100 hits in a month was Yves Prairie's "Evaluating the Predictive Power of Regression Models," which deals with a subject of interest beyond the field of aquatic science. This suggests that electronic publication makes it far easier for people to find relevant information in publications outside their field. In other words, electronic publication improves dissemination by compensating for the filtering that occurs when an author elects to publish in a particular journal.

Figure 2
Access to Full-text Articles in *CJFAS*

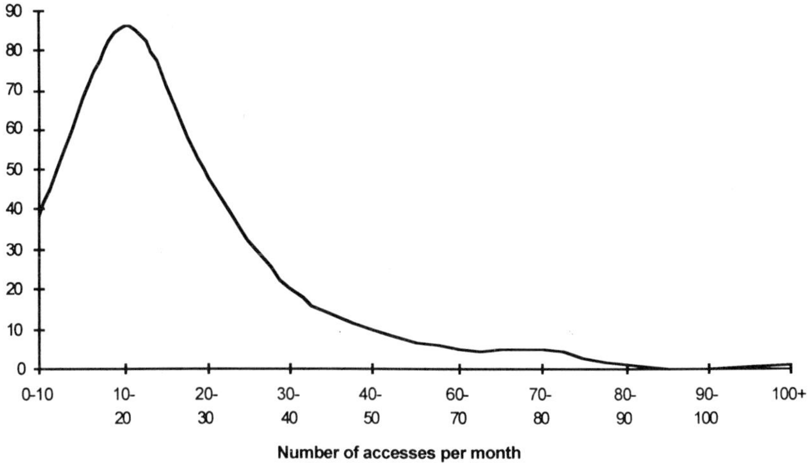

Cost considerations

Peer review

NRC Research Press is a not-for-profit publisher, publishing 14 scientific and technical journals. Our production process is fairly typical of those of medium-sized, high-quality publishers. Costs are incurred at each stage by the various parties contributing to the scholarly communication process. Three major categories of activity incur costs: filtering, accessibility, and dissemination. The components of these activities are shown in Table 1.

Table 1
The Elements of Scholarly Communication

Filtering or validation	Authoring costs Peer-review costs Editors, referees
Accessibility	Preparation for publication Copy editing, layout and file preparation, indexing
Dissemination	Publication/Dissemination Printing, distributing, loading on the networks, provision of reader access, archiving and storage for long-term dissemination

These activities have to be undertaken regardless of the format of communication. If any one of these activities is overlooked, the process of communication from author to reader is inhibited. In the various models of scholarly communication under discussion at this conference, the effect of changing models is to move the costs incurred for each activity in the process from one participant to another in the hope that someone will undertake the activity on a volunteer basis, thus absorbing the costs and reducing the burden on the institutional budget as it is presently structured.

The authors' costs

As a publisher, I have no direct knowledge of the costs incurred by authors in preparing a paper. We receive papers from around the world and see only the reaction to a request to submit in particular electronic formats. It is a relief to know that, for about 95% of the papers submitted, we can get diskettes in major software packages that we can read. There are still some problem areas in the world, and we have to face the fact that for some time yet we may have to bear the cost of rekeying some papers to create an electronic version suitable for the publication process. We are increasingly able to get electronic files of images; these too facilitate publication. In fact, we are continually challenged to keep our own hardware and software up to the levels of some leading-edge authors who submit material to us; had we fewer titles, this investment would be hard to justify. How would the authors' costs change in an electronic publishing environment? I can only speculate that the pressure to have the best possible equipment and connectivity, or the ability to produce material in formats acceptable to publishers or attractive to readers, would become as intense as the pressure to secure funds for the research itself.

The author is responsible for the first stage of filtering the information when he selects the vehicle for publication that is most likely to reach the audience with whom the information is to be shared. There may be other reasons for selecting a particular publication, such as prestige or ease of acceptance, but these are matters of ethics for the scholarly community and not for public comment by a publisher.

The peer-review process

At NRC Research Press, we do not generally pay editors, but we do contract with the editor's institution to pay for the office support necessary to run the peer-review process. The costs of these editorial offices have increased 61% in the last 10 years. In comparison, inflation as measured by the Consumer Price Index has been approximately 34% over the same period. The reason for this cost increase seems, on examination, to be that the institutions are unwilling to donate as many services and facilities as they were in the past. Once, the universities would willingly donate free office space, furniture, and postage, but this is changing rapidly; all institutions expect the publisher to cover the cost of postage, computers, and equipment for the office, and an increasing number are requesting that space be rented from the institution. So far we have had two requests to fund editors, either directly or indirectly by funding replacement teachers. This may be indicative of a future trend. The community of scholars, or their institutions, is becoming less willing to support the validation process without financial recompense. These expenses all relate to the peer-review process. If the integrity and accuracy of scholarly communication are to be maintained, the peer-review process must continue to be funded regardless of the format of communication. The electronic review process can save postage but someone has to ensure that all reviewers have machines and connections powerful enough to receive and view the large, complex files that make up some scientific articles. In the electronic world, the demand to include MPEG files in scientific publications is just emerging. Addressing the problems does not require technology, but rather investment in the infrastructure to support electronic publishing, particularly the peer-review process. Is it appropriate to restrict the review process to those peers who have the necessary hardware on their desktops? If connectivity and hardware play a key role in the success of electronic publications, those costs will not be borne by the publisher or the library, but by the departments that pay for the computers and by the administration that provides the connectivity. On the American Association of Higher Education Newsgroup (AAHESGIT), a recent discussion on the cost of computer technology at the desktop came up with a figure of U.S.$5,000 to $7,400 as the direct cost per year per machine in an academic environment (Bantz, 1996). The cost of postage to ship manuscripts around for peer review (an average of $21 per manuscript for a full review with a minimum of two reviewers) has just been shifted from the publisher to the reviewer's institution, which provides the communication infrastructure.

Preparing material for publication

Once a paper has gone through the peer-review process, the author has made all the necessary revisions to the content, and the paper has been accepted for publication, that is, it has passed through the second stage of filtering, the material then has to be prepared for publication. Despite titles such as *New England Journal of Medicine*, *Canadian Journal of Forest Research*, *Journal of the American Chemical Society*, STM publications are typically global in nature. The first language of the author may not be the language in which he or she is publishing. Of the papers NRC publishes, 53% originate outside Canada. Figure 3 shows the sources of articles published in all 14 titles.

While the use of either British or American spelling may not impede communication, it may impede access (Ito, 1996). The use of unusual or colloquial grammatical structures can slow a reader down. For an international readership, the language of the article must be internationally comprehensible. This is where the work of copy editors comes in. These are highly skilled people; it takes about nine months to train a scientific copy editor to NRC Research Press standards. This quality-upgrading function is independent of format.

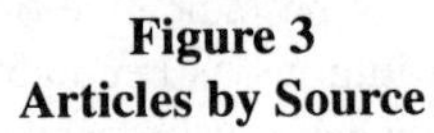
Figure 3
Articles by Source

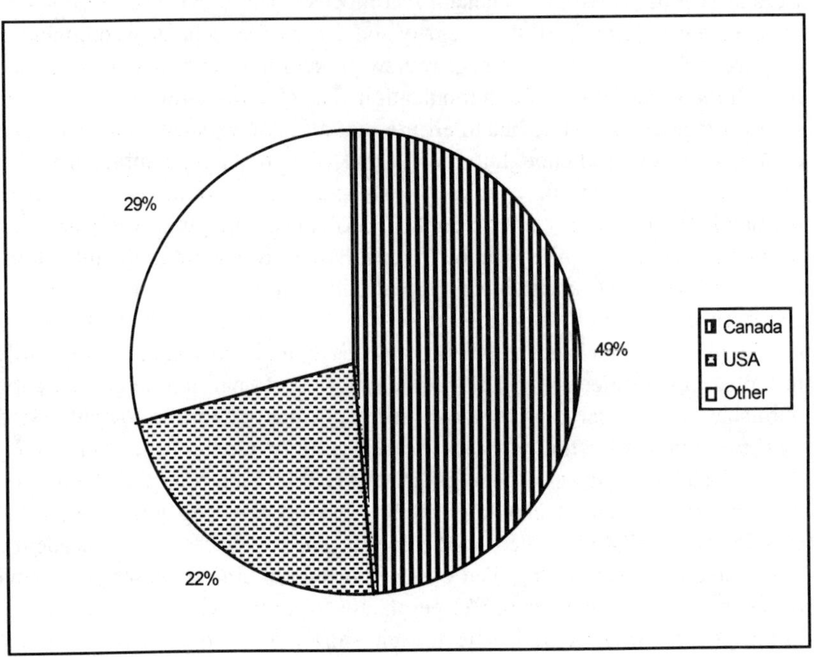

It is at this point that the costs of producing an electronic versus a paper journal start to diverge: the prepublication processes differ for electronic and paper publication. Nor are these processes stable; they are constantly being re-engineered to take advantage of technology. The average costs of publishing in paper and paper plus electronic formats, based on eight months' financial data for 14 scientific journals, are summarized in Table 2. These data include all the costs associated with the learning curve involved in the transition from paper to electronic format and the re-engineering of existing processes, and may not be indicative of the long-term costs. They do, however, highlight the possibility of economies of scale when overhead is spread over more titles or pages.

Based on the subscription prices for 1996, the average revenue per journal page was $306.18, which when compared with the costs in Table 2 shows the extent to which NRC currently subsidizes scholarly communications. NRC has been gradually reducing its subsidy to the publishing operation; in 1995, the average cost per page was $376.16, for average revenue per page of $275.12. As we gain experience in the production of electronic journals, we have observed that the lines between the tasks blur as individuals take on different tasks to make the process more efficient. The goal is always to get papers out as quickly as possible without any loss in quality.

The publisher provides the authoring community with editing and layout services, and also deals with the business aspects of distribution, protecting authors' rights to the material by handling copyright, and also by passing the material to secondary publishers for indexing and abstracting to increase the accessibility of the work. These services facilitate scientific communication by making the work easier to read, on screen or on paper, and increasing access to it. Ease of access and reading allows information to be transferred from author to reader as expeditiously as possible.

Table 2
Average Cost Per Published Page in 1996

	Paper ($)	Paper and electronic ($)
Editorial office costs	41.80	41.80
Distribution (to an average of 1,400 subscribers)	6.90	6.90
Editing/pre-marking/coding or tagging[a]	41.23	39.11
Layout/typesetting[a]	30.59	53.32
Printing	49.41	49.41
Total direct cost per page	169.93	190.54
Overhead per page[b]	161.56	161.56
Total publication cost per page	331.49	352.10

a. Coding and tagging is integrated with editing when material is prepared for contract typesetting, but is performed by layout staff in the in-house process. More extensive coding and tagging is required for the electronic product.

b. Includes management, facilities, maintenance, business systems, sales, marketing, subscription fulfillment, equipment, hardware, software, connectivity, and network support.

Access and dissemination

Once the electronic files are ready for publication, the dissemination process for electronic products diverges totally from that for the paper versions. For electronic publications, the file has to be further processed to facilitate access. The table of contents has to be prepared in HTML format; this is still onerous for titles with Greek characters, subscripts, and superscripts. Technology is catching up and simplifying the process, but whether readers will have the high-level browsers that enable them to see the special characters remains to be seen. Simple bookmarks are added to the articles and, as technology allows the process to become more automated, more internal links will be added. The file for each article has to be linked to the table of contents. The value added is limited only by the cost of adding it! The files are loaded onto the Web site, which, along with the links to the various indexing sources, have to be maintained. A whole new area of marketing is necessary to get links to and from other related sites, no mean task when one is dealing with titles in 14 different disciplines.

For publication on paper, the files go to an image setter and then plates are loaded on the printing press. Up to this point, the costs are all independent of the number of copies produced and distributed. The press operates and the copies are bound, packaged, and distributed. As shown in Table 2, printing and distribution costs account for between 15% and 17% of the total production costs of NRC's scientific journals. Commercial publishers are able to charge their overheads to a much wider range of publications, some with high profit margins.

Savings

There are widely divergent views on the savings to be achieved by moving to electronic publication. Harnad claims that the true cost of electronic publishing offers a 75% saving over paper (Okerson & O'Donnell, 1995). However, his electronic-only publishing model has serious limitations for international journals that aim to serve the whole community and not just those connected to the Internet. Science publishers such as the American Chemical Society (Okerson & O'Donnell, 1995) and the American Physical Society (Lustig, 1996), who recognize the need to keep paper versions of their journals available in order to reach the full international community and so are publishing in parallel formats, produce cost breakdowns similar to those of NRC Research Press. Because of the complexity of the technical terms and mathematics in STM publications, copy editing seems to take more time and skill than are being invested in the same process in humanities and social science journals. It is impossible to determine if this is a function of the language skills of the authors, the international sources of the material being processed, or the standards being set by individual disciplines. The *Canadian Journal of Communication* is claiming savings of 25% by going electronic; however, savings in distribution and printing costs of the paper version are offset by the increased costs of the expertise required to support the electronic product (Brandao, 1996).

Based on less than one year of producing electronic versions of only two titles, NRC Research Press has found that the electronic versions, produced in parallel with the paper versions, are costing an extra $20.61 per page, or 6%

more than a paper-only journal. This compares with the American Physical Society's figure of U.S.$10 per page quoted by Lustig (1996). As the processes are refined, costs will be reduced, but it seems unlikely that the spread will change, as many of the technological improvements made in order to produce the electronic version can be equally applied to the paper version.

Potential problems of electronic distribution

The instability of electronic products leads to the risk of valuable research being lost to future generations. The early electronic journals did not keep up their archives, they changed URLs (Harter & Kim,1996), and generally became invisible. NRC hopes to be able to assist the small Canadian STM scholarly publishers to move into the electronic world by providing advice and electronic distribution. Concern has been expressed that commercialization of the Internet will limit its availability to scholars. Already congestion is not unknown. As we work to solve the challenge of putting electronic publications on the shelves of the virtual library for NRC scientists across the country, we see an opportunity to add other titles to our collection by sharing our expertise in electronic publishing with other Canadian publishers. We are already discussing issues surrounding the legal depositing and archiving of electronic publications with the National Library. The systems for depositing electronic journals are in their infancy. National libraries around the world are confronting the issue of making these archival electronic publications available for the next hundred years. There is no cheap, easy solution, except perhaps to download the electronic file onto paper! Without publishers and librarians, who will ensure that scholarly research is recorded and stored for posterity?

Conclusion

The various steps that take STM information from the scientist and prepare it for sharing around the world have costs attached to them. Changing the format may change the cost structure but is unlikely to reduce costs significantly. It is more likely to transfer the costs from the publisher to the institutions of the author and reader. This implies that the large prolific research institutions will carry a much greater share of the cost of scholarly communication than the teaching institutions, where the readers are primarily located. Will the investment by research institutions in the information infrastructure become greater and be made at the expense of the library budget? If the economic infrastructure for scholarly communication is destroyed, the vehicles of communication will be eliminated. The not-for-profit publishers will be among the first to disappear. Will the individual disciplines be well served if the various societies can no longer afford to sponsor publication?

References

Bantz, D. (1996, December). *Full cost of information technology*. AAHESGIT Newsgroup.

Brandao, C. (1996, Winter). Rewiring the ivory tower (Putting scholarly journals online) [Special issue]. *Canadian Business Technology*, pp. 61-64.

Harter, S. P., & Kim, H. J. (1996, September). Accessing electronic journals and other E-publications: An empirical study. *College and Research Libraries*, *57*(5), 440-456.

Ito, K. (1996). Letter to the Editor. *Nature*, *382*(6593), 666.

Lederburg, J. (1996, February). Options for the future. In D. Shaw & H. Moore (Eds.), *Electronic publishing in science: Proceedings of the Joint ICSU Press/ UNESCO Expert Conference* (pp. 122-126). Paris: UNESCO and International Council of Scientific Unions.

Lustig, H. (1996). The finances of electronic publishing. *APS News* [Supplement], *5*(10), 2.

Okerson, A. S., & O'Donnell, J. J. (Eds.). (1995). *Scholarly journals at the crossroads: A subversive proposal for electronic publishing*. Washington: Association of Research Libraries.

An Evaluation for Scholarly Societies and Non-profit Associations: Self-publish or Go Commercial—Critical Issues for Boards and Managers

Walter Ludwig
The Prospect Group, Washington, DC

Abstract: The historical relationship between societies and commercial publishers is coming under increasing scrutiny, and for good reason. This paper discusses the issues of branding, content, finances, and stewardship in the context of non-profit-organization publishing. The arguments and tactics of commercial publishers in securing societies' publishing business are dissected, and the economics of commercial versus self-publishing are presented. A strong case is made that scholarly societies have both market and legal reasons to examine closely the blandishments of commercial publishers.

Résumé: Le rapport historique entre société et éditeurs commerciaux suscite un examen de plus en plus attentif, et pour cause. Cet article discute des questions de marques de commerce, de contenu, de financement, et de responsabilité dans l'édition à but non lucratif. Il examine les raisonnements et les tactiques des éditeurs commerciaux qui accaparent la charge d'éditer la grande part des publications dans notre société, et compare le financement de l'édition commerciale à celui de l'édition à but non lucratif. L'article soutient fortement que les sociétés savantes ont de bonnes raisons autant commerciales que légales de mettre en question les cajoleries des éditeurs commerciaux.

Introduction

It is no longer news that the governing boards and professional managers of non-profit organizations, even the most prosperous ones, are under increasing pressure to increase non-dues income. Demand for member services is

Walter Ludwig is Managing Partner of The Prospect Group, 1621 Connecticut Avenue, N.W., Suite 550, Washington, DC 20009. E-mail: walter@prospect-group.com

***Canadian Journal of Communication*, Vol. 22, No. 3/4 (1997) 117-125**

constant, often coupled with vehement resistance to higher membership fees. Not surprisingly, boards and managers often look to the organization's publishing program as a potential source of relief. In the majority of non-profit groups, publishing is the second-largest source of revenues behind dues, and for many scientific, technical, and medical (STM) societies, journals, books, and other media provide over half of the organization's income.

However, despite the obvious possibilities, many organizations continue to assign their potentially lucrative publishing operations to commercial companies. In doing so, they often needlessly deprive themselves of hundreds of thousands of dollars in revenue they could retain by asserting direct control over their publishing programs. The reasons for such decisions can vary from inertia to ignorance to fear. As well, commercial publishers use pressure tactics, play on the valid concerns of boards and managers, and have even used money to suborn editors of journals, undermining legitimate governance roles.

In this paper, I intend to examine the broad state of scholarly publishing today, discuss the issues involved in strategic management of publishing in non-profit organizations, and provide a rational framework that boards and managers of non-profits can use in making decisions about their publishing programs.

Publishing versus publishers

Since the Enlightenment, the system of reviewed publication to ratify information has evolved. Through the exposure of ideas to comment and response and eventual consensus, publication is the gold standard for data and the gateway for intellectual debate—and it will likely remain so.

Regardless of evolution in methods, modalities, and media, it is the information transmitted—the content—that is primal in the advance of ideas. In the face of Mr. McLuhan's thesis, in scholarly publishing the message is the message, and the medium really is just a delivery system.

Content is king

In 1997, scholarly publishing—really, all publishing—is in a situation much like that of commercial broadcasting 15 years ago. According to the Nielsen ratings, in 1980, the aggregate viewership of the big three U.S. networks—NBC, CBS, and ABC—was around 800 million people a week. At the same time, the new cable networks had a weekly viewership of just under 900,000. Less than two decades later, in a population about 15% larger, the Big Three's weekly aggregate viewership is down, around 740 million, and the cable companies draw around 400 million. Overall, more people are watching TV, and they have apparently become easily accustomed to the concept that the big providers are not necessarily the best judges of what they want to see. They want what they want, and it does not matter to them whether it is on Channel 4 or Channel 84.

As this model teaches us, content is king: the intrinsic value of an intellectual property is the information/content inside. (An example is David Letterman's television show, whose fans switched viewership allegiance in the millions from NBC to CBS without any consideration except that of content.) No one says, "Let's go see the new Paramount movie." People say instead, "Let's go see the new Stallone flick" or "I want to catch Woody Allen's new movie."

In its own way, the same is true for scholarly works. The non-profit society provides the brand name—and its journals and books provide the information value. Just as with movies, no one ever says, "I've gotta get the library to order that new Elsevier journal." They say, "I need the *Journal of Elbow Reconstruction*." More to the point, quick, can you name the publisher of *JAMA*? *Science*? The *New England Journal*? Whether you can or not, do you care? (All three are self-published.) The fact is that if your society, your journal, or your books have sufficiently important information, then a commercial publisher needs you a lot more than you need them.

Commercial scholarly publishing today

Today, commercial scholarly publishers ignore the above truth and operate on the premise that it is their imprint that confers credibility on the information they publish, rather than the other way around. This conceit embodies the outdated business model of current commercial scholarly publishing, and that antiquated model informs such companies' "pitch" to non-profit organizations.

Any nineteenth-century economist would recognize scholarly publishing as practised by commercial publishers today—Karl Marx could make it a case study. It is premised on, and hard-sells to, non-profits, a nineteenth-century version of the world. This version says that scholarly publishing requires huge amounts of capital, first and foremost to create and maintain facilities for physical production and, second, for the establishment and maintenance of elaborate distribution infrastructures.

These maxims may well have been true in 1792, when Lippincott was established; or in 1807, when Wiley was founded; or even as late as 1901, when Mosby began, but they are no longer true in the 1990s.

(The commercial companies are still competent at production and distribution—I have no arguments with them over methods of publishing. The Lippincotts, Wileys, and Mosbys do make the trains run on time, but the cost of their expertise is dear, as will be shown below.)

One might quibble over this or that mechanical aspect on this or that journal. But those are the legitimate kinds of differences that professionals might have over approaches. That is the point—that despite the impression commercial publishers try to leave, for many years now publishing professionals in all disciplines have existed, even flourished, outside commercial publishing companies.

Harbour no illusions that commercial publishers own plants full of third-generation employee-craftsmen wearing company patches on their shirts. Like everyone today, these publishers buy services on the outside—copy editing, typesetting, printing, mailing, warehousing—from companies and free-lance individuals who specialize in such services. Why? Because they have, internally and consequent to consciousness of their own bottom lines, realized that the physical part of publishing—the services part—is available on a competitive, global basis.

At the end of the day in 1997, all a commercial publisher provides is a clearing-house method to procure a variety of services—editorial office management, redaction, pre-press, printing, all the way to list maintenance, and marketing—which they buy on the open market, at open market prices.

Under this model, commercial publishers act as banks with Yellow Pages. They flip though the phone book, find the right vendors for this and that and the other, and front the money to the vendors for each service. What is that extension of credit worth?

The commercial publisher as bank: A metaphor

Suppose you had a credit card, and it offered what the bank called a "telepathic" shopping service. For a fee, the bank would do all your shopping and remembering and make all your payments for you—house, clothes, food, transportation—and everything would be delivered to your house. No trips to the mall. No remembering in August that school is going to start in a week and that you have to buy crayons and book bags. This credit card requires no payments; there are no monthly statements; and there is no nagging balance. But the bank gets your whole annual pay cheque, directly, at the beginning of the year, as well as the money that your mother pays you to do her taxes, and the Christmas bonus, and the kids' lawn-mowing money. Everything goes straight to the bank. Certainly this is an uncomplicated financial situation. The bank takes all your income, but they do all the shopping and pay for everything. All just for a fee.

If the bank is a commercial publisher, that fee is going to be around 65% on top of the real price of the goods or services. A typical commercial publishing contract provides for an extra "overhead" fee of $65 for every $100 of actual purchases. In terms of that magic credit card, your $1,000 house payment turns into $1,650; food is $250 a week instead of $150; and the car costs around $6,000 a year, not $3,500. But you worked hard all year, and you make a lot of money; even with these fees, surely there is something left from all those pay cheques and all those lawn-mowing fees. However, the fine print says that the bank gets to keep most of the money left over after all the bills are paid. Typically, commercial publishing deals split profits—money left over after expenses (plus overhead)—60% to the publisher, the balance to the sponsoring society.

An example

This typical structure of a deal between a commercial publishing company and a society can have dramatic effects on the finances of even a modest journal, as you will see below. Table 1 shows the actual financial analysis of a real journal we have worked with, fictionalized here as *The Journal of Elbow Reconstruction*.

Table 1
Annual Journal Subscriber/Revenue Base

Item	Amount	Rate per unit ($)	Revenues ($)
Subscriptions			
U.S. Institutional	1,971	75	147,825
U.S. Individual	1,071	46	49,266
U.S. Student	297	24	7,128
All Foreign	997	75	74,775
Totals	4,336		278,994
Advertising pages	36	350	12,600
125-page supplements	2	200	50,000
Total annual revenue			341,594

With revenues of nearly $350,000, this journal should be profitable to the society. But Table 2 shows the numbers for the commercial publishing deal previously agreed to by the society.

Under this arrangement, the sponsoring society actually lost money on its own journal when editorial costs were included, while the publisher had revenues above direct expenses of over $150,000. But, as Table 3 shows, when the journal was society-published, there was a dramatic difference, even after factoring in significant one-time costs.

Over five years—the typical length of a contract with a commercial publisher—self-publishing the *Journal of Elbow Reconstruction* will positively affect the society's "bottom line" by over $580,000, even if circulation and subscription rates remain static. Most important, it will do so without increasing dues or decreasing member services.

Given numbers like these, which again are strongly typical, why do societies with clearly valuable publishing properties and defined audiences give them away to commercial publishers? Unfortunately, publishers use a number of scary arguments and questionable tactics to frighten societies and, in some cases, undermine their legitimate interests in order to make these deals.

Table 2
Annual Revenue and Expenses for a Commercially Published Journal

Total revenue	$341,594
Expenses	
Services procured by publisher	
Production (redaction, pre-press, printing, binding)	105,000
Mailing/Postage	20,000
Marketing	20,000
Renewal/List maintenance	12,500
Total for services	157,500
Publisher's overhead charge (65% of total services)	102,375
Profit (Services + overhead − revenues)	81,719
Publisher's share (60% of profit)	49,031
Net to society	32,688
Editorial office expenses (society-paid)	78,000
Net revenue to society	–45,312
Net revenue to publisher	151,406

Table 3
Annual Revenue and Expenses for a Society-Published Journal

Total revenue	$341,594
Expenses	
Services procured by society	
Production (pre-press, printing, binding)	105,000
Mailing/Postage	20,000
Marketing	20,000
Renewal/List maintenance	12,500
Total for services	157,500
One-time transition costs	25,000
Profit (Services less transition costs)	159,094
Net to society	159,094
Editorial office expenses (society-paid)	108,000
Net revenue to society	51,094
Net revenue to society after one-time costs	76,094

Fear, uncertainty, and doubt: How publishers scare societies

1. The value-added argument

Publishers routinely tell renewing or prospective non-profit clients that it is only the intrinsic value that the publisher has added or will add that makes the society's journal worth anything at all, and that, without this publisher-added value, subscription rates will dwindle, advertising will evaporate, and contributions wither.

It is continually surprising to me that societies accept this absurd argument. A commercial publishing company does not take on a society's publishing program as a charitable act. Commercials only go after programs with either a well-established audience or clear potential.

2. The distribution argument: Only big guys have access

Physical distribution channels are well established and generally separate from the publishers themselves. There are no fleets of Elsevier planes, boats, and trucks speeding journals and books around the globe. Over half of journal subscriptions—more in the library market—are delivered by subscription agencies, who really do not care where the journal comes from as long as it comes on time. Besides this, the inevitable trend is toward electronic distribution. It is by no means clear how long that will take to happen, or in what form or forms it will happen, but the fact is inescapable. However it happens, electronic distribution will be cheaper and more democratic. As Nicholas Negroponte (1995) says in *Being Digital*:

> Most media companies . . . add most of their value to . . . content in one way: distribution. . . . The distribution of atoms [for which read journals] is far more complex than that of bits and requires the force of an enormous company. Moving bits, by contrast, is far simpler, and, in principle, precludes the need for these giant corporations. (p. 83)

On this same theme, I have heard the argument made by commercial publishers that only they will be able to harness new technology in the service of scholarly information. Based on the efforts I have seen so far, I am reminded of the joke told during the gas shortage of the 1970s that if there was money to be made from solar power, Exxon would buy the entire state of Arizona, cover it with mirrors, and figure out a way to blow it up.

3. The marketing argument: Yet another "size counts" approach

To market the next John Grisham book requires nothing more than the money to buy the ads announcing its publication date; to market the next John Irving book probably requires a lot more—review copies, author tour, and thoughtful placement. Despite the differences, each of these projects is well suited to a large, multinational company with large amounts of capital and a savvy publicity staff with good media contacts.

But do those strengths translate into superior marketing power for *The Journal of Elbow Reconstruction*? Marketing STM journals is micro-marketing—finding and talking intensely to the 300 or so American Medical Association members who reconstruct elbows, and spending as little as possible on the other tens of thousands who do not. The information playing field is level today. Thanks to the advance of commerce and technology, any of us can have access to the same sliced-fine lists of prospective subscribers (and contributors) to our journals that the big guys have.

You will hear from time to time about cross-marketing—another size-counts argument. When publishers talk about cross-marketing, they are often talking about spending your money—as always multiplied by that overhead factor—to cross-market their journal on wrist reconstruction to the audience created by your journal and your content. (And no doubt in reverse, which is probably futile, unless you are collecting a premium on both ends of such a cross-marketing effort, as they are.)

4. The prestige argument

Commercial publishers will often talk to a society about their prestige—their lengthy corporate history, the well-reputed journals they publish, even the number of Nobel Prize-winners whose articles "their" journals have published (as though the publisher conveyed some Nobel halo effect). What they do not like to talk about is the considerable "negative charisma" effect that conglomerate publishing companies, especially those whose ultimate parent company is based outside North America, are experiencing in the marketplace.

Scholarly publishing divisions of several foreign-owned companies have instituted repeated and significant year-to-year price increases mandated by their home offices—sometimes on the order of 40% a year. These companies have been publicly targeted by librarian groups and buying consortia for across-the-board reductions in subscriptions, regardless of the merits of individual journals.

If I owned a valuable publishing property today, I would be more concerned with the notoriety of a given commercial publisher than their prestige.

5. The infrastructure argument

The argument is frequently made that if a society takes on its own publishing, it will have to add staff and even whole departments. This has not been my experience. Some societies choose to add new staff members in order to exert better control over a given function. One society found that it needed to increase its accounting staff because of large amounts of additional revenues.

But most societies elect to do exactly what commercial publishers do—buy services outside. Certainly this may cost a little bit more than if the same service was performed by a staff member, but not 65% more.

6. The risk argument

The most insidious and unfair argument made by publishers has to do with risk and financial liability. This argument posits that the society will find itself with large exposure and liability if the publishing program loses subscribers or buyers. However, it is far more likely that a society in such a situation would respond just as a commercial house would, by adjusting print runs, refining marketing plans, and restructuring content. There is no intrinsic reason why a society would be more exposed financially, and it is safe to assume that if a property became permanently moribund, a commercial publisher would shed it as fast as it could.

Stewardship: Why boards and management must consider self-publishing

I do not intend to suggest that the decision to undertake self-publication is one to be taken lightly by a society. It requires realistic research, careful planning, and organizational will. Nonetheless, it is an option that must be examined by almost any non-profit that is not already doing so.

There is an ethical consideration involved, that of stewardship. A society's board and management are stewards of the properties of the organizations, its assets. A healthy publishing program is one of the most tangible assets such an organization can own. As well, it serves the outreach and education mandates all scholarly societies were originally formed around more fully and clearly than almost any of its other assets. It is plainly an open question whether such stewardship can be adequately maintained by a commercial publisher whose management has, as its duties, the maximization of profit, generally in the shortest time possible.

From this ethical framework grows a legal consideration as well. Managers, and boards in particular, all have legal responsibilities as fiduciaries to husband the real assets of their organizations. I think it is only a matter of time before a suit is brought by the members of a society charging breach of such duties over the management of publishing by a commercial house. While such a charge might or might not be sustained, the fall-out either way would be devastating to such an organization.

Reference

Negroponte, Nicholas. (1995). *Being digital*. New York: Alfred A. Knopf.

Here there Be Tygers: Profit, Non-Profit, and Loss in the Age of Disintermediation

Michael Jensen
Johns Hopkins University Press

Abstract: Scholarly publishing and access to high-quality information may in fact be threatened, rather than improved, by the revolution in communications, particularly in a fully commercial Internet. The effects of the political revolution in Eastern Europe on scholarship and quality publishing are used as a touchstone of the dangers that occur when naïve revolutionaries make swift changes without fully recognizing the impact upon delicately balanced social institutions such as non-profit organizations.

Résumé: La révolution en communications, particulièrement en ce qui regarde un Internet commercialisé, plutôt que d'améliorer l'édition savante et l'accès à de l'information de haute qualité, pourrait en fait poser une menace pour ceux-ci. Cet article examine comment la révolution politique en Europe de l'Est a influé sur la recherche et l'édition de qualité. Il utilise cet exemple pour examiner les dangers que peuvent courir certains révolutionnaires naïfs quand ils instaurent des changements rapides san songer à leur impact sur des institutions sociales à équilibre délicat comme les organisations à but non lucratif.

The first version of this paper was a rant about the dangers of naïve revolutionaries; the second a dark overview of the consequences of capitalistic scholarship made likely by the advent of micropayments in a disintermediated world. This third is, I hope, a more balanced expression of my concerns.

I want to address the dangers of digital publishing rather than the delights. It is an odd role for me. I am an electronic publisher, and I have been encouraging digital publication for a long time. I believe strongly in the value of digital publishing and I am of the opinion that it is already transforming scholarly communication, frequently for the better.

Michael Jensen is Electronic Publisher at Johns Hopkins University Press, 2715 N. Charles, Baltimore, MD 21218. E-mail: michael.jensen@jhu.edu

Canadian Journal of Communication, Vol. 22, No. 3/4 (1997) 127-134

The Internet is still very much a child, or perhaps more accurately an adolescent—gangly, uncertain of its size and abilities, unwieldy—but all of us can see that its power and influence will only increase. We are still in the wonderful volunteerism phase, where individual labours of love and institutional experimentation into electronic publishing is occurring. Volunteerism is reaching its limits, however, as the complexities of publishing begin to demand cost-recovery mechanisms. Cost recovery is destiny in the non-profit publishing world, and the models we choose, the models we encourage, will change the economic underpinnings of the digital ecosystem, which in turn will change the resulting scholarly community.

I hope that we all can agree that scholarly publishers—specialists in the selection, preparation, presentation, and dissemination of scholarly material—are a valuable and necessary part of scholarly communication. There are some who are still under the false impression that publishers are not necessary, just as there are others under the false impression that libraries are soon to be moot, or that universities are outmoded institutions. There is some truth to all of those points in a disintermediated world, where all intermediaries are potentially erasable by the direct producer-to-end-user contact made possible through the Internet.

It is true that professors could, in a few years, teach students without a university's intervention, or with only one big university's accreditation, or that scholars could spend the time producing the complicated presentational structures required for effective on-line publication, without the need for a publisher. Or that universities could contract with mega-information providers for just-in-time provision of scholarly content using contractual agents, replacing the need for an active library.

But I hold that having specialists do what they do best is the most efficient model in general, and that intermediaries, though not required, will nonetheless be preferred. None of the intermediaries I mentioned—the universities, the scholarly community, the scholarly publishers—will become moot in our lifetime, if for no other reason than the inertia of the credentialing culture.

It is clear that to do electronic publishing right is not simple: it takes time and personnel and organization and a business infrastructure and stability and cost-recovery systems, which require managers, which require some structural institution. This sounds to me a lot like a university press, or a non-profit publisher.

There are circumstances where digital publication is cheaper than traditional print, but on the whole—and certainly for the next three to four years—its full-scale production is at least as expensive as the traditional mechanisms. Publishing is a huge gamble—an investment of time, energy, and capital into a project with a completely uncertain return—but traditional mechanisms are known gambles, sort of like counting cards, rather than the crapshoot that is the current state of electronic publishing.

How scholarly publishers deal with these gambles—what stakes the house requires—will have a significant impact on the quality and long-term value of scholarly publishing. The policy decisions made in this venue and in others will have direct impact on me and my kind, and so my message—among other things—is that if the non-profit publishers' forays into electronic publishing are not supported by library purchases, then we may endanger a valuable institutional foundation of scholarly discourse, which may result in a purely capitalist information marketplace and even endanger the library's integral role in the intellectual arena.

I am a non-profit publisher and have been all my professional career. Most non-profit publishers are not in it for the money, they are in it because they love the intellectual process. As a non-profit publisher, I have to say that I am always disquieted when I find—especially in policy or position papers—homogenizing terminology that conflates scientific, technical, and medical (STM) publications with humanities publications; that equates for-profit publishers with non-profit publishers (like associations and university presses); or that does not discriminate between scholarly communication and scholarly publishing. Each of these have different goals, different means, and different methods for survival, which should be analyzed separately before we throw out the good in an attempt to dispense with the bad.

I have watched a revolution in scholarly communication that did some of that—a surprisingly little-studied phenomenon in Eastern Europe, in the years immediately after the fall of the Soviet Empire. Between 1990 and 1994, I either participated in or organized seminars for scholarly publishers from Estonia, Latvia, Lithuania, Poland, Hungary, and other countries. By far the deepest experience was in Czechoslovakia, before it split. I spoke with publishers and scholars from throughout the country during that period, and watched as the totalitarian socialist model—which had strengths as well as significant weaknesses—was replaced by an amateur's understanding of a capitalist model, with significant weaknesses as well as perhaps a few strengths.

The Eastern European model had every university publishing its own stuff—introductory biology course books, collections of essays, lecture notes, monographs, research—at the professor's behest. There was heavy subvention from the universities, which was of course subvened by the state. There was no economic feedback system, because there were no cost-recovery systems beyond a token fee of a quarter or so per *scripta*, as the class publications were called. Hardbacks cost the equivalent of a pack of Czech cigarettes.

Editorial selection hardly entered into the matter. Every year, a few works were designated as worthy of being put in hardback, usually in an attempt to give their universities a medium of exchange for publications in the outside non-Soviet world. Often they were lavishly produced, but there was never any relationship between price and publication costs. The system separated to the point of immeasurability, by massive bureaucracy, all indirect costs and in fact discouraged any cost containment systems based on merit or audience. Instead, decisions were based on old-boy status. An important professor could insist on having 50,000 copies of his book on the aerodynamics of bat wings printed, in Czech; this was to his advantage because his royalty was based on numbers printed, rather than numbers sold.

Other state-run publishing houses also published scholarly work in philosophy, science, metaphysics, etc.; they had more freedom of choice of what to publish, but their work was also heavily subsidized, and prices and print runs were at the whim of "important" people.

When the Soviet Union collapsed, there were warehouses with hundreds of thousands of copies of the writings of Stalin which nobody would buy even at the minuscule prices charged in the Soviet days, much less in the post-Soviet economic crises. And about 49,800 copies of that bat-wing book.

In the pre-revolution days, a socially supported, exceedingly expensive publishing industry created very inexpensive books and that deeply affected the Czech culture. New books came out every Wednesday, and the bookstores were like flowers in a field—every square had bookstores, every tram stop had a card table selling books. When I first spent time in Prague just after the revolution, I saw everyone—the butcher and the hard-hat and the professors—reading on the trams, the metro, the street corners, and lining up to pay a few crowns for new titles. These were not Danielle Steele trash, but philosophy, history, science, metaphysics. This system of subvention created a highly literate, well-educated populace, who read for fun, all the time.

When the revolution came, suddenly universities, whose subventions were being completely reconsidered by new governments, were telling their presses that they had to become self-sufficient in two years, and many were told they had to start giving money back to their universities—make a profit—in the third year (much like several major university presses have recently been asked to do). For most of the Czech university policymakers, their naïve recipe for capitalism was a pinch of slogan-level ideas picked up from *Dallas* reruns and the *Voice of America* and a dash of Hayek, spiced with understanding gleaned from dinner table conversations.

Their consequent policies had no consideration of the realities of publishing costs and cost recovery; no understanding of the infrastructure (like distribution and warehousing, not to mention computers, databases, and predictive knowledge) required to have a viable publishing market; no comprehension of the place of scholarly publishing in the educational system; and no recognition that, in a revolutionary economy, nobody would have spare money to make discretionary purchases.

Four years after the 1989 revolution, the prices for books had become 10 to 50 times higher than they used to be. The publishers who were succeeding were subvening their own translations of Derrida by publishing—literally—soft-core pornography.

Bookstores closed down everywhere. Publishers closed down everywhere. People stopped reading every day. By 1995, nobody was reading metaphysics on the tram. A quarter of the university presses I knew of were closed, over half of the small scholarly publishers I had known and well over half of the bookstores I knew of in Prague were closed, and the scholars I had befriended were telling me that they could not get anything published anymore—there were fewer outlets than ever.

Neither model was right. Though the result was frequently a marvelously high level of intellectual discourse, the absurd redundancies and inefficiencies of the Soviet system were far too costly. The follow-on naïve-capitalist system was far too brutal and had consequences that the citizenry are still feeling—far fewer high-level publications in their own languages, far fewer high-quality scholarly publications in general (a significant problem in a small language group), and cultural costs that are hard to quantify but easy to identify as causing a sort of poverty in the intellectual culture.

What this has to do with the current revolution should be self-evident, though the parallels are indirect. We are in a revolutionary period, and we must be careful not to damage the valuable qualities of the current system based on a naïve understanding of the coming state of scholarly communication based on a few visionaries' description of what is inevitable. We must carefully assess what qualities we want to maintain and be sure that we create evolutionary pressures that encourage a scholarly communication biosystem that serves scholarship well.

In the U.S., the post-World-War-II funding system for scholarship, the GI-Bill, catalyzed explosion in institutions, in library-building, in encouragement of scholarship in general, creating the current non-profit scholarly publishing environment. Universities and colleges got federal, state, and private monies to build, and to fund the development of libraries, who purchased books, which gave university presses the impetus to publish works that were valuable because there were 800 to 1,000 nearly guaranteed sales. With that kind of certainty, the prices on books could be kept lower, both for the libraries and for the non-institutional purchasers.

That began changing with the STM crisis (a term I see as more accurate than "serials crisis"). Monographs are not being purchased as dependably. Instead of 800 to 1,000 library sales, we are lucky to sell 400 to 500 copies to libraries. This raises the proportion of the first-copy costs that every sale must carry, thus raising the per-unit cost even more.

Publishing in the social sciences and humanities is suffering dramatically because that is the blood being squeezed to pay for the STM journals.

Earlier, I said that unless you support the electronic publishing forays of non-profit publishers, libraries themselves would be endangered, and so far I have not made clear why I made that statement. It was not just to wake you up, I assure you.

There is a trend I am very unhappy with: I am on the board of directors of the Association of American University Presses, and at a quarterly board meeting in February, as always, we gave our reports on what we term our "parish calls," in which each board member talks with a dozen or so presses. We ask how sales are, how returns from the bookstores are, if budget and projection targets are being met. The reports were bleak in a peculiarly dismal way, and are worth mentioning.

In general, the only university presses that were experiencing even static sales were those that had enlarged the number of trade titles at the cost of scholarly monographs. One important mid-sized university press (UP) director, whose list of titles has won more awards in his fields than any others—over a third of his new titles in the last year won a scholarly award of some kind—is experiencing a 17% decline in sales compared with last year. Conversely, another largish UP is doing quite well, but has only published a few scholarly monographs in the last two seasons. Instead, intellectually stimulating trade titles, or flat-out trade titles like a coffee-table book on vegetables, are keeping them solvent. Nobody likes it, but the market is quite evidently requiring these sorts of choices: winning awards does not keep your staff employed and your press operational, sales do. If the institutional market gets smaller and smaller, greater selectivity will result, along with greater insistence on saleability as a primary criterion for publication.

Sales to institutional libraries have become less and less significant to the success of an individual title, which has affected the selection of titles for publication. As a consequence, scholarly titles—in the humanities and social sciences, at least—have been cut back at many scholarly presses. These are simply market pressures. Few of us believe that scholarly communication is well served by an exclusively capitalist model, but that is the world in which we find ourselves.

The important books that are important only to a small number of scholars are failing to find publishers because publishers cannot afford to publish something that will sell less than 600 copies. The price per unit becomes too high, resulting in 400 staying in the warehouse.

Will electronic publishing solve this? Let me report from the front: at Johns Hopkins University Press (JHUP), the oldest university press in North America, we have Project Muse (URL: http://muse.jhu.edu), which provides a digital version of 42 journals at less-than-paper prices to institutions for campus-wide access. We also have two on-line reference works currently in beta testing with our Project Muse subscribers. These are *The Johns Hopkins*

Guide to Literary Theory and Criticism Online (Groden & Kreiswirth, 1997) and Walker's *Mammals of the World Online*, 5th edition (Nowak, 1997), each with the same campus-wide domain access framework. They are not priced less than paper, because they are used differently—classroom and desk copies are purchased by students and scholars, and that loss of sales must be acknowledged and dealt with.

All of these projects are being published as campus-domain purchases—in which the entire campus has access to it 24 hours a day. They all have significant advantages over paper—they are not just page images, but are full recastings in digital form, reconceptions of how the material can be used which takes advantage of digital access and digital presentation. The reference works are so much more useful in the digital form that they are transformed into something else—something which can be continuously updated with new material, enhanced with new navigational mechanisms, improved with contextualizing material and links (all of which take money).

Project Muse—at two years old, a granddaddy of digital journals projects—was made possible by a grant from the Mellon Foundation and the NEH and was developed in partnership with the Johns Hopkins Library. It was consciously designed as a library- and institution-friendly model. We have discounts for consortia, deeper discounts for community and small colleges, and deeper discounts still for public libraries. We allow interlibrary loans (ILL) of printouts of articles, printing anywhere on campus, saving for campus use, and linkages for class use; we expect and encourage its use as an always-available reading room. Once distance-learning authentication standards are established, we will enable that. We provide several years' back issues at no extra charge for most of the journals. We have tried to make it as institution-friendly as possible. Project Muse currently has over 260 subscribing campuses and over 75 public libraries. We are still only about a quarter to a third of the way to sustainable cost recovery, especially when paper subscriptions begin being cancelled.

If the Johns Hopkins University Press cannot make broad, easy access succeed on a campus-wide basis, much less have the wherewithal to do the deeper development work to integrate our publications with others', then publishers are going to shy away from this type of model—including the Johns Hopkins University Press.

If we shy away from the institutional-access model because we cannot survive within it, then we will begin to change our publication model: raise prices, make back issues available on a document delivery basis, apply micropayment and restriction software to individual articles, and aim predominantly at individual access.

That constitutionally limits our dreams for digital libraries, and for easy integrated fair use, not because the publishers disallow it, but because if the material is not available easily on a campus, if it becomes time-consuming and complicated to integrate, it becomes too damn troublesome for everybody. And, further, it creates an environment in which libraries are relegated to being archives of paper, rather than integral actors in making access to digital material available to the students, faculty, and scholars in their institutions.

This hardly serves the greater good of scholarship in its broadest sense, but scholarship is even more poorly served by not having digital access to this material, which would happen if publishers cannot make cost-recovery mechanisms work. Even if each institution builds a digital publication centre, pays the staff enough to keep them from being bought away by the commercial sector, and provides assistance to all scholars and professors to make their research and product available for free—and I hope that happens too—the validation and prestige and promotion value conferred by "real" publishers will not disappear. The on-line environment will be perceived, rightly or wrongly, as the place where the less worthy material is available for free (you get what you pay for), while the top-flight material will be available only to those individuals willing and able to pay for it.

Scholarship will not be well served by such a phenomenon, and I fear that this is a real danger.

I am not saying that if you do not purchase Johns Hopkins University Press's on-line publications you will not be living up to your responsibilities. Rather, I am using us to explain my belief that non-profit publishers must be encouraged by institutional purchases to provide the broadest access to the material. Without such encouragement, the non-profit publishers will continue to make the best material available at the lowest possible price, but the scholarly communications system will be weaker than it could be. Non-profit publishers are not in it to profiteer—we want readers, we want impact in the scholarly world, but we also want to keep our jobs. Non-profit publishers should not be seen as antagonists in this new environment, but as partners.

If libraries and institutions consciously try to encourage, by their market clout and purchasing power, the non-profit publishers' natural match with its primary audience, then we can strengthen the non-profit scholarly communications community's natural partners: the scholars, the students, the libraries, the institutions, and the non-profit scholarly publishers.

References

Groden, Michael, & Kreiswirth, Martin (Eds.). (1997). *The Johns Hopkins guide to literary theory and criticism online*. URL: http://www.press.jhu.edu/books/guide

Nowak, Ronald. (1997). *Walker's mammals of the world online*. URL: http://www.press.jhu.edu/books/mammals/

On-line Journal Publication: Two Views from the Electronic Trenches[1]

Jonathan Borwein & Richard Smith
Simon Fraser University

Abstract: Scholars are using new technology to communicate more widely, more efficiently, and more quickly than ever before. The authors report on their experiences at several scholarly publications, including the *Canadian Journal of Communication*, the *Canadian Mathematical Bulletin*, and the *Canadian Journal of Mathematics*, during the adoption and deployment of new electronic media. The authors draw on first-hand experience in creating these Web-based journals and provide insight into the technical, commercial, administrative, and scholarly implications of such a move. The paper concludes with a discussion of a paradox in the move to electronic publication and of a possible solution.

Résumé: Les chercheurs aujourd'hui profitent des nouvelles technologies pour atteindre un public plus vaste, de manière plus efficace et rapide qu'à toute période antérieure. Les auteurs décrivent leur participation à plusieurs publications académiques, y compris le *Canadian Journal of Communication*, le *Canadian Mathematical Bulletin,* et le *Canadian Journal of Mathematics* au moment de l'adoption et l'installation de nouveaux médias électroniques. Les auteurs décrivent chacun leur propre participation active dans l'établissement de ces journaux, et réfléchissent sur les implications techniques, commerciales, administratives, et académiques d'une telle transition. Cet article conclut en soulignant un paradoxe dans le passage à la publication électronique et en indiquant une solution possible.

Jonathan Borwein is Shrum Chair of Science and Director of the Centre for Experimental and Constructive Mathematics (CECM) at Simon Fraser University, Burnaby, BC V5A 1S6. E-mail: jborwein@cecm.sfu.ca
Richard Smith is an assistant professor in the School of Communication in the Faculty of Applied Science and Associate Director for Management of Technology in the Centre for Policy Research on Science and Technology (CPROST) at Simon Fraser University at Harbour Centre, 515 West Hastings Street, Vancouver, BC V6B 5K3. E-mail: smith@sfu.ca

***Canadian Journal of Communication,* Vol. 22, No. 3/4 (1997) 135-152**

Introduction

Scholarly communication has long been an international undertaking. Computers and computer networks have merely accentuated that tendency. With the advent of personal computers in the 1980s, many scholars got their first taste of electronic manuscript preparation and distribution by creating and submitting papers on disk. These disk files were then used to create traditional print publications. More recently, scholarly communication has begun to move directly to its audience through the creation of document servers that allow direct access by readers.

Electronic scholarly communication received a significant boost with the advent of a hypertext distribution mechanism known as the World Wide Web (WWW) and its subsequent popularization by the availability of easy-to-use browser or client application software, such as Mosaic and Netscape. The history of this process has been widely reported elsewhere (Okerson & O'Donnell, 1995; Peek & Newby, 1996) and the many financial and scholarly implications have been broadly debated (Odlyzko, 1995). In this paper we use our own experience with electronic publication at the Canadian Mathematical Society and *Canadian Journal of Communication (CJC)* to draw out implications for some of the many participants in the scholarly publication process.

The on-line addresses for the three publications that are the major focus of this paper are:

- *Canadian Journal of Communication*—URL: http://www.ccsp.sfu.ca/calj/cjc/
- *Canadian Journal of Mathematics*—URL: http://www.camel.math.ca/CMS/CJM
- *Canadian Mathematical Bulletin*—URL: http://www.camel.math.ca/CMS/CMB

(On-line versions of both the *Canadian Journal of Mathematics* and the *Canadian Mathematical Bulletin* are available by subscription only.)

Background

Canadian Journal of Mathematics/Canadian Mathematical Bulletin

In the transition from print to electronic publication at the Canadian Mathematical Society (CMS), several intervening events have had significant impact. The first is the evolution of the field itself and its emergence as a modern, research- and publication-focused discipline. The second is the choice by the society to move most aspects of journal publication in-house. The third is the emergence and subsequent acceptance of the TeX (pronounced "teck") programming language for user typesetting of mathematical text/formulae. (TeX was developed by Donald Knuth, the author of many books and articles about mathematics, computer programming, and computer typesetting. He has made his TeX language freely available to the world.) The fourth and most recent event has been the emergence of open-standards-based network communication, most notably the World Wide Web. These forms of communication are well suited to the work of mathematicians. Contextual factors, such as the financial resources of the CMS, also played a factor.

The *Canadian Journal of Mathematics* (*CJM*) has been published by the Canadian Mathematical Society since its founding in 1945. Before 1945, mathematical research in Canada was largely limited to a few principally foreign-trained mathematicians at the University of Toronto (Filmore, 1995, 1996a, 1996b). Since 1945, research and teaching in Canadian mathematics programs have grown dramatically. Currently mathematicians and statisticians account for close to 10% of federally (Natural Sciences and Engineering Research Council [NSERC]) funded researchers, are present in more than 65 university and colleges across the country, and publish widely around the world. In fact, in terms of scholarly publications per capita, Canada is by far the most math-intensive country in the world. (See Borwein & Davidson, 1995).

Since its founding, the Canadian Mathematical Society has managed the publication of *CJM*, and later the *Canadian Mathematical Bulletin* and other material, as a central undertaking of the society. Prior to 1982 all publication responsibilities other than editorial were handled by the University of Toronto (U of T) Press. In the later 1980s the society underwent a transition to full control of its publication process, and now delivers camera-ready pages to the U of T Press for printing and mailing. Editorial and typesetting functions are carried out in-house in Winnipeg and Halifax.

Mathematics is one of the most ancient and fundamental of the scientific disciplines. One of the distinguishing aspects of mathematical communication is its reliance on a very large number of specialized symbols. A highly refined mode of communication has evolved through the use of such symbols in addition to or in place of words. An equation can be used both to communicate a complex thought and to present ideas in a provable and logical format. For example, Isaac Newton's method of calculating the diameter of a circle, or *pi*, is displayed in the following concise integral equation:

$$\pi = \frac{3}{4}\sqrt{3} + 24\int_0^{\frac{1}{4}} \sqrt{x - x^2}\,dx$$

(For a demonstration of how the graphic was created, see URL: http://www.cecm.sfu.ca/~jborwein/newton/newton.html).

While it has always been possible to represent these symbols in handwritten manuscripts, the results are messy and prone to errors in copying. The advent of textual computer systems provided a mode of communication that initially lacked equation capabilities entirely and then later allowed only limited and idiosyncratic solutions for home and scholarly users. In the early 1980s, there were those who argued that computers were a hindrance to effective scholarly communication in mathematics. They opined that computers brought with them numerous opportunities for confusion and mis-entry—because of incompatible formats and lack of suitable methods to represent symbols—and that they imposed an artificial linearity on symbolic representation and so, on mathematical thought processes.

The world of mathematical electronic publication was greatly influenced by the emergence of Knuth's TeX publishing language, which he described in *The TeX Book* (1984). TeX made it possible for the individual scholar to create accurate, legible, and symbolically rich documents without the use of a dedicated typesetting machine. More importantly, as a procedural language in the public domain, TeX allowed mathematicians (and all others dependent on symbols and equations) to exchange computer files almost independent of the equipment used and be confident that their ideas would arrive intact. Although its dominance was not predictable at the outset, TeX has become the de facto standard for electronic document preparation among mathematicians, computer scientists, and physicists around the world.

As a procedural text-processing language, TeX is very well suited to the types of document processing involved in moving information onto the World Wide Web. The Web, as it is widely known, is built upon several foundation technologies, including hypertext markup language (HTML), a text-processing markup language. (For more information about HTML, see URL: http://uts.cc.utexas.edu/~churchh/htmlqref.html.) Documents prepared in TeX can be readily moved to and around the Web and, perhaps more importantly, can be manipulated easily by computers in ways that allow the electronic formats to provide additional value to scholars. A simple example of this is a listing of all the papers where a particular individual is first author. By virtue of its embedded tags, a TeX document allows this type of rich internal reference even after conversion to a web format. (TeX, like HTML, is essentially a markup language in which one has preserved a great deal of information about the underlying semantics and syntax.) Although many writers are making use of tools such as latex2html, robust public domain or commercial tools for putting documents on-line are still more of a prospect than a reality.

TeX, as HTML, is also an open standard, freely available to any who might wish to adopt and use it, and it is standardized in the form of a set of rules governing its use and evolution. Although an open standard is not sufficient to ensure widespread adoption of a technology, in the case of scholarly communication, the TeX's low cost and ease of customization were certainly factors in ensuring broad use. The complexity of TeX suggests that a user base will adopt difficult new tools that have a clearly proven advantage over existing methods. As many as 90% of submissions to diverse mathematics journals are now made in TeX.

Beyond the use of TeX, high-quality, easily generated computer graphics and animations have helped to extend the understanding and communication of complex (or simple) concepts beyond what can be quickly assimilated symbolically. Multimedia interfaces such as the Web provide a way for colleagues and students to apprehend the process as well as the outcome of an algorithm, for example. At the Centre for Experimental and Constructive Mathematics (CECM), these types of visual demonstrations provide powerful and compelling arguments for the extension of mathematical visualization. These interface advances provide scientists with the chance to go beyond presentation of results and invite readers to participate in an exploration of the process of scientific undertakings. For illustrations of mathematical visualization, see a recent MathLand column at the Science News Web site (Peterson, 1997) or the images provided by CECM (Products and Byproducts, 1997).

The Canadian Mathematical Society has made at least two significant decisions that have given the society the financial basis to experiment with new mechanisms. The first was a bit of foresight on the part of the society's early leadership in the form of an endowment fund. This fund, and an even more significant return on publications, currently provides a six-figure return that allows the society to entertain new ideas that less-well-established societies could not consider. The second decision was the hard business decision, made in the late 1980s, to dramatically increase prices for the journal in an effort to move toward a more bottom-line operation. This occurred at the same time the society moved most of the editorial and publishing details in-house, allowing them to reduce costs significantly. The combination of reduced costs and increased subscription rates, coupled with the fact that subscriptions did not fall off the way they were feared/projected to (the journals were still relatively cheap by comparison with the commercial houses), resulted in a much more economical journal publication system, which in turn has been able to underwrite entry into new media publication.

A salient feature of the CMS's experience has been its coming to terms with publishing as an enterprise with a significant research and development (R&D) component. Electronic publishing bears more and more resemblance to software engineering, especially since one intent is to provide fully interactive journals, allowing for computation and manipulation of data within. At the time of writing, the problem-solving journal *CRUX with Mayhem On-line* (Sato, 1997) is available by subscription in various forms (Postscript, DVI, GIF, PDF), and readers are already providing feedback as to its function and form. Additionally, the new medium is starting to generate new subscriptions. The society also maintains an electronic repository for the *Mathematical Comptes Rendu* (URL: http://camel.math.ca/Epub/CR/) of the Royal Society of Canada.

The *Canadian Mathematical Bulletin* and *Canadian Journal of Mathematics* have abstracts and a full index available on-line, with the complete journal formats in development and expected to be fully released in 1997 (*CMS Publication Indices*, 1997). Other on-line resources offered by the Canadian Mathematical Society include the Canadian Mathematical Electronic Services (Camel) (URL: http://www.camel.math.ca/home.html), which provides a full gamut of electronic services (for example, registration for meetings, society business, job advertisements, etc.), as well as the entire on-line indices of its two research publications *CMB* and *CJM* as noted above, whose construction represented a sizeable undertaking in its own right. The two main research journals maintain a common editorial policy and accept roughly 20% to 30% of submissions (which are still initially made in hard copy). Both journals have faced enormous challenges achieving a balance and co-ordination between conventional and new media publication.

Canadian Journal of Communication

The *Canadian Journal of Communication* (*CJC*) began publication in 1974 as *Media Probe*. The current name was adopted in 1977. Although there have been discussions over the years of making the *CJC* an official Canadian Communication Association (CCA) journal, it remains independent, owned by its subscribers. The CCA, which was founded in 1979, offers members a discount on subscriptions to the *CJC*.

The *CJC* is edited at the Canadian Centre for Studies in Publishing at Simon Fraser University, under the editorship of Rowland Lorimer. The publisher is Wilfrid Laurier University (WLU) Press, based in Waterloo, Ontario. Since the journal came to Vancouver in 1993, the editorial work has been done on computer, using microcomputers and word-processing programs. The resulting files are sent to Waterloo for conversion to a typesetting format for proofs and final output. The final editorial work is currently done based on the proofs from WLU Press. The actual flow of articles is as follows: Articles move from the author to the managing editor by post as disk copies with printed versions included. The editor sends out printed copies to anonymous reviewers and makes the decision to publish or revise. If revisions are requested, this is co-ordinated by the managing editor under the supervision of the editor. Once a manuscript has been accepted for publication, it is sent to the copy editor in disk version. The copy editor prepares the files for submission to the Press, including basic formatting and style corrections, as word-processor documents. These files are sent by disk or electronic mail to the Press, which converts them to a markup language (based on SGML) and produces page proofs. The page proofs are returned to the copy editor, who sends them both to professional editors/proofreaders and to the author for review. Any revisions are consolidated by the copy editor, who returns the proofs to the Press for implementation of the changes, as well as printing, binding, and mailing.

Authors must submit their material on disk, although some who are submitting shorter articles do so by e-mail. The journal accepts files in the two major word-processing formats (Microsoft Word and WordPerfect) and from Macintosh or IBM computers. Most of the editorial (academic and copy editing) correspondence is also conducted by e-mail. The journal accepts 30% to 40% of articles it receives, publishing five or six major articles per issue and four issues per year.

The *CJC* began its experiment with electronic publication in 1994. The experiment has been through several generations. The first was very informal. A graduate student converted some of the managing editor's word-processing files from a recent issue into Web (HTML) format by manually tagging the documents. These were placed on a server at Simon Fraser University under a text-based table of contents and advertised on a very limited scale to members of the editorial board. Other items converted to electronic format at this time were the guide to authors, subscription information, and the masthead information. While the journal did have an on-line presence, at this point it was extremely limited in scope. Also, there were differences between the electronic and final printed version of the journal because the files available for this experiment were created before the final copy edit in Waterloo. These early examples are still available on line (URL: http://edie.cprost.sfu.ca/cjc/cjc-info.html).

The second experiment was based on a graduate student project in the Canadian Centre for Studies in Publishing. The student sought to learn more about the possibilities of hypertext and multimedia design and used an article from the *CJC* for the experiment. The student's objective was to create a mode of presentation that maximized the value to be added by the non-linear elements of the medium. In this case, a single article was selected for intensive post-publication processing, which included hypertext links to Web-based resources not anticipated by the original authors, such as coloured backgrounds and graphical elements (see Acheson & Maule, 1995). The original authors were aware of and were consulted for this experiment. The project did result in a more colourful and entertaining presentation but demonstrated the dependency for understanding and the significance of a point in context that a (linear) argument creates. When major points were featured each on a separate page, they lacked credibility and force.

With the help of professional publication designers associated with the Canadian Centre for Studies in Publishing, the next step in the journal's on-line evolution was to acquire a graphic front end, complete with a logo evocative of the print publication and a style suited to multimedia delivery. The designers implemented a style that focused on consistency, ease of navigation, and an uncluttered look. The Web site was also moved to a production server at this point, ensuring that there were regular back-ups and sufficient computing power and network bandwidth to serve multiple simultaneous users (see URL: http://www.ccsp.sfu.ca/calj/cjc).

At the same time that the *CJC* look was being improved, the quality and quantity of on-line materials took a major leap ahead by the shift from word-processor files to the use of typesetter-input files as the source material for the conversions to HTML. The publisher, Wilfrid Laurier University Press, uses a markup language (based on SGML) that is remarkably similar to HTML. As a result, it was relatively straightforward to write a computer program to automate the conversion process. By changing to this mode of conversion, it was hoped that the *CJC* would be able to reduce the time and increase the accuracy and consistency of its on-line versions. Using the same input sources as were used to produce the final proof pages for printing meant eliminating the inconsistencies caused by the use of the word-processing files that were later sent to Waterloo for copy editing. The tagged format of the typesetting files also allowed the computer program to automatically create tables of contents and author lists, much the way other journals have been able to do with TeX documents.

By going to "machine translation" of print materials, the *CJC* was confronted with some significant challenges, however. For example, it was only after several rounds of comparison and conversion that it was discovered that the typesetting files were not, in all cases, the latest versions and certain editorial changes had obviously been made to the version in the typesetter and were not reflected in the disk files that had been received. Tabular and graphical material was not included in the typesetting files, and a gradual evolution in the tags used by the typesetters meant that the conversion program had to be adjusted many times. Footnotes and bibliographic items also presented conversion challenges, especially when the program encountered uncompleted tags.

The sensible solution to these problems is to bring the typesetting and the hypertext setting processes closer together. Toward the end of 1996, in the latest stage in the *CJC*'s electronic evolution, this is precisely what we started to do. The programmer at Wilfrid Laurier University Press recreated the conversion software on his own system and linked the print production computer system with the electronic production computers using the Internet. Although this process is still not complete, the next issue of the journal should have simultaneous production of the two versions and therefore eliminate questions of different versions on the different media. Even so, a certain amount of "hand tuning" is still required after the automated conversion is completed. As a result, the journal continues to explore other options, including the use of portable document format (PDF) files created out of the typesetter's Postscript files. An experiment using this technology will be conducted in 1997 with the co-operation of Wilfrid Laurier University Press.

Observations

Our experience as facilitators of electronic journal publication has provided us with many rewarding and satisfying achievements. It has also led to many instances of unexpected and unsettling outcomes, some of which have been described above. We explore a few of these in more detail below and include our suggestions or observations on the role of amateurs and experimentation, the impact of the highly competitive computer software and hardware industry, managing expectations of users in terms of interface, access, and archiving, billing, and other financial issues.

Amateurs

These early days of electronic publication are like the early days of other media of communication such as radio: there is a great deal of experimentation and extensive participation by amateurs. Amateurs bring with them a curiosity about the media, a love for the topic (mathematics, communication studies, etc.), and an autonomy or idiosyncrasy in modes of expression that traditionally has not been accommodated in mass publishing. Furthermore, amateurs frequently undertake their projects as labours of love and do not draw salaries, sometimes supporting the electronic publication with resources drawn from other projects.

We are concerned that the current diversity of form in electronic scholarly publication will not last as amateur burnout occurs, and amateurs are replaced by traditional publishing companies. In an effort to reduce costs through economies of scale, publishing firms tend toward homogeneity in the form of their Web publication projects. While some homogeneity is probably inevitable, it is not at all clear that the modes of presentation currently in use are the best available or possible. Some formats, such as PDF, are very closely tied to existing paper production systems, to the extent that page images are distributed electronically. While these may be comforting as bridging technologies between existing and future standards, they only touch the surface of what is possible in electronic publication.

Computer industry

It appears that practices from the computer hardware and software industries have begun to affect the form of scholarly electronic publication. Unfortunately, the changes are not driven by the needs of scholars but rather the very short product cycles in the computer hardware and software industries. So much of the work of electronic publishing is tied up in equipment and software that the relentless pattern of change and obsolescence inevitably works its way into the scholarly publication process, even without us realizing or anticipating it. This experimentation, however, does not seem to be driven by the communication needs of scholars but more by the competitive pressures in the computer industry itself. For example, the release in mid-1997 of a new version of Java (a type of building-block software for on-line multimedia) may render obsolete large amounts of software written as part of scholarly publications in mathematics. Java is a product of Sun Computers, which is locked in a competitive battle with software giant Microsoft.

These changes in Java are at the host or production side of electronic publishing. Similar changes have been occurring in the client software. Subtle but important differences exist between the two most popular graphical WWW browsers. For example, the two most popular browser producers, Netscape and Microsoft, differ in their use of internal scripting protocols such as JavaScript and ActiveX and how they interact with client computers. There are also dramatic differences between earlier and later versions of each of these programs, and there are differences between the Macintosh, Windows, and UNIX versions of the clients. Finally, there are differences in how they may be set up at a user's site, including variables such as screen size and resolution, colour depth, window size and position, graphic-loading options, and font and colour selection (a user choice most of the time). All of these require that scholarly communication adopt an unprecedented level of attention to commercial and technical issues that may stand between authors and readers.

At the same time, some of these advances do hold promise for scholars. When these new technologies emerge, there will be a strong temptation to adopt them quickly—even though doing so may leave some readers behind. According to our Web-site maintainers, one of the major issues is this lowest-common-denominator approach, wherein the publishers must sacrifice technological improvements in order to be accessible by a larger audience. Coupled with that is the time it takes to ensure compatibility: in order to ensure maximum use, designers spend considerable time testing different formats on the plethora of different platforms. At the CRUX mathematics site (URL: http://www.camel.math.ca/CMS/CRUX/), these issues of compatibility and availability have been an enormous concern. Finally, there is the frustration that comes with being close to perfection but not quite there. As one designer put it: "Even though we are able to offer aesthetic and entertaining journals, we find that we cannot. Thus the experimentation that we have conducted in design and new ideas are extremely slow to materialize as so few people could actually enjoy them!" (Sinclair, 1997).

Managing expectations

A further related experimentation concern is the focus on user interface changes at the expense of usability. There is the temptation, at least in these early days, to reinvent the wheel at each Web site. While computers are gradually becoming more similar, with a common trend to a WIMP (windows, icons, mouse, and pointer) interface, Web pages rarely look or act alike (in fact, uniqueness is a point of pride among designers), forcing users to rediscover navigation and interaction skills at each site. To exacerbate this problem, some sites update their user interface frequently to make the site seem fresh but at the expense of further confusing readers.

In our experience, electronic publishing carries with it a halo effect from other computer-provided information, from video games to business software, making it seem necessary to create scholarly products that are lively and engaging in the manner of multimedia or, for that matter, television. The question emerges: How much does a scholar or scholarly publisher have to invest in look and feel in order to keep the reader's attention on the content? There is at least some obligation on the part of authors, editors, and publishers to present material in an engaging manner, but those materials that are not easy to use or perhaps do not have a pleasing appearance may fall into disuse, to be overwhelmed by the attractive and functional. Is there not some intrinsic worth to intellectual products?

Concern over page design also affects updates and timeliness. Frequently a trade-off must be made between the amount of effort that is put into adjusting the user interface and the effort that goes into updating or monitoring the content on a Web site. From what we have seen, too often the balance falls on the "looks good" side, resulting in flashy graphics, many broken links, and many "under construction" sections.

Several other timing-access issues come from early release of materials. At the Canadian Mathematical Society, abstracts are now, in principle, posted to the Web as soon as they are received. The electronic version of CRUX arrives before the print copy goes to the printers. Both of these practices have the prospect of involving authors and the rest of the audience more directly in the publishing process. The frequency of posting takes on the aura of a dialogue and fosters a sense of community, especially among teachers and other non-professional users who might not ordinarily feel as connected to the society.

Now that final drafts are posted to the Net just prior to printing, the CMS has noticed another benefit from electronic publication: a small army of proofreaders. Frequently, members of the society now catch small errors that the editors are able to resolve before the issue is printed and mailed, reducing corrections and retractions. As always, there is a downside in the temptation to rely on those eyes rather than one's own.

The army-of-proofreaders phenomenon brings with it another issue, how to "freeze" an electronic publication. There is a famous story among mathematicians about one eminent, dedicated author who, over a lifetime, visited libraries around the world, located copies of his articles, and corrected various minor errors. While electronic publishing would obviate the need for the travel, several things are lost in a revisable form. For one, there is the connection with the author's spirit in the form of holograph marginalia. While that may sound fanciful, a more serious issue is the possibility of unauthorized corrections. Who holds the key that ensures your words are published as written? Although such technology exists, neither the *CJC* nor the CMS have implemented digital signatures or similar devices to ensure authenticity.

"Access" implies continued access. Electronic publication is something that is deceptively easy to initiate but difficult to sustain. As the *CJC* quickly found out, a small experimental Web site based on volunteer and amateur labour can quickly grow to significant proportions and public expectations soon mount. Archiving and access are two areas that posed immediate problems in these circumstances. Mathematicians are accustomed to a very high level of reliability in their literature. Even minor issues of font substitution can mean that the printed and electronic versions no longer correspond. Informal archives have the effect that a theorem may exist in preliminary versions that circulate widely but not in the definitive print version. Increasingly, journals publish articles electronically as soon as they have been approved, weeks and perhaps months before they appear in print.

Managing archives is another aspect of managing expectations. Publication of a paper journal is often regarded as simply a larger version of personal publishing. For the scholar or editor, the practical side of journals, especially the maintenance of back issues, 24-hour availability, and so on, is simply someone else's problem—usually the library's. With electronic publishing, however, these are frequently problems that have to be considered by the journal itself. In the heady atmosphere of taking control of one's own journal, practical issues like backups, back issues, access, and indexing can get pushed aside or forgotten—forgotten, that is, until the user community starts to demand these services. At the *CJC* it is not uncommon for electronic readers to write to the Web-site maintainers looking for further information, provide feedback on material, or ask for back issues. While it is difficult to quantify so far, there are some preliminary indications that electronic access is resulting in more widespread use of the *Canadian Journal of Communication* than was heretofore thought possible. The *CJC* has relatively few overseas subscribers other than in major centres; however, in recent months, requests from Austria and Italy have come in based on people browsing *CJC*'s Web site.

New forms of communication

Technical product limitations may be limiting our modes of expression as scholars. Here electronic publication has great potential to make up for the limitations of print that we have grown to accept and even assume are natural. Why, for example, should we communicate in black and white? Although the *Canadian Journal of Communication* does not contain colour material, this is less a reflection of the interests of communication scholars than it is a reality of a limitation of funds. A recent special issue of the *CJC* that focused on television was republished using significant quantities of graphic material. Although widely regarded as a success, the special issue nonetheless reflects only the advances of desktop publishing, a 1980s phenomenon, and none of the potential of multimedia publication. An equivalent treatment of the topic for Web or CD-ROM publication could have been much more effective with embedded video instead of, for example, the flip-book effects in the page margins as the desktop publishing (DTP) version had to create.

As noted above, the mathematics community has already incorporated significant numbers of colour images into their electronic versions of journals. The Institute of Physics publishes selected electronic versions of articles for subscribers (URL: http://www.iop.org/Journals/na/), in which concepts "come alive" in multimedia appendices. A recent eight-page article, titled "Molecular Dynamics Simulations of Carbon Nanotube-based Gears," includes MPEG movies that show these tiny gears in action (Han, Globus, Jaffe, & Deardorff, 1997).

Billing and other financial issues

At present, the CMS journals provide abstracts and "teasers" of articles via the Web. The society depends on the subscription revenues from traditional print journals, and especially (almost exclusively) the subscriptions from institutional (library) subscribers. How these subscribers will pick up and use an electronic version remains to be seen, although many experiments are under way around the world. In our experience, those journals that have a large infrastructure and a profit-making publication enterprise under way, like the Canadian Mathematical Society, potentially would have a great deal to lose if they gave away their electronic versions.

The *CJC* began its electronic publishing project with virtually no financial support or budget. As a result, the initial experiments relied on unpaid or low-paid student programmers who did not, as a rule, document what they were doing or put a high priority on correcting errors or deficiencies.

Copyright

Copyright issues, of course, are always significant but there are aspects of electronic publishing that raise copyright issues in unusual ways. A custom symbol font designed for CMS's print publications may not be available for on-line use or such use must be negotiated separately. The creators of fonts are naturally reluctant to have them distributed electronically as they argue the fonts may be reverse engineered out of embedded files, such as portable document format (PDF or Adobe Acrobat) files. In one instance, at one of our journals these fonts could not be used in electronically distributed documents.

Conclusions and policy recommendations

Market and technological changes beyond the control of journals or their publishers underlie many of the issues facing scholarly publishers. Our experience with browser evolution and corporate use of technology standards as a way to achieve competitive advantage suggests that these activities mitigate against robust, reliable, and, most importantly, user-friendly electronic publishing standards. Moreover, the initiative or drive for experimentation is frequently left to software developers and not journal editors or publishers. One solution may be policy initiatives that encourage publisher or journal-driven experimentation across a wide range of disciplines.

Payment schemes remain one of the most intransigent problems, and until an accepted industry practice emerges many of us will find ourselves reinventing the wheel in this area, a waste of resources for both publishers and subscribers. Current proposals for payments leave a lot to be desired from the publisher's perspective. Per-use payment schemes typically do not result in a viable business model for small-circulation publishers. The current practice of institutional subscribers paying for most of the cost of producing and distributing journals will inevitably continue, but we would argue the electronic version contains significant value-added when compared with the print version. The possibility of multiple concurrent users, for example, suggests that subscriptions will not be only on a per-site basis but on a per-user basis as well. Even the potential of multi-user, multi-location (home, office, library) access to a journal has a value and it will be up to the journal publisher to construct a pricing scheme that is fair to both user and information provider. Building the mechanisms for this, however, is a complex task and clearly beyond the traditional billing systems most publishers utilize. Scholarly journals, which traditionally rely on volunteer or low-paid staff, who work on the journal because of an interest in the topic, are unlikely to find the networking, computation, and business modelling skills implied by a move toward per-use billing of on-line products within their existing organizations.

Recent initiatives, such as the Canadian Association of Learned Journals (CALJ) Web site (URL: http://www.ccsp.sfu.ca/calj/), suggest that this enormous task may be mitigated somewhat by spreading the burden over multiple users. A combined software development project to address billing and payment schemes from the publishers' perspective would be an ideal vehicle for co-operation and joint funding and should be regarded as a policy priority by the scholarly communication community, including journals, government, and funding agencies. Such initiatives may be extremely important if the scholarly communication industry is to avoid further concentration of ownership—driven by the costs of developing custom billing systems—just when these new technologies present the opportunity for scholars to take control of the dissemination of their works.

It can be argued that electronic publishing technology brings with it a paradox: on the one hand this technology offers greater control over the production and dissemination of scholarly communication for a greater number of people, but on the other it requires a greater reliance of complex technological and business systems that are typically beyond the capabilities of a small journal and may, in fact, result in greater, not lesser concentration within the industry.

This paradox is neither unique nor unprecedented, and numerous scholars who have addressed technological change and society have commented on the flawed character of technologies. The Greek god of technology, Prometheus, is called "the god that limps" (Norman, 1981). From our perspective, this flaw should not be viewed as fatal nor a source of despair. On the contrary, it is a perfect example of the tension that exists between human society and new technologies. Out of this tension come solutions, either new technologies or new ways of using them.

In the case of billing systems, for example, the answer may lie within the very practices that have made hypertext publishing technology possible. We refer to the use of "open systems" as a means of developing highly reliable, inexpensive, shared tools.

The evolution of the Internet, from the earliest agreements on networking protocols and software applications to the present day of the World Wide Web has been closely linked to the emergence of robust, publicly available, user-created software.

Various groups have co-ordinated these activities in order to ensure that new applications inter-operate, and standards are set with maximum participation from those who wish to do so. The Internet Engineering Task Force (IETF) is an example of a volunteer group which sets standards and fosters innovation in Internet technologies.

This open environment has been credited with much of the widespread adoption and innovation of Internet communication systems. This movement toward publicly available and publicly developed standards can be seen as an example of open-systems computing and software. In practice, open systems can mean two quite different things. On the one hand there are the community-based (community of expert users, that is) emergent standards that typify Internet technologies. On the other hand are the officially mandated open systems designed to allow greater competition in the supply of technology to public bodies. The U.S. government's Government Open Systems Interconnection Profile (GOSIP) standard for information technology is an example of the latter.

Open-systems technologies like the Web have created a significant opportunity for the publication of scholarly works without the need for large capital-intensive systems for the creation, transportation, and sale of artifacts (that is, paper journals). This would, at first blush, appear to be an opportunity for smaller independent publishers. But if the movement of ideas is enhanced by new technologies, what about the movement of money? To date, only large corporations have been able to underwrite the development and maintenance costs of a financial network that is secure and efficient enough to use for commercial transactions, just as earlier multimedia efforts were expensive and limited. As a result, informal or small-time publishers face awkward hurdles.

But what if the forces of open-systems development were to be shifted from content production and transmission to transaction processing? Would we see a new level of smaller, independent, but financially viable publishers? Recent developments in open-systems standards for financial matters may hold the key to these next steps (Smith, 1996).

On the side of official open systems, the activities of the X9F group (which sets standards for financial networks) and the HLSG (High Level Strategy Group within the European community's information and communication technology industry) committee provide examples that may indicate the way in which open standards will play a role in future small- and medium-sized enterprises' access to electronic commerce (Shannon, 1996). The HLSG, for example, has recently set out requirements for "Electronic Commerce for SMEs," which will be presented to the European Union for discussion and implementation (Gann, 1996).

The real action may come in the informal standards, however. Recent developments among Internet commerce interest groups, and the e-cash system in particular suggest a possible solution for informal or society-based publishers. E-cash could provide authors and publishers with a medium of exchange with very low transaction costs and low barriers to entry, something traditional electronic payment systems have been unable to do. At present we have only possibilities and hints of solutions. Nevertheless, the recent history of rapid evolution among Internet content delivery software providers (for example, Netscape) is a vivid example of the potential that exists in software built to set de facto standards.

Some would argue that traditional models of scholarly publishing, which rely on an artifact that can be created, transported, and sold, are under threat from electronic technologies fostered by open-systems standards. These same open technologies may in turn redress the balance once again with the delivery of low-cost public-domain electronic payment systems that create opportunities for smaller publishers or even academics themselves to disseminate works.

If billing systems can be opened up and evolve as rapidly as hypertext transport and display systems, then there may be hope for those who see within the World Wide Web a chance for scholarship to return to its unmediated origins (Sirbu, 1997).

Note

1. An earlier version of this paper is also available on-line: URL: http://edie.cprost.sfu.ca/scom/

References

Acheson, Keith, & Maule, Christopher. (1995). Copyright and related rights: The international dimension. *Canadian Journal of Communication*. URL: http://edie.cprost.sfu.ca/cjc/amb/

Borwein, J. M., & Davidson, K. R. (1995). The future of mathematics in Canada 50 years later. In P. Filmore (Ed.), *The Canadian Math Society 1945-1995* (Vol. 1, pp. 231-248). Ottawa, ON: Canadian Mathematical Society.

Canadian Journal of Mathematics. (1997). URL: http://www.camel.math.ca/CMS/CJM/

Canadian Mathematical Bulletin. (1997). URL: http://www.camel.math.ca/CMS/CMB/

CMS Publication Indices. (1997). URL: http://www.camel.math.ca/vault/J-TOC/

Centre for Experimental and Constructive Mathematics (CECM). (1997). *Products and byproducts of ongoing research*. URL: http://www.cecm.sfu.ca/images/images.html

Filmore, P. (Ed.). (1995). *The Canadian Math Society 1945-1995* (Vol. 1). Ottawa, ON: Canadian Mathematical Society.

Filmore, P. (Ed.). (1996a). *Selecta* (Vol. 2). Ottawa, ON: Canadian Mathematical Society.

Filmore, P. (Ed.). (1996b). *Invited Articles* (Vol. 3). Ottawa, ON: Canadian Mathematical Society.

Gann, D. (1996). HLSG releases electronic commerce recommendations. *Open Systems Standards Tracking Report*, *5*(3). URL: http://www.europe.digital.com/info/osstr/tr0796.htm#A8

Han, Jie, Globus, Al, Jaffe, Richard, & Deardorff, Glenn. (1997). Molecular dynamics simulations of carbon nanotube-based gears. *Nanotechnology*, *8*(3), 95-102. URL: http://www.iop.org/Journals/na/

Knuth, Don. (1984). *The TeX Book*. Reading, MA: Addison-Wesley. URL: http://www-cs-staff.stanford.edu/~knuth/abcde.html#texbk

Lorimer, Rowland (Ed.). *Canadian Journal of Communication*. (1997). URL: http://www.ccsp.sfu.ca/calj/cjc/

Norman, C. (1981). *The god that limps: Science and technology in the eighties*. New York: W. W. Norton.

Odlyzko, A. M. (1995). Tragic loss or good riddance? The impending demise of traditional scholarly journals. *International Journal of Human-Computer Studies*, *42*, 71-122. URL: http://hyperg.iicm.tu-graz.ac.at

Okerson, A. S., & O'Donnell, J. J. (Eds.). (1995). *Scholarly journals at the crossroads: A subversive proposal for electronic publishing*. Washington, DC: Association of Research Libraries. URL: http://cogsci.ecs.soton.ac.uk/~harnad/subvert.html

Peek, R. P., & Newby, G. B. (Eds.). (1996). *Scholarly publishing: The electronic frontier*. Boston: MIT Press.

Peterson, Ivars. (1997). MathLand [Column]. *Science News*. URL: http://www.sciencenews.org/sn_arc97/2_8_97/mathland.htm

Sato, Naoki (Ed.). (1997). Mayhem On-line. *CRUX*. URL: http://www.camel.math.ca/CMS/CRUX/

Shannon, S. (1996). X9F, the accredited standards subcommittee, data and information security for financial services. *Open Systems Standards Tracking Report*, *5*(3). URL: http://www.europe.digital.com/info/osstr/tr0796.htm#A7

Sinclair, N. (1997, February). Lowest common denominator dominates Web publishing [Interview]. Burnaby, BC.

Sirbu, M. A. (1997). Credits and debits on the Internet. *IEEE Spectrum*, *34*(2), 23-29.

Smith, J. L. (1996). Let's collaborate on global standards. *Open Systems Standards Tracking Report*, *5*(7). URL: http://www.europe.digital.com/info/osstr/tr1196.htm#A1

Promoting Electronic Scholarly Publishing in Canada: Initiatives at Industry Canada

David Beattie & David McCallum
Industry Canada/SchoolNet

Abstract: As part of its internationally acclaimed SchoolNet project, Industry Canada is supporting major initiatives in the area of electronic scholarly publishing. This paper provides a brief introduction to Industry Canada's activities related to universities, academics, and students, and describes SchoolNet's efforts to promote electronic publishing of scholarly information in Canada.

Résumé : Avec son projet SchoolNet acclamé autour du monde, Industrie Canada est en train d'appuyer des initiatives majeures dans le domaine de l'édition savante électronique. Cet article donne une brève introduction aux activités d'Industrie Canada se rapportant aux universités, aux académiques et aux étudiants, et décrit les efforts du SchoolNet à promouvoir l'édition électronique de recherches savantes au Canada.

Industry Canada initiatives of interest to the Canadian academic community

Industry Canada's (URL: http://info.gc.ca/ic-data/ic-eng.html) principal objective is to help make Canada more competitive by fostering the growth of Canadian business; by promoting a fair, efficient marketplace; and by encouraging scientific research and technology diffusion. A major policy document, *Building a More Innovative Economy* (1994) recognized the emerging knowledge-based global economy and emphasized the advancement of education and research as essential means of strengthening Canada's competitive position.

The policy also recognized the rapid evolution of the "information highway," as well as the need to take full advantage of its potential as an educational tool. This thrust was reinforced in *Science and Technology for the*

David Beattie is Director of the Virtual Products Group at Industry Canada/SchoolNet, 4th Floor, 155 Queen Street West, Ottawa, ON K1A 0H5. E-mail: beattie.david@ic.gc.ca
David McCallum is Principal Consultant to the Electronic Publishing Promotion Project, Industry Canada/SchoolNet. E-mail: mccallum.david@ic.gc.ca

***Canadian Journal of Communication,* Vol. 22, No. 3/4 (1997) 153-160**

New Century (1996), which called for making full use of networking technology to connect Canadian communities, including schools, universities, and colleges.

SchoolNet (URL: http://www.schoolnet.ca) is one of several Industry Canada programs aimed at helping students build skills that will allow them to be more marketable, to transfer from their studies to employment as quickly as possible, and to be well positioned as entrepreneurs in the new global economy. A multifaceted World Wide Web site, SchoolNet is composed of vetted content for use by the Canadian educational community.

The mandate of SchoolNet is to facilitate the linkage of the 16,000 schools and 3,400 libraries in Canada as well as the 447 Native communities that fall under the federal government's jurisdiction. Access to SchoolNet is completely free of charge to students, teachers, and the general public.

Although most SchoolNet applications are oriented to the Kindergarten-to-Grade-12 levels, some are aimed squarely at the post-secondary sector. One example is the recently launched National Graduate Register (NGR) (URL: http://www.schoolnet.ca/ngr). A companion service to the Electronic Labour Exchange (ELE) (URL: http://ele.ingenia.com) of Human Resource Development Canada, the NGR allows students at Canadian universities and colleges to place their resumes on-line and to have them accessed by employers within and outside the country. This will effectively create an electronically searchable national labour pool, thereby allowing firms, even small ones, to do on-line campus recruiting across Canada.

Electronic scholarly publishing initiatives

Dissemination of new knowledge is an essential aspect of the research process. In a knowledge-driven economy, cost-effective methods for the distribution of scholarly information are vital, particularly in a time of reduced financial support for universities and their libraries.

To date, SchoolNet's work in the area of electronic scholarly publishing can be grouped under three headings: studies; demonstration projects; and active promotion. The program is currently exploring the establishment of a virtual centre for on-line scholarly publishing to facilitate large-scale conversion of paper-based journals to on-line publication.

Studies

In order to explore the viability of electronic publications, in 1995 SchoolNet contracted for two studies concerning the economics of scholarly publishing: *The Cost and Revenue Structure of Academic Journals: Paper-based Versus E-Journals* by Vijay Jog (1995) and *Funding Electronic Journals on the Internet* (Phoenix Systems Synectics, 1995).

Jog's study identified savings as high as 50% in the costs of on-line publication compared with paper-based publication; the savings rose to 90% if publication could be undertaken and managed centrally. The Phoenix study showed the technical feasibility of charging usage fees on-line, and described methods by which journals could charge for access to their publications.

Demonstration projects

To develop practical data on the operational aspects of electronic scholarly publishing, SchoolNet assisted the electronic publication of three journals, chosen by means of a formal competition. One was an upgrade of an existing electronic journal; two were conversions of existing paper-based journals, one of which continues to publish in its original form. Although support for these projects by SchoolNet has come to an end, all three journals continue to be published on-line.

SchoolNet provided support for the multilingual on-line journal, *Surfaces* (1997), Canada's oldest and most respected on-line journal, now in its fifth year of publication. Activities include the systematization of the production process, standardizing on-line pagination techniques, and conversion to standard generalized markup language (SGML), all of which have the objective of upgrading the technical platform of the journal to the highest common denominator in electronic scholarly publishing. *Surfaces* will shortly become the first on-line journal to be published by a Canadian university press, Les Presses de l'Université de Montréal.

A parallel publishing project (paper and on-line) with the *Canadian Journal of Behavioural Sciences (CJBS)* (1997) is another of SchoolNet's initiatives. This assessed the impact of parallel publishing on readership of the journal, on subscriptions to it, and on issues such as copyright. According to the Canadian Psychological Association (personal communication, 1996), reaction from authors and readers has been positive to date; in fact, paid subscriptions to the paper-based journal actually increased following its availability on-line.

Finally, SchoolNet supported the total conversion of a journal from paper to on-line publication with the library-reviewing journal, *Canadian Review of Materials* (*CM*) (1997). Published by the Manitoba Library Association, *CM* ceased paper publication late in 1994 and is now only accessible on-line. The journal experimented with various methods of maintaining revenue and has now determined that its principal source of revenue will come from advertising.

The demonstration projects with *Surfaces* and *CJBS* have yielded a great deal of information on the management, policy, and technical issues concerning the publication of an on-line scholarly journal. Both journals have written up their experience to date (Guédon, 1996; Hickox, 1996). This information will be an invaluable record of experience for those considering electronic publishing.

Promotional activities

To help break down barriers to the acceptance of electronic publishing of scholarly information, in the spring of 1996, SchoolNet contracted with David L. McCallum (URL: http://www.schoolnet.ca/vp/cesn/mccallum.htm), on sabbatical from his position as executive director of the Canadian Association of Research Libraries, to head up the Electronic Publishing Promotion Project (EPPP).

EPPP has the following objectives:

1. To raise awareness in the Canadian academic community of the soaring costs of traditional scholarly communication methods and the potential for electronic publishing to address them. Key messages being communicated include:
   (a) The Internet has become a bona fide medium for academic information exchange and publishing.
   (b) Electronic communication of research information allows many advantages over print publishing, including ease of searching, multimedia functionality, and global accessibility.
   (c) It is not difficult for Canadian academics to become Internet users.
2. To seek endorsements from Canadian academic associations and related organizations of peer-reviewed electronic publications as valid outlets for scholarly material.
3. To encourage both the transition of existing Canadian scholarly publications from paper to electronic format and the creation of entirely new electronic scholarly products.

Objectives 2 and 3 relate directly to recommendations 21, 22, and 23 of the final report of the AUCC-CARL/ABRC Task Force on Academic Libraries and Scholarly Communication (AUCC-CARL/ABRC, 1996, p. 10).

Outreach activities

Initial presentations on the EPPP were made at the Canadian Learned Societies Conference, June 1996, at Brock University in St. Catharines, Ontario. In the fall of 1996, full information packages were prepared and distributed to Canadian academic organizations. The packages contained a detailed description of the project; excerpts from the project Web site, the Canadian Electronic Scholarly Network (CESN) (URL: http://www.schoolnet.ca/vp/cesn); information on how academics could become computer literate and go on-line; and a request for the organizations to endorse electronic scholarly publishing in principle.

Feedback on these mail-outs has been most encouraging. The project is being publicized in the newsletters of various associations, and in response to numerous requests, presentations on the project are being made to associations, government organizations, and universities across the country.

Endorsements of electronic scholarly publishing

Recognizing that Canadian academics will be hesitant to publish electronically unless their publications are officially recognized both by their peers and academic institutions, Canadian scholarly associations and related organizations have been approached to consider formally adopting the following statement: "This organization recognizes the legitimacy of scholarly material published in electronic form when such information conforms to broadly accepted standards of peer review."

The proposed resolution is based on a similar resolution passed in 1994 by the Higher Education Funding Council for England (HEFCE, 1996) (URL: http://www.hefce.ac.uk): "In the light of the recommendations of the Joint Funding Councils' Libraries Review Group Report, refereed journal articles published through electronic means will be treated on the same basis as those appearing in printed journals" (Joint Funding Council, 1993).

The statement of endorsement, or a close variant, has been adopted by the Humanities and Social Science Federation of Canada (HSSFC) (URL: http://www.hssfc.ca); an umbrella group composed of over 50 scholarly societies; by the Canadian Association of University Teachers (CAUT) (URL: http://www.caut.ca); and by the Canadian Association of Research Libraries (CARL) (URL: http://aixl.uottawa.ca/library/carl). It is expected that other organizations, including the Association of Universities and Colleges of Canada (AUCC) (URL: http://www.aucc.ca), will follow suit in due course.

The director general of Industry Canada's Science Promotion and Academic Affairs Branch has written to the presidents of the three Canadian granting councils (the Medical Research Council, Natural Sciences and Engineering Research Council, and the Social Sciences and Humanities Research Council) requesting that they develop equivalent policy statements. Initial reaction has been positive; in fact, the Medical Research Council has officially adopted this policy.

Canadian Electronic Scholarly Network (CESN)

CESN is a Web site on SchoolNet (URL: http://www.schoolnet.ca/vp/cesn) that groups all EPPP information in one place. It also identifies and allows access to full-text, peer-reviewed Canadian electronic scholarly publications, links to related activities throughout the world, and provides information on the Forum for Electronic Scholarly Publishing in Canada (FESPIC) discussion group.

Electronic scholarly publishing principles

Electronic publishing is still too new to have established generally recognized standards. Development of, and adherence to, such standards should accelerate the acceptance of electronic publishing within academia. At the same time, electronic availability is no guarantee that a publication will be equitably priced; reasonable pricing policies are also essential.

A draft set of principles intended to describe the characteristics of high-quality electronic scholarly publishing projects was developed by David L. McCallum (1997) and will shortly be issued to a variety of electronic publishing and related Internet discussion groups. The principles cover archival, bibliographic, economic, legal, and technical aspects, and reflect an academic library perspective.

The concept of the principles has been well received, and audience members at presentations have submitted helpful feedback in the form of suggestions and e-mails.

A virtual centre for on-line scholarly publishing

A fleeting comment in the study by Jog (1995) opened the door to an exciting new development. Basing his conclusions on work performed at Virginia Tech, Jog noted that significant benefits should be realized by clustering production and proficiency around a common electronic publishing centre. These benefits can be made possible through:

- Greater savings from efficiencies in publication markup and preparation;
- A critical mass of expertise in such management issues as copyright, digital integrity, maintenance of subscription revenues, and journal operations;
- A co-ordinated capacity to locate or develop, then to apply, the latest technologies.

Efforts are under way by Industry Canada/SchoolNet to establish a self-sustaining virtual centre for the on-line publication of scholarly journals, to be formed through a partnership between university presses and journals, with the goal of creating a national network of on-line publishing resources for peer-reviewed, non-profit scholarly journals.

Over the initial period of this project, the partners will publish 20 or more journals on-line, and will promote on-line publishing within the journals community. The intention is to expand the number of presses participating as the project develops and new partners are found. New technologies developed will be freely accessible to the partners and ultimately to the Canadian scholarly community. Progress and results from the project will be published on the CESN Web site.

Industry Canada/SchoolNet estimates that the overall cost of the project over three years will be about $1 million. SchoolNet is seeking financial participation from other federal programs, provincial governments, and educational institutions, and possibly the sponsorship of private-sector organizations.

Results from this project will support several government objectives:
- employment in new technologies;
- retention of highly qualified personnel within Canada.
- lower costs to government and universities (especially libraries), as journal costs decline;
- construction of research infrastructure; and
- creation of commercial opportunities for exploitation of technologies and expertise developed.

Next steps

EPPP's founding partners hope that financing for the Virtual Centre will be in place shortly so that activities can begin no later than late 1997 or early 1998. Over time, they anticipate expansion in the number of university presses participating in the project. The CESN Web site will report the results of their work on a regular basis.

The Electronic Publishing Promotion Project has the potential to significantly change the face of scholarly communication in Canada, creating what we hope will be an affordable publishing environment that takes full advantage of new technological capabilities, while at the same time respecting the values of the traditional system.

References

AUCC-CARL/ABRC Task Force on Academic Libraries and Scholarly Communication. (1996). *The changing world of scholarly communication: Challenges and choices for Canada*. Ottawa: Author.

Building a more innovative economy. (1994). Ottawa: Industry Canada. URL: http://xinfo.ic.gc.ca/ic-data/economy/BAMIE/summary-e.html

Canadian Journal of Behavioural Sciences (*CJBS*). (1997). URL: http://www.cycor.ca/Psych/ac-main.html

Canadian Review of Materials (*CM*). (1997). URL: http://www.mbnet.mb.ca/cm/

Guédon, Jean-Claude. (1996). *Meta-surfaces or ends and means to grow a viable electronic journal*. URL: http://tornade.ere.umontreal.ca/~guedon/

HEFCE. (1996). Research assessment exercise. URL: http://www.gold.ac.uk/history/hyperjournal/rae.htm

Hickox, Stuart. (1996). *Guidelines for the conversion of scholarly journals to electronic form*. URL: http://www.cpa.ca/project/guide.html

Jog, Vijay. (1995). *Cost and revenue structure of academic journals: Paper-based versus e-journals*. Ottawa: Industry Canada. URL: http://www.schoolnet.ca/biz/economics/vijayjog.html

Joint Funding Councils' Libraries Review Group. (1993). *Report*. Bristol: Higher Education Funding Council for England. URL: http://ukoln.bath.ac.uk/follett/follett_report.html

McCallum, David L. (1997). *Principles of electronic scholarly publishing* [Draft]. URL: http://www.schoolnet.ca/vp/cesn/princips.htm

Phoenix Systems Synectics. (1995). *Funding electronic journals on the Internet*. Ottawa: Industry Canada. URL: http://www.schoolnet.ca/biz/economics/phoenix/index.html

Science and technology for the new century. (1996). Ottawa: Industry Canada. URL: http://canada.gc.ca/depts/science/english/strat-e.html

Surfaces. (1997). URL: http://tornade.ere.umontreal.ca/~guedon/Surfaces/index-a.html

Faculty Perspective on Scholarly Communication

Kenneth Field
Trent University

Abstract: The means and method of scholarly communication are changing as new and faster forms of communication become accessible to scholars. The potential for electronic scholarly communication via the Internet and the World Wide Web to positively affect the current state of affairs is very good. It may provide the means to address the hegemonic tendencies of the large for-profit scholarly publishers. Many matters need to be addressed though. Some of these are: copyright and ownership of intellectual property; the methods used for assessing the work of scholars; development of the communications infrastructure, both within and among institutions; and provision of equipment and services to those in the scholarly community. This paper examines these issues in the Canadian context.

Résumé: Les moyens et méthodes de communication savante sont en train de changer à mesure que des formes de communication nouvelles et plus rapides deviennent accessible aux chercheurs. La communication savante électronique à l'Internet et au World Wide Web a un très fort potentiel d'avoir un impact positif sur l'état actuel des choses. En effet, la communication électronique pourrait permettre aux chercheurs de contrebalancer les tendances hégémoniques des grandes maisons d'édition académiques à but lucratif. Il est nécessaire dans ce contexte d'adresser plusieurs questions. Parmi celles-ci, il y a: le droit d'auteur et l'appartenance de propriétés intellectuelles; les méthodes utilisées pour évaluer les ouvrages académiques; le développement d'une infrastructure pour la communication, autant au sein d'institutions qu'entre celles-ci; et la fourniture d'équipement et de services à la communauté savante. Cet article examine ces questions dans un contexte canadien.

Kenneth Field is Chair of the Canadian Association of University Teachers Librarians' Committee, Microforms and Photoreproduction Librarian at Trent University, and Principal of Lady Eaton College, Trent University, Trent University, Lady Eaton College, 1755 West Bank Drive, Peterborough, ON K9L 1Z6. E-mail: kfield@trentu.ca

***Canadian Journal of Communication*, Vol. 22, No. 3/4 (1997) 161-178**

Introduction

Scholarly communication begins with the desire of scholars to communicate the results of their work to peers in the scholarly community. Gutenberg's development of mechanized printing using movable type led to wide distribution of research findings, which previously was limited to those with access only to handwritten manuscripts. The monograph soon became the primary vehicle for the communication of scholarly work. With the establishment in 1664 of the *Philosophical Transactions of the Royal Society*, research writers acquired another means of disseminating the fruits of their labours, the print journal. This is not so huge a leap in the development of vehicles for scholarly communication as one might think. James O'Donnell provides an explanation of the difference between monograph and article: "It is crude but effective to say that a monograph is an article that is too long for any journal to accept it, and so it must be printed and bound separately" (1993, p. 29).

This system of scholarly communication has remained practically unchanged since the time of Gutenberg. But things are changing and rapidly. Enormous advances in information technology over the past three decades present new ways of communication independent of paper-based systems. The established practices of peer review, publication in prestigious journals, and the surrender of copyright are all coming under close scrutiny as scholars explore the uncharted waters of scholarly communication in an electronic environment. The potential for vastly enhancing scholarly communication is very great, but there are also costs involved in shifting from a firmly established system to one still in embryo.

The urgency with which those in the scholarly community are moving to utilize these new tools and channels of communication is only partially due to the new means and media of communication—hypertext, multimedia, and a degree of interconnectedness among academics that until recently was unheard of. Another element that is creating a climate of urgency is the continuing erosion of funding for post-secondary education in many countries, particularly in Canada. The costs of information are not falling but rising. This is most evident in the continuing escalation of serial prices. As funding to universities has declined so has the purchasing power of university libraries. Libraries have thus been forced to cancel journal subscriptions in order to stay in line with overall university budget decreases. This crisis has fueled much activity in electronic publication of scholarly journals and also in the repatriation of copyright in scholarly works—initiated in order to loosen the stranglehold journal publishers have on the market for communication of scholarly research.

New developments in electronic and information technologies are having a variety of effects, including the impact of electronic information exchange on scholarly communication; shifts in government funding away from support of post-secondary institutions toward private sector development of information technology; and the adjustment of scholars and institutions to the changing demands of the new information environment.

The ironies are numerous. The new technology is popular, but only uncertainly effective. Indeed, the more it spreads, and the more it is used in the chaos of the Internet, the less effective it becomes—or so some would like to say. And the obvious irony is that a device for saving money has become a permanent reason for spending ever-larger amounts. This paper will have served its purpose if it has put flesh on the bones of these ironies.

Publish or perish

Although these words may seem *démodés*, for academics the publish-or-perish imperative is an important motivating factor in their professional lives. In an article published in the journal *Nature*, John Maddox writes:

> People's research programmes, even their careers, may depend on what their sponsors or employers see in print. It is not surprising that within reason authors will go to endless trouble to meet conditions laid down by journals and their editors. In the process, they are moulding accounts of their research in response to external demands. (1989, p. 657)

The pre-eminence of paper-based journal publishing in providing the fora for this aspect of career development is well established. Publication of scholarly work in journals respected by one's peers is critical to the establishment and maintenance of one's career. It is almost a rule of thumb that consideration for tenure and promotion includes an examination of one's record of publications, either of monographs or articles, by publishers or in journals that are considered the most important in the particular field of study. It is not surprising, then, that many academics give little thought to the implications of this kind of system. This imperative provides the perfect environment for a profit-making publishing industry working with an audience that is captive and thus more or less immune to market pressures.

Some think universities ought to de-emphasize the number of publications in tenure review and promotion, with several beneficial effects. Firstly, it might slow the flood of scholarly writing fueling the expansion of the scholarly publishing industry. It would also limit what Paul Ribbe, in his paper on cost/quality in academic journals calls "fragmentation and 'shingling' of research reports," which allows researchers to get more "bang for the buck," as it were, out of their research publications (1990, p. 133). This is not to say that publication of research results would cease to occur. Rather, as a result of this and with aid of other aspects of electronic communication, it might stem the flood of scholarly writing.

The carrying out of research is an integral part of the scholarly endeavour and will continue whether or not there is a strong emphasis on it for tenure and promotion. This de-emphasis may also create an environment that is more conducive to doing research at a natural pace, rather than at a speed driven by the demands of institutions, thus further assisting in stemming the flood of scholarly writing and returning it to a more natural flow.

For academics in Canada, a change in the emphasis placed on publication for tenure review and promotion will be accomplished only with systematic changes in the collective agreements of some 75 universities. After all, rules for evaluation of professors are laid out in those agreements, as indeed they should be. In a university system where academic senates cannot be expected to evaluate professors' research and teaching, and where administrators have proven themselves incapable of balanced judgments of teaching and research, there is only one way to do the job: through peer review, openly and freely conducted on a regular basis. (Senates are not suitable for evaluating the teaching and research of academics for one primary reason, senates are the academic policy-setting bodies of our universities and as such are responsible for setting the policies on teaching and research consequent on the mission of the university. They are not well placed to carry out evaluations of the teaching and research of individual faculty; rather they work at the levels of course offerings and above.)

Peer review must continue to play a role in the area of scholarly communication. It is through review and criticism that knowledge expands and increases. Ideas first presented by one or a group of academics in the form of research results are placed in the academic arena where fellow peers can examine and analyze the work, incorporating it where appropriate into the body of knowledge in the discipline.

The perception among scholars that work published electronically is less legitimate from a scholarly standpoint than work published on paper in a prestigious journal is diminishing. As scholars become connected to the Internet and involved in electronic communication they see the enormous benefits to be had. One stumbling block to broad acceptance of electronic scholarly communication is the view, whether valid or not, that work published in an electronic journal will not be given as much weight by those reviewing a scholar's work, as work published in an established prestigious journal.

Industry Canada through its Virtual Products Division has been actively promoting the development and use of electronic communication for the dissemination of scholarly work. In addition, the Canadian Association of University Teachers (CAUT) has taken the position that work published electronically should be viewed on the same level as work published in paper-based journals in cases of tenure review and promotion, provided that the electronic journal has a rigorous peer review system. The issue then is not one of the medium used for publication, but rather whether there is peer review. There will, of course, always be journals with reputations that put them above all others in a discipline; however, the ease and efficiency of Web-based communication means that other, perhaps marginalized, voices will have an opportunity to be heard.

Peer review in the electronic environment

Whether the current form of peer review remains in place for long is of importance only inasmuch as it remains a viable measure of the life of the scholarly community. It is widely agreed that the current scholarly communication system of editorial boards, reviewers, and publishers will continue in place for at least another decade and probably much longer. Although the number and variety of scholarly publications that are exclusively electronic has grown tremendously since the late 1980s, there has not yet been the kind of fundamental change that would spell the end of the current regime and the start of a new regime. Rather, there is a gradual transformation. As more scholars establish their own communication networks and the credibility of the work being disseminated grows, the efficacy of this new means of communication will become evident and attractive.

Stevan Harnad, the publisher of the electronic journal *Psycholoquy*, characterizes scholarly communication on the Internet as the "fourth cognitive revolution" (Harnad, 1992, p. vii). He argues that two of the previous three cognitive revolutions have had the effect of slowing the natural tempo of the brain. These brakes on brain activity, handwriting, and the reading of print require more time than speech (the first cognitive revolution) to carry out, and therefore they force the brain to slow down to an unnatural tempo (Harnad, 1992, p. vi). Harnad likens paper-based scholarly communication to handwriting and reading print in that it slows down creative scholarly activity. It can require months, if not years, for a piece of research to be disseminated to the scholarly community, and then it may take a year or more for the community to respond, at which point the author of the original research has probably gone on to other things. With scholarly communication on the Internet, the time from dissemination to response is greatly reduced, allowing the creative process to occur in a more timely and natural fashion, similar to the speed and fluidity of conversation.

In the case of articles submitted to *Psycholoquy*, authors are not expected to submit fully formed accounts of research, but rather preliminary or partially completed reports. These reports are vetted by a member of the editorial board of the journal in order to insure a high level of quality. But here the similarity ends between this journal and other more traditional journals, for the vetting is expected to be done within a few hours of the receipt of the submission. Once vetted, the article is posted to the electronic journal and the "scholarly skywriting'' (1992, p. ix), as Harnad calls it, begins. Harnad states quite plainly that

> Scholarly skywriting in *Psycholoquy* is intended especially for the prepublication "pilot" stage of scientific inquiry in which peer communication and feedback are still critically shaping the final intellectual outcome. This formative stage is where the Net's speed, scope, and interactive capabilities offer the possibility of a phase transition in the evolution of knowledge. (1992, p. ix)

Harnad's system does not remove the necessity for vehicles in which to publish the finished work of a particular project. However, his scheme, if widely accepted, would reduce the numbers of print journals, providing another forum in which to communicate and discuss ongoing work, leaving print journals to publish the final reports of the completed work.

This model of pre-print publication on the Net has taken on even greater importance in the communication of research findings in the area of high energy physics. Paul Ginsparg (1994), the developer of the e-print archives at the Los Alamos National Laboratory, states that preprints, even in hard-copy form, have "largely supplanted journals as [the] primary communication medium." The growing popularity of e-prints as a means of getting reports of research out quickly is understandable. Once a network of scholars has been established and a way of managing it has been found, then the Internet becomes the ideal channel for disseminating and discussing scholarly work.

Rather than a radical shift away from the scholarly communication system that we know, we see an expansion and enhancement of the system, mitigated by the speed and interconnectedness of the Internet and by the recognition of scholars that this is a medium providing a forum for global scholarly exchange. This globalization of scholarly communication via the Internet is having the effect of tearing down national borders and blurring the lines of attribution of scholarly work to specific individuals. There is much greater opportunity for far-reaching collaboration in the development of ideas, manifesting itself in more frequent interdisciplinary exploration of ideas. This particular outcome of the globalization is placing stress on the classical idea of copyright as it applies to academics.

Copyright

The purpose of copyright in Canada is, among other things, to insure the *droit d'auteur* or the natural-law right of an author to his/her work. This includes both an economic right and a moral right. In the first case, the author or creator has the right to remuneration for the use of her work. In the second case, the author or creator has a right of integrity in her work such that it cannot be modified in any way which damages the reputation of the author/creator.

In the scholarly community, well-established common practices guard against the improper use or appropriation of another scholar's work. In the very recent past, the three Canadian granting councils, the Natural Sciences and Engineering Research Council of Canada (NSERC), the Social Sciences and Humanities Research Council of Canada (SSHRC), and the Medical Research Council of Canada (MRC), required that all universities obtaining grants from them have policies on academic fraud and misconduct in order to further guard against unscrupulous use of the work of others. It is reasonably safe to say that in the scholarly community there is zero tolerance for this type of behaviour. A scholar's career is dependent on the work that he/she has published. All academics know this and most respect the work of others. For those instances where such respect has broken down procedures in policies on fraud and misconduct in research come into play.

Scholars also want their work to be widely disseminated in the scholarly community. If this requires that some photocopies be made, then so be it. The fact that the work is being circulated is of far greater importance than the making of a few copies. An important point to remember is that in the world of scholarly publishing, with the exception of monographs, authors surrender the copyright in their work to the publisher. The publisher is then free to sell the work of scholars for whatever price the academic community is willing to pay and reap all the benefits from the sales.

In his paper examining the issues of cost/quality and the proliferation of academic journals, Paul Ribbe, series editor of *Reviews in Mineralogy* and professor of mineralogy at Virginia Polytechnic Institute and State University, wrote, "Nearly every professional paper is written by someone whose salary is paid by someone else and who is provided with a place to work. Thus the concept of 'unsupported' research is mythical in the absolute sense" (1990, p. 129).

The benefit, then, to the scholar of having a paper published in a prestigious journal is one of enhanced career opportunities and greater scholarly recognition. There is little or no direct monetary gain for the scholar. However, the hegemony that scholarly journal publishers hold over the academic community means that, as noted above, academic libraries, which are required to provide access to the resources necessary to support the research and teaching at the university, are at the publishers' mercy when it comes to buying back the very research that scholars have provided free—particularly when the contributors have surrendered their copyright to the publisher.

The interim report of the AUCC-CARL Task Force on Academic Libraries and Scholarly Communication suggested that

> Institutions must revisit the current model in which they forgo or ignore *their* statutory ownership of scholarly output. The new model could still yield to the interests of the scholar, but might require automatic granting of non-exclusive licences for using the intellectual property within an institution, within a group

> of institutions, or within the national or international scholarly community. (1995, p. 5)

The emphasis under "their" is mine. It is important to remember that the person in whom copyright resides is the author/creator and not the institution. This principle has recently been recognized at the international level by the World Intellectual Property Organization (WIPO), of which Canada is a member. In the WIPO Copyright Treaty, Article 6 states:

> (1) Authors of literary works and artistic works shall enjoy the exclusive right of authorizing the making available to the public of the original and copies of their works through sale or other transfer of ownership.
> (2) Nothing in this Treaty shall affect the freedom of Contracting Parties to determine the conditions, if any, under which the exhaustion of the right in paragraph (1) applies after the first sale or transfer of ownership of the original or a copy of the work with the authorization of the author. (1996, Article 6, p. 3)

Although this Article refers to the transfer of ownership and not permission to copy without remuneration, it reinforces the fact that authors and creators are the rightful holders of the copyright. Parenthetically, this treaty is directly related to the Berne Convention, to which Canada is signatory.

Clifford Lynch makes a somewhat convincing argument against the AUCC-CARL proposal:

> While this would probably make a major impact on the economic bind facing libraries, it seems highly unlikely that such a shift could be accomplished. Faculty would besiege university administrations, and publishers (and others) would challenge such policies in the courts and legislatures. . . . If nothing else, the bureaucratic ineptitude of many large institutions would threaten to become a major barrier to the dissemination of new knowledge. (1993, p. 15)

One can well imagine the reluctance of faculty to give to their administrations one more element of control over their professional lives. This control could conceivably mean that an author would not be free to choose the place in which he/she wished to have their work published, but would have to seek permission from an administration. If the aim of this type of arrangement is to gain greater control over the publishing process, then that permission may well not be given. As noted above, academic careers are built, in part, on a record of scholarly publishing in the right places and this would seem to undermine a scholar's efforts at establishing and maintaining a career. There may also be a natural reluctance on the part of publishers, who have for a long time reaped the benefits of a scholarly publishing system that gives them all the opportunities for making profits from the very people that provide them with the means. Lynch concedes that a move of this type would have a major effect on the budgetary crisis that university libraries have been experiencing for at least five, if not ten, years.

One possibility not discussed by Lynch is the retention of copyright by the authors of the works, that is, the scholars. If scholars retained copyright to their work, then publishers would probably not be as anxious to raise prices exorbitantly or to divide their journals into areas of greater and greater specificity in order to get more "bang for the buck" from the articles being published.

This last possibility raises interesting questions about what scholars might demand if they retained owners' rights. Some may decide that they should receive royalties from the publication of their work. This could have a considerable impact on the costs to users for making use of this material. This may well sound attractive to a copyright collective such as CANCOPY, which would view the inclusion of scholars in their collective as a means of extracting more money from all manner of institutions with which they have licences. Therefore, the savings to libraries that Lynch refers to in the quotation above may not amount to much, as the profits would simply be shifted from the publisher to the creator. As equitable as this may seem, it would defeat the cost-saving purpose of author retention of copyright.

Still, practically speaking, no unsupported research occurs in the scholarly community. The benefits scholars receive for their efforts, one hopes, are tenured appointments and increases in prestige, and thus the incentives to reap greater profit from one's research may be minimized. However, it is the right of the authors/creators to grant or not grant, as the case may be, "non-exclusive licences" for the use of their work.

It is current CAUT policy that

> The general principle of a proper copyright policy is that the copyright should belong solely to the creator(s) but that where the university has commissioned a work dealing with the operations of the university itself or where it requests the member to edit a university publication, the university and the member may make alternate arrangements. (1987, Preamble)

The policy goes on to stress the importance of language in faculty contracts that ensures that copyright—not only in books, but also in films, videos, works of art, lectures, and computer programs—does reside with the creator and not the institution, because the language in the *Copyright Act* permits employers to claim copyright in the work of their employees (CAUT, 1987, Preamble). Entrenching this principle in faculty contracts makes substantive recognition of the scholar as creator.

The issue of copyright and who holds it is a difficult one to manage as the section above illustrates. All of the scenarios suggested have advantages and disadvantages. It is critical, therefore, that more work be done by all the Canadian organizations involved in post-secondary education on a fair and equitable system of copyright—a system that recognizes and rewards the creators and, at the same time, facilitates use of research material.

Bill C-32

The new amendments to the *Canadian Copyright Act*, found in Bill C-32, provide an opportunity to address this issue by means of exceptions for copying of single articles for the purposes of research and study by those associated with libraries, museums, or archives. Unfortunately, these exceptions are fettered by restrictions on what type of material can be copied, that is, only articles from scholarly, scientific, or technical periodicals, excluding other types of periodical literature not of a scholarly nature, for a period of a year after publication. In addition, language has been added to qualify the applicability of some exceptions by requiring that institutions be members of copyright collectives before exempt copying can take place.

The first of these limitations can be dealt with by providing broad definitions of scholarly, scientific, and technical periodicals, thus capturing the greatest variety. The second of the restrictions places libraries, museums, and archives at the mercy of copyright collectives. All of these institutions will have to be members of a copyright collective in order to avoid prosecution. This will require that more money be spent on making research material accessible, placing further strain on already severely reduced budgets, and benefiting not only the collective but also the publishers. The only solution to this problem is removal of this qualification from the Bill.

Funding of technological development

The increasing ease of network communication and the growing number of people utilizing it are precipitating the development of electronic scholarly communication. Practically all those involved in scholarly communication, from government to publishers to the universities to scholars, are looking closely at the medium as a means of answering pressing financial and political questions.

For government, the issues are manifold. Canada, like others in the G-7, is active in building and maintaining a Canadian communications infrastructure that will be able to support the growing use of electronic network communication. In the report of the Information Highway Advisory Council (IHAC), the prevailing theme is private-sector development of not only the infrastructure but also the products disseminated on it. One can only think that the reason for this particular perspective is the now commonly held position of many politicians that people want less government and more free-market capitalism.

This certainly seems to be the case with funding for post-secondary education. The federal government is actively decreasing the post-secondary education funding it provides to the provinces, which in turn are looking for ways to shift the cost of operating universities away from themselves and onto the individual institutions, and encouraging greater use of private sector funding. Therefore, it appears less and less likely that government will provide funding to develop a system of electronic scholarly communication when other spending on education is being reduced.

The federal government has not yet officially accepted the recommendations of the IHAC. Yet, over the past few years, it has been systematically commercializing its information-providing services. In its 1994 brief to the IHAC, CARL made a number of valuable points about government funding policies and the rising cost of information.

> The collections and services of the National Library have been severely reduced due to federal budget restrictions; CISTI has been obliged by federal policies and those of its parent body (the National Research Council of Canada) to become a commercial information provider whose rates are so high that the use of its excellent services by non-profit organizations is in jeopardy.
>
> It should be added that the trend to view information primarily as a commercial commodity has led to drastic increases in the cost of Statistics Canada data, information essential to research on how rapid social change is reshaping the country. And as government departments move from paper to electronic publishing, the Depository Services Program is finding it increasingly difficult to carry out its mandate of providing federal information to the nation's libraries. (Canadian Association of Research Libraries, 1994, p. 5)

Since CARL made these points, the federal government has continued to divest itself of its information-providing services with the privatization of the Canada Communications Group, the body responsible for publication and dissemination of most government information.

On the infrastructure side, if one uses the Canadian Network for the Advancement of Research, Industry and Education, Inc. (CANARIE) (originally started as a government-funded organization that supported network communication technologies by both public and private sector institutions) as a bellwether of the government's direction, then the recently initiated Technology and Applications Development (TAD) Program is an indicator of the move toward private sector development.

The TAD has been established to assist the private sector in the development of "Canada's communications infrastructure" (CANARIE, 1996). The condition for being an applicant for funding from TAD is:

> Lead Contractors must be incorporated under the laws of Canada, a province or a territory, at the time the application is submitted. CANARIE requires for-profit corporations to lead projects, since they normally will be in the best position to commercialize the results of projects.

The Frequently Asked Questions (FAQ) document goes on to say that "public sector corporations which receive an appropriation from the Canadian government and public sector corporations such as hospitals, universities or school boards are not eligible as a Lead Contractor."

These two statements alone show that the government intends to assist the private sector, before all others, in developing "Canada's communications infrastructure." The reason is that commercialization of the communications infrastructure will encourage the private sector to do the development work and to reap the benefits, while the public sector and universities, in particular, are to play a merely supporting role.

In its final report, IHAC recommends privatization of CANARIE, which is now under way (IHAC, 1995, p. 152). In addition, the IHAC report recommends that research and development carried out by universities, in particular, be of the kind that eases the use of new information technologies. If IHAC's recommendation is followed, these technologies will have been developed by the private sector for private-sector gain (IHAC, 1995, p. 160). IHAC has also recommended to the federal government that private industry be provided with incentives to develop the communications infrastructure in the form of tax breaks for the purposes of R&D, deregulation in order to remove barriers to greater competition, and the relaxation of foreign ownership limits to give businesses better access to foreign capital.

From what is described above, it seems a safe bet that the development of the national communications infrastructure will very probably be carried out by the private sector. It is abundantly clear from the IHAC final report and from the initiatives of CANARIE that the profitability of any development will be a major consideration. As a result, the Canadian government will have succeeded in shifting the costs of the publication and dissemination of information, and the development and maintenance of the information highway, to the private sector. In doing so they will have compounded the difficulties for universities seeking to cope with issues around the fast-evolving world of information technology.

Given (a) that the federal government and many provincial governments are reducing their funding to post-secondary institutions, (b) that they are creating a communications infrastructure, and (c) that publication and dissemination of government information is fertile for exploitation by the private sector, we in the scholarly community should be worried that a class structure among and within institutions will develop. Some will be able to make the transition from the current system of scholarly communication and some will not.

The private sector will see profit margins and the bottom line as important in the development and use of the communications infrastructure. Karen Hunter, vice-president and assistant to the chairman of Elsevier Science Publishers, notes that the rules governing the development and implementation of electronic communications are

> . . . being established by others. Those others include *our authors and readers* on the one hand and such megapowers as the government, the telephone and cable companies, and . . . perhaps even power companies. All have the potential

> to control computerized access to the home and, via the home to every individual. (Hunter, 1994, p. 127)

The emphasis is mine, pointing to the proprietary attitude of this publisher to creators and readers.

In the final report of the AUCC-CARL/ABRC Task Force (1996) it is recognized that governmental support is essential to "help [universities] build the technological infrastructure needed to network their campuses" (p. 13). It is of critical importance that government not only support the internal development of network capability in universities, as AUCC and CARL suggest, but that it also ensure that access to the national communications infrastructure be affordable and equitable. In order to accomplish this, an independent federal agency should be established to regulate the development and costs of the communications infrastructure, with, inter alia, a specific mandate that public educational institutions be charged substantially reduced rates. Of equal importance is an increase in governmental support of the publication and dissemination of government information. In this latter case the government produces information with public money, then it is sold back to the very people that supported its creation. This system seems remarkably similar to that currently practised in scholarly journal publication, a system that obtains, free of charge, information produced with public money, publishes it, and then sells it back to those who supported its production. If one of the goals of a new scholarly communication system is to deal with the buying back of information provided free of charge, then we must work to ensure that the inequity of the current system is not replicated in a new one. Government should therefore take back its publishing function in order to provide all Canadians, at a reasonable cost, with information produced with public funds.

Publishers

Publishers, both commercial and not-for-profit, are actively working to incorporate the latest enhancements in computer and information technology into their publications. The embedding of hypertext links in texts, allowing instant access to cited articles and three-dimensional illustrations and graphs, is greatly enhancing the utility of articles published electronically. In addition, as noted above in the description of *Psycholoquy* and the Los Alamos National Laboratory (LANL) e-print archives, the speed with which reports of research can be disseminated and responded to is mitigating the move of scholars, particularly in the sciences, away from a reliance on paper-based journals for publication of their works to the electronic environment.

However, the transition from paper to electronic formats is slow by today's standards, where computer software manufacturers come out with new versions of their software about every six months. Part of the reason for this, as

Karen Hunter says, is a result of the unevenness of the development of the information infrastructure.

> In full-text scholarly publishing, the necessary electronic infrastructure is growing but is far from uniform, particularly outside of the United States and in less well-funded parts of the country. It is certainly not such that one can shift existing products from paper to electronic form only. That means parallel publication of both paper and electronic formats, increasing overall costs. (Hunter, 1994, p. 128)

From the commercial point of view there is another reason:

> Consider the much touted "multimedia revolution." Publishers privy to the truth know that with very, very few exceptions, sales of a multimedia bestseller number in the (low?) four digits. That is very small relative to the cost of creating such products. Increased market readiness will be the catalyst to product introduction. (Hunter, 1994, p. 128)[1]

The first of these points is important considering the commercial development of the information infrastructure. If profit is to be the driving force behind network development, then it is fairly easy to imagine a scenario where network service in major urban centres is excellent, but as one moves away from those centres to areas where there is a smaller population base, service declines. For these areas with smaller populations probably the main means of accessing the network will be over long-distance communications lines, at long-distance rates. Under these conditions there will be a gap between those who have ready access to network communication facilities and those who do not, the haves and the have nots. It is essential that governments establish regulations to ensure that access to communications networks is equitable and affordable both for individuals and universities. Here again an independent federal agency could regulate access and costs.

There is yet another aspect of unevenness in the establishment of the electronic infrastructure in institutions. The AUCC/CARL Task Force report recommends that governments support internal network development in universities (1996, p. 15). This is crucial given that many universities do not provide the basic tools for electronic communication, that is, personal computers, to their faculty. Most faculty have to rely on personal research funds to purchase such equipment or one-time-only start-up funds available to new faculty upon being hired. This is fine for those few faculty who, in these days of fiscal restraint, are lucky enough to get a tenure-track position, but it ignores the needs of established faculty.

University libraries are also struggling to develop the necessary electronic infrastructure in order to provide access to these new forms of communication. Karen Hunter's comment about parallel publishing of both paper and electronic versions is especially pertinent to libraries. She notes that publishers are incurring additional expenses to maintain this parallel system. There can be little doubt that some of these additional costs are being passed on to the subscribers, the bulk of which are academic libraries. In addition, the costs of equipping university libraries with the necessary hardware and software to access and use electronic publications is enormously expensive. With funding to libraries being cut as a result of the trickle-down effect and libraries having to undertake massive serial cancellation programs in order to balance the books, it is fairly easy to see a time in the not-too-distant future when access to information through libraries will be severely limited.

Government and the universities should, in brief, provide the necessary support to assist the libraries in establishing an electronic infrastructure and at the same time maintain paper subscriptions where necessary.

The mechanics of publishing

Whatever savings a publisher might experience by shifting from paper to electronic will be offset by decreases in revenue of one sort or another. In a cost/benefit analysis of paper-based versus electronic journals done by Vijay Jog (1995) for the Virtual Products Division of Industry Canada, it is quite clear that the savings from the conversion would be offset by a loss in revenues from subscriptions.

Jog divides the costs of publishing a journal into two groups. The first group he labels "first copy" costs (1995, p. 5). These are the costs associated with the writing and peer-review stage of the scholarly communication process. As noted above, there are minimal costs associated with this phase of the process. Scholars rarely do unsupported research and referees usually volunteer their services in exchange for the added prestige of serving on an editorial board as an expert in the discipline. Sometimes this service is rewarded with a small honorarium.

It is in the second phase of the publishing process that the main costs of journal production are found. Jog identified six tasks, divided into two groups, which are required for a journal to be published: administration, editorial management, promotion, typesetting, printing, and shipping (distribution) (1995, p. 8).

The first three form the first group; he has identified these as fixed costs. In other words, the tasks of administration, editorial management, and promotion will occur regardless of whether a journal is paper-based or electronic. He does make the point though that currently, for the electronic journals that he examined, these costs were considerably lower because "there seems to be a strong spirit for making the [electronic] journals work, and those involved are donating their time (or their University's) due to their 'love' of technology and their interest in using the technology in an innovative manner" (1995, p. 11).

Included among these volunteer editorial managers and journal administrators are systems experts who are necessary to keep the computer hardware and software running effectively.

However, he goes on to say: "This cannot continue to be the case and must be accounted for in the incremental analysis. The estimates are that for a typical E-journal, these system related efforts would require one or two days a week of a system specialist" (1995, p. 11).

The second group of costs—typesetting, printing, and distribution—includes those that Dr. Jog, among other commentators, has identified as the places where savings can be found in the move from paper to electronic. This is easy to see, as electronic publications do not require typesetting, printing, or distribution in the same way that paper journals do. In the electronic environment, word processing becomes the equivalent of typesetting, and that is normally done by the author. And, because the distribution is done over telephone lines, there is no need for centralized printing or for labour-intensive distribution, as the information can be distributed to all the subscribers with a few keystrokes.

In his analysis, Jog found the average costs of these two groups to be 57% and 43% of the costs of production, respectively. He also found the average distribution of revenues to be 42% subscriptions, 4% advertising, 1% back-issue sales, 12% association support, 34% government grant, and 8% other funding (1995, p. 9). These figures were obtained by an examination of the financial statements of a sample of five Canadian scholarly journals. In a conversion from paper-based to electronic, Jog points to a number of choices effecting revenues. First, will the journal be offered free of charge on the Internet to a limited group, such as members of a supporting association, while all others pay, or it will be free to everyone? He estimates losses in revenue from a decline in subscriptions as a result of a free offering to individuals who drop their association membership and a decline in advertising, as well as back-issue sales. He assumes, however, that institutions, who in the case of association journals provide much of the subscription revenue, would continue to buy subscriptions to the electronic version. In his conclusion Jog posits that the most likely savings from a switch from paper-based to electronic would be about 7% of expenses (1995, p. 12).

One should not assume therefore that a shift from paper-based to electronic will produce large savings. There are too many variables that offset savings in typesetting, printing, and distribution.

Conclusion

The development of computers and networks opens marvelous opportunities for enhancing scholarly communication. Scholars already use the Internet and the WWW to facilitate research, and the speed of dialogue in the scholarly community greatly encourages the exploration and expansion of knowledge.

However, some legal and political problems have arisen to bedevil the sensible development of an electronic scholarly communication system. These include copyright and the ownership of intellectual property, continuing government support of learning institutions so they can fulfill their missions, and equal and affordable access to the communications infrastructure for all Canadians.

The trend in Canada and the United States is toward privatization of the information infrastructure. Coupled with this is government action helping the private sector in this development to the detriment of the general public good. The information rich are pitted against the information poor.

However platitudinous it may sound, if we are to benefit and prosper as Canadians from the information society, then our government must continue to support the scholars and institutions they work in so that people will have the opportunity to learn and become a part of the information society.

Note

1. The number of sales of multimedia products was obtained by Karen Hunter from Hawkins (1993).

References

AUCC-CARL/ABRC Task Force on Academic Libraries and Scholarly Communication. (1995). *Towards a new paradigm for scholarly communication* [Discussion paper]. Ottawa: Author.

AUCC-CARL/ABRC Task Force on Academic Libraries and Scholarly Communication. (1996). *The changing world of scholarly communication: Challenges and choices for Canada*. Ottawa: Author.

Canadian Association of Research Libraries. (1994, September). *Brief to the National Information Highway Advisory Council*. Ottawa: Author.

CANARIE, Inc. (1996.) *Technology and Applications Development Program, 1996 Competition, Frequently Asked Questions (FAQ)*. Ottawa: Author. URL: http://www.canarie.ca

CAUT. (1987, September). Policy statement and model clause on copyright. In *CAUT Information Service* (45-1) [Preamble]. Ottawa: Author.

Ginsparg, Paul. (1994, October 14). After-dinner remarks at American Physical Society (APS) meeting at the Los Alamos National Laboratory (LANL). URL: http://xxx.lanl.gov/blurb/pg14oct94

Harnad, Stevan. (1992). Post Gutenberg Galaxy: The fourth revolution in the means of production of knowledge. In *Directory of electronic journals, newsletters, and academic discussion lists* (pp. v-xi). Washington, DC: Association of Research Libraries.

Hawkins, Donald. (1993, October). *Is there a Telecommunications Company in Your Information Future?* Speech at ASIDIC 25th anniversary meeting, Newport, RI.

Hunter, Karen. (1994, June). Issues and experiments in electronic publishing and dissemination. *Information technology and libraries*, *13*(2), 127-132.

Information Highway Advisory Council (IHAC). (1995). Connection community content: The challenge of the information highway. *Final report of the Information Highway Advisory Council*. Ottawa: Ministry of Supply and Services Canada.

Jog, Vijay. (1995). *Cost and revenue structure of academic journals: Paper-based versus e-journals*. Ottawa: Industry Canada. URL: http://www.schoolnet.ca/vp/cesn

Lynch, Clifford A. (1993). The transformation of scholarly communication and the role of the library in age of networked information. *Serials Librarian*, *23*(3/4), 5-20.

Maddox, John. (1989, June 29). Can journals influence science? *Nature*, *339*(6227), 657.

O'Donnell, James J. (1993). St. Augustine to NREN: The tree of knowledge and how it grows. *Serials Librarian*, *23*(3/4), 21-41.

Ribbe, Paul H. (1990). A scientist's assessment of a microcosm of the serial universe. *Serials Librarian*, *17*(3/4), 133, 121-142.

World Intellectual Property Organization (WIPO). (1996, December 20). *WIPO copyright treaty* (Article 6, p. 3). Adopted by the Diplomatic Conference.

And What About Students? The Forgotten Role of Students in the Scholarly Communication Debate[1]

Richard Nimijean
University of New Brunswick

Abstract: This paper has two major goals: to explain why students matter in the scholarly communication debate and to explore the student's role in selected issues surrounding that debate. Students, often neglected in the scholarly communication literature, have a potentially significant role in the evolution of the system, both politically and culturally. Academic and government decision-makers will need to address student-related issues as part of their strategic planning.

Résumé: Le but de cette communication est double: reconnaître la place des étudiants dans les débats sur la communication savante, puis explorer comment ils peuvent contribuer à quelques thèmes importants dans ce domaine. Les étudiants, trop souvent négligés dans les discussions consacrées à ce sujet, ont potentiellement un rôle significatif—autant politique que culturel—à jouer dans l'évolution de la communication savante. Les décideurs académiques et gouvernementaux devront adresser la question étudiante dans la formulation de leurs stratégies.

The changes in our system of scholarly communication are well known. They involve a growing body of published scholarly knowledge that far exceeds our capacity to consume this knowledge; the dramatically rising costs of acquiring this knowledge; the mushrooming of electronic communication networks and the costs of supporting such networks; new issues concerning intellectual property; a reassessment of the academic reward system; and so forth. These changes are taking place in an environment where a fundamental re-examination of the university's role and mission in an era of greater fiscal restraint is taking place.

Richard Nimijean is a doctoral candidate in the Department of Political Science at Carleton University, 1125 Colonel By Drive, Ottawa, ON K1S 5B6. E-mail: rnimijea@ccs.carlton.ca

***Canadian Journal of Communication,* Vol. 22, No. 3/4 (1997) 179-196**

While the outcome of these changes remain unknown, the parameters of the debate are being established, and the questions that must be asked are becoming clearer. But while academic administrators, librarians, and scholars are debating the changing world of scholarly communication, students—with the notable exception of teaching and the Internet—are at best haphazardly involved and referred to only in passing in the literature. For example, *Scholarly Communication in an Electronic Environment* (Martin, 1993) is the product of a conference on scholarly communication, yet in a section called "Reactions from Scholars," students do not merit consideration.

This is not to say that students' roles and needs are not understood, nor that individual universities undertaking strategic planning do not address them. If students were to become part of the debate, we would be better able to examine the changes in our system of scholarly communication and ultimately be in a better position to implement reforms within the context of the restructuring of our university system. In this sense, Canadians should follow the lead of the Follett Report (Joint Funding Council, 1993), which reviewed the state of British libraries in the context of the changing world of scholarly communication and clearly acknowledged the impact these issues are having on students. The Canadian academic community must also undertake such an examination, so that governments and university administrators can make more informed choices as we inch toward fundamental change. Students will have a major role in this, both as consumers of scholarly knowledge and, increasingly, as producers of scholarly knowledge.

In some areas, such as electronic publishing, students will be agents of change. However, in areas such as the academic reward system (namely, hiring), they are likely to be forces of conservatism. The mixed outcomes are due in part to the fact that, like scholars, students are a heterogeneous body, divided by status (undergraduate and graduate) and area of study (social sciences and the humanities versus the medical, physical, and natural sciences and engineering). As such, students do not possess uniform career expectations, are subject to different research programs, and thus have different roles to play in, and expectations from, their university experiences.

The central message of this paper is that meaningful and effective changes to our system of scholarly communication will occur only if students are brought into the debate and are involved in the process of reform. Failure to do so can lead to two possible, though not mutually exclusive, outcomes: further uncertainty in enrolment levels, which will force the university system to radically redefine itself, and/or a perpetuation of one of the root causes of the crisis in scholarly communication, namely, the development of a new generation of prolific scholars. Following an examination of the role of students in the system of scholarly communication, this paper will examine the implications of these roles.

Students and scholarly communication

If we accept the premise that the evolution of our system of scholarly communication is linked to the evolution of our university system (AUCC-CARL/ABRC, 1996), then the interests and roles of students must enter into the debate. These interests relate to the current conjuncture our university system finds itself in, namely, a massive rethinking of all aspects of the system, from finances to autonomy to expectations associated with a university education.

The nature of the changing university library, for example, has been well documented (AUCC-CARL/ABRC, 1995, 1996; Senate Library Committee, 1995). Under budgetary constraints, the library is expected to maintain levels of acquisitions despite rising prices and the growing body of published knowledge; balance the diverse needs of the university community; and keep pace not only with the traditional print-based materials but also with the growing body of electronic resources and databases (as well as provide the accompanying infrastructure). This has led to systematic journal cancellations and the transfer of funds from monograph acquisitions to the serials budget in order to lessen the impact of journal cancellations. In response, the university library is moving from a "just-in-case" model to a "just-in-time" model, placing greater emphasis on providing timely access to teaching and research materials outside the library.

Inquiries into the impact of these changes, such as the Association of Universities and Colleges of Canada–Canadian Association of Research Libraries/l'Association des bibliothèques de recherche du Canada (AUCC-CARL/ABRC) Task Force on Academic Libraries and Scholarly Communication (1996), have addressed issues such as the ability of universities to support the activities of their scholars and the ability of scholars to conduct research in this changing environment. However, the impact of these changes on students, who will also be affected, has not been adequately examined. In their traditional role as consumers of scholarly knowledge, students will be affected by changes in the university library, notably in terms of relatively decreasing holdings in the university library as the body of published knowledge increases. As future scholars in a tight labour market, students will contribute to the growing body of published knowledge.

Students as consumers of knowledge

Students are consumers of the information and knowledge generated by scholars. Students require access, particularly at the undergraduate level, to a readily available literature in order to complete course assignments and obtain course credits. Requirements vary by level. Undergraduate students normally require access to materials initially recommended by faculty, although they are usually expected to perform additional secondary research. Graduate students, however, are expected to perform more thorough searches in their academic work. In both cases, however, faculty participate in the development of the library collection in order to assure some congruence between course offerings and requirements and the needs of students to fulfill these requirements.

Increasingly, students are using non-print materials in their work, materials often not found in their university libraries. Electronic databases, CD-ROMs, and the World Wide Web (WWW) are increasingly important sources of information for many students. This is due in part to the fact that these sources, particularly information obtained via the World Wide Web, are not restricted to one user at a time. As a result, the range of information available to students has increased dramatically, thereby raising expectations that this material can or should be found in the university library.

However, many students, particularly undergraduates in the social sciences and humanities, appear to be comfortable with the just-in-case library. Facing multiple assignment deadlines and, increasingly, working in part-time jobs to support their studies, students face time constraints when performing research. A quick search of the stacks is often the most efficient, though not necessarily the most effective, method of obtaining source material, particularly for part-time students, who do not spend as much time on campus and do so for shorter intervals than their full-time colleagues. As described in the *Times Higher Education Supplement*, "For the part-time student, a library visit is often a question of grabbing as many relevant books as fast as possible before dashing to the next lecture" (Tysome, 1994, p. vii). Indeed, as the importance of part-time and continuing-education students increases, their needs will deserve closer scrutiny, especially since they have historically not received the same treatment as other students (Williams, 1995, p. 34).

New forms of data and holdings may not be alleviating this problem. A recent survey of two American universities found that even if they are aware of the existence of CD-ROM and on-line databases: "Few students used them for needed information" (Hsieh-Yee, 1996, p. 165). Undergraduates in particular are in-library customers who largely use on-line catalogues to search for information. Hsieh-Yee suggests that the most important factors for students are convenience, quality of data, ease of use, and availability: It appears that the "traditional" is indeed comforting to students.

It is tempting to extend this characterization of students to how they actually find and use source materials for their assignments. My Canadian Politics students at Carleton University would always use classics such as John Porter's *The Vertical Mosaic*, first published in 1965, and other old (albeit important) works. They would get upset when I would comment that their work would be improved if they used the most recent literature, until one particularly frustrated student told me that it was just not accessible. The most recent monographs (of which there is often only one copy) are either checked out or on reserve (if the library has them at all). A quick check of the catalogue was revealing: At Carleton, there were 28 copies of *The Vertical Mosaic* (which does not include copies in departmental reading rooms), yet rare was the book on the shelves that had been published within the last few years. (See Advisory Committee on Information Technology, 1996, p. 33, for a vignette that captures the problems facing undergraduate students when performing research for their assignments.) Recent data appear to confirm this observation. Acquisitions per student in ARL libraries continue to decline (30% fewer monographs and 8% fewer serials per student in 1995 than in 1986) (Association of Research Libraries, 1996, p. 13).

Addressing this situation necessarily leads to the issue of whether students possess the skills to adequately use the just-in-time library. While students tend to see library problems in terms of the lack of resources and not in terms of their own search skills (or lack thereof), it remains that many undergraduates are not trained properly to conduct searches, and many do not know how to use or search for journal articles. Indeed, training students how to use journals would greatly increase journal readership, for one of the paradoxes of the current system of scholarly communication is that, despite their great cost, journals actually have a very low readership (Senate Library Committee, 1995, p. 6). Given the increase in non-print resources and the focus on access to material held outside the library, students will also need to be trained in searching for electronic resources in databases, the Internet, and the Web, because "... the organization of the information must be tailored to the search requirements of persons searching for references. It is no longer a matter of arranging the shelves; instead it is arranging bytes" (Boynton & Creth, 1993, p. xvii).

Students as producers of knowledge

Increasingly, students are becoming producers of information, as the development of new communications technologies reduces the gap between the consumption and production of knowledge (Advisory Committee on Information Technology, 1996, p. 9). Moreover, the students of today are the academics of tomorrow. They are influenced by the mentoring aspect of education and research and ultimately contribute to the shape of our evolving system of scholarly communication. This is due primarily to advances in communication and computing technologies, increases in graduate enrolment, and a tight academic labour market.

The dramatic growth in publication outlets, including the proliferation of electronic journals, will increase student publishing. As Marchionini & Maurer argue:

> Digital libraries offer greater opportunity for users to deposit as well as use information. Thus, students and teachers can easily be publishers as well as readers in digital libraries. The number of student-produced [WWW] home

> pages continues to grow as teachers and students not only bring digital information into the classroom but move the products of the classroom out into the digital libraries (1995, p. 73).

In other words, the traditional filtering system that has kept the published contributions of students to a minimum no longer works in the digital world. As the TULIP final report notes (1996), unlike undergraduates, graduate students appear to be the greatest users of electronic journals and on-line systems, in part because of their propensity to perform wider searches of the literature as well as their research functions for faculty. Thus, for example, while some mainstream prestige journals have explicit conflict-of-interest policies that prevent graduate students from publishing book reviews and rarely publish articles by students, the proliferation of electronic listservs and the rise of the electronic book review offer new avenues for student participation. For example, H-Grad is a listserv specifically for graduate students, and it has a Web site as part of the H-Net initiative, which sponsors more than 75 listservs for scholars in history and the humanities. It allows for discussion on employment searches and will eventually offer a graduate book-review service.

However, in terms of the crisis in scholarly communication, we must focus on more than just increased publication opportunities: We must also examine the factors which are driving students and young scholars to publish more. Graduate students—at least those who are likely to become academic or non-academic researchers and scientists—will help determine the future evolution of our system of scholarly communication. They will contribute to the stock of published knowledge; they will be subject to new or reformed hiring and promotion systems; and they will be responsible for teaching new generations of students. The increased publishing activity of these students is influenced primarily by the current nature of the academic job market and the mentoring system.

In Canada, the number of doctoral degrees awarded continues to increase, with 3,552 doctoral degrees granted in 1994. However, fewer and fewer teaching jobs are available. In fact, the total number of teaching jobs declined by 1% in both 1993 and 1994 (Association of Universities and Colleges of Canada, 1996, chaps. 3 and 5). Thus, at a cursory level, it appears that there is a surplus of qualified candidates for the academic jobs available.[2]

A few decades ago, when there were fewer graduate students and the university system was expanding, mentors might easily advise promising scholars, "Keep up the good work, and a job could be yours." While scholars continue to be hired in 1997, an increase in graduate student enrolment has made competition incredibly severe. However, the advice commonly given out remains essentially the same: "Finish the dissertation, get it published, and develop a research agenda." Indeed, what responsible supervisor would tell a student, "Not publishing or publishing 'responsibly' is going to get you an academic job, and you'll have the additional satisfaction of helping to address the crisis of scholarly communication!" Moreover, universities and departments continue practices that perpetuate the crisis of scholarly communication, such as seminars for graduate students outlining publication and job search strategies. These practices help ensure that future scholars develop the same mores that have contributed to the explosion of published knowledge. Furthermore, this issue is compounded by efforts to overcome long-standing inequities in the university, with the development of strategies to help those historically discriminated because of gender or ethnicity to learn how to work in the system. This includes, clearly, a publishing strategy (Frank Fox, 1985, pp. 13-14).

Hiring committees also contribute to this aspect of the scholarly communication crisis. As usually indicated in job ads, those with promising research and publication agendas and an ability to teach make the best candidates. Hence we are witnessing doctoral candidates who focus on broader horizons than the completion of the dissertation: articles and book projects are increasingly undertaken simultaneously while the dissertation is under way, as a means of distinguishing themselves from other candidates. If these are the candidates who are being hired, then this will only compound the problem of the growing body of published knowledge. As Mary Frank Fox has argued, while there is a significant attrition in research productivity following completion of the PhD, "Early publication is associated with continued productivity." Indeed, she states:

> Of those who publish and receive citations to their work in the five years immediately after receiving their Ph.D., the majority continue to be active in publication . . . and to be cited in a subsequent period. . . . Correspondingly, those who fail to publish early on continue to be nonproductive in publication. (1985, p. 7)

So if universities are only hiring candidates with proven or potentially strong publishing records, then how does the problem of the growing body of knowledge get resolved? By hiring people who are not ambitious, who have a small research agenda or do not want to research?

Implications for changing our system of scholarly communication

If efforts to reform our system of scholarly communication are to be successful, the role of students as both consumers and producers of scholarly knowledge must be recognized. As consumers of knowledge and major users of the university library, students expect the library to adequately support their academic work, particularly in an environment of rising tuition. As more important producers of scholarly knowledge, it is necessary to see if the pressures leading to increased production can be addressed. This will be discussed below in terms of the changing university library, digital scholarly resources and the computing infrastructure, the academic reward system, and intellectual property.

The changing university library

That the university library is changing is no longer in doubt. In an environment of restrictive budgets and rising costs of published knowledge, the body of published knowledge is growing. At the same time, universities and their libraries are also expected to provide an infrastructure for computing and communication technologies. Balancing these pressures is a Herculean task that will not satisfy all interests. Scholars, through their representatives on senate library committees and their direct access to university administrators, can and do regularly express their various (and sometimes parochial) concerns on these matters. Students, on the other hand, certainly at the individual level and even at the organizational/representational level, do not have the same ability to participate in these important discussions and decisions regarding choices that the library makes.

Why should we even be concerned with what students think or want? As the Follett Report notes, two student surveys in Britain indicated that adequate access to library facilities, resources, and library staffing are among the most important factors in the overall undergraduate student experience (Joint Funding Councils' Libraries Review Group, 1993, p. 37). Assuming this to be true of the North American experience as well, the ability of any one university to offer library services is likely to be a major factor in how students "vote with their feet"—the one trump that students have in an environment of change and uncertainty. Particularly in light of the heightened importance given to such issues, such as the annual *Maclean's* survey of universities, students have greater information about the universities they wish to attend. Universities can no longer assume that they have a captured market. Unstable enrolment levels, distance education, the Internet and the World Wide Web, the rise of virtual universities, the increasing differentiation between universities (including curricula and fees), and the increasing popularity of community colleges ensure this.

Universities and their libraries therefore must address or at least understand the needs of this major client group and provide the resources they expect. For example, the preponderance of on-line catalogues and CD-ROMs increases student expectations that a university provide such resources (McCarthy, 1995, p. 222). At the University of Rhode Island, she argues, student satisfaction is linked more to whether students find the resources they want than to their own abilities to estimate the strength of their search skills.

University libraries therefore must, if they have not done so already, measure the needs of their students, for as Williams notes, while the literature is replete with calls to evaluate the library needs of students, little data actually exists (1995, p. 33). These surveys must be broad-based and focus on the diverse needs of all user groups, not simply faculty.

However, it remains difficult to satisfy the needs of students. The price increases in scientific and technical journals and the institutional commitment to these journals hurts the acquisition of social science and humanities materials, particularly monographs (Manoff, 1996, p. 220). In CARL/ABRC libraries, serials expenditures accounted for 21% of library expenditures in 1993-94, while monograph expenditures accounted for only 8%. Furthermore, expenditures on serials continued to increase, but monograph expenditures peaked in 1991-92 (Canadian Association of Research Libraries, 1996). Pricing trends suggest that the serials budget is mostly devoted to scientific and technical journals and not to journals in the social sciences and humanities.

This affects students in two ways. First, the great majority of Canadian undergraduate (72%) and master's (63%) students are in the social sciences and humanities (Association of Universities and Colleges of Canada, 1996, p. 9). Secondly, undergraduate students, particularly in the first and second years, are dependent on monographs for their research. With student numbers at all levels increasing significantly over the years and library expenditures per full-time equivalent (FTE) student falling dramatically (22.4% in constant dollars from 1980 to 1993) (Association of Universities and Colleges of Canada, 1996, p. 4), student dissatisfaction is likely to increase. This likely dissatisfaction links to a direct correlation between increased library use and increased perceptions of problems or dissatisfaction with the library's collection (Williams, 1995, p. 41). In other words, students who use the library regularly are more apt to complain about its inadequacies.

Will the just-in-time library, with its growing emphasis on interlibrary loans (ILL), document delivery, and networked resources adequately serve the needs of students? First, how frequently do students use ILL and document delivery services? For example, of 70 students informally surveyed in my first-year Canadian politics class in 1996-97, none could either explain what the services were or report that they had used them. This admittedly unrepresentative sample nevertheless suggests that access to the growing body of knowledge is potentially restricted. Document-delivery systems are effective when you know what you are looking for, but are far less effective without a good bibliographic search tool (Greenberg, 1993, p. 18). Even if we were to teach students new search skills, ILL and document-delivery services raise questions of cost and logistics. Will students or their libraries willingly pay for document delivery? Can the de facto lender libraries (the major research libraries) support a system predicated not on the demand of a relatively small number of researchers but of a significant proportion of the Canadian student body? Can students working on tight deadlines effectively use document delivery even if these other factors are addressed? And, finally, as the University of British Columbia has asked: Who pays? (Senate Library Committee, 1995, p. 18).

An increase in non-print resources might not adequately address the needs and concerns of students, for the rise of electronic journals is likely to diminish serendipitous reading (Silverman, 1996, p. 60). This hurts students who face time constraints, tend to browse less than faculty, and possess less-developed search skills. On the other hand, there is also a positive side. As students develop electronic search skills, they will learn to use non-library sources found on the Web and through the Internet. For example, Andrew Heard of Simon Fraser University has recently reported that one third of his first-year students effectively used the Web in his first-year Canadian Politics course (Heard, 1997).

The university community must therefore re-evaluate its approach to teaching research skills. The various disciplines, in conjunction with the university library, will need to re-evaluate their courses on research methods to include the new dimensions of the scholarly communication debate and the Internet. Such is the case at Dalhousie University in Halifax, for example, where medical students are trained, as part of their curriculum, to perform electronic searches (Birenbaum, 1995, p. 7). Given the constant turnover of students and a faculty that is somewhat untrained in electronic search methods, universities might consider offering library courses for credit or include them as part of a common first year curriculum since most new university students do not possess adequate research skills and thus place huge demands on reference librarians (Adams & Morris, 1985, p. 5). (See Adams & Morris, 1995, chaps. 1 and 2, for an overview of the major issues and details in offering such courses.) The constant turnover in the undergraduate ranks ensures that this problem will not disappear, particularly as we move increasingly toward the digital library (University of California, 1996). On an encouraging note, however, instructional sessions in Association of Research Libraries (ARL) institutions are significantly on the increase (Association of Research Libraries, 1996, pp. 8-9).

Digital scholarly resources and computing

The new computing and communication technologies are radically transforming the student experience. Access to remote data and resources and the ability to work interactively with faculty, even in classrooms, are but two examples. However, we are far from the scenario where students have computers in each classroom and all faculty are able to offer coherent multimedia instruction. Thus, it is imperative that universities examine their information technology infrastructures, policies, and practices to ensure that they can best capture the democratic potential of electronic resources (AUCC-CARL/ABRC, 1996, pp. 5-6). In other words, universities can aid the transition to the just-in-time library.

Access to the computing infrastructure is an important issue. Only 29% of Canadian families own a home computer, and not all of them have Internet access. Moreover, there is a class discrepancy. Families in the top 20% income bracket are four times as likely to own a personal computer as a family in the bottom 20% (Statistics Canada, 1996, pp. 18-20), thus undermining somewhat the notion of universal access to post-secondary education in a computerized learning environment. Even when students do own computers, off-campus access to university networks is uneven across the country due to the great costs involved.

Until and unless all universities adopt the Acadia University strategy of building a fully wired campus with obligatory student leasing of computers, they will need and will be expected to provide adequate computing resources for students as part of tuition fees. A common excuse for late submission of papers is that students cannot spend sufficient time on the university computers to search the Internet and Web, to do word processing, or to print documents. The Advisory Committee on Information Technology (ACIT) at the University of British Columbia (UBC) reports that in computer and library labs "demand far outstrips the supply" (1996, p. 11), an experience that is likely representative of the situation across the country. The ACIT report also suggests other factors that must be addressed: equitable access across faculties; the wiring of student residences and graduate student offices; and the level of adequate and sufficient training in the new technologies offered by universities to students, faculty, and staff.

Smaller and more remote universities face a dilemma. While the new technologies might allow for an increased democratization and decentralization of knowledge production and consumption, as suggested by the AUCC-CARL/ABRC final report, inadequate investment in these technologies (due to their high costs, including the cost of technical support, training, and maintenance) places the capturing of these benefits at risk, leading to a potential scenario of both impoverished libraries and electronic infrastructure. How can such universities address this challenge?

Going the "wired" route also carries its own risks. Given the growing questioning of the value of a university degree, the skills developed for using computing and communication technologies are one of the tangibles that students identify with their education. Increasing tuition or ancillary fees to cover leased computers has not been a popular idea with many students, given the substantial increases in tuition in recent years. In fact, one of the concerns of protesting students who occupied the president's office at Carleton University in Ottawa in February 1997 was that the university not introduce "technology fees." Thus, access to the computing infrastructure becomes an equity issue within the university.

One method for addressing this issue is to set targets. ACIT, for example, recommends that UBC set a target of one public computer for each 50 students (Advisory Committee on Information Technology, 1996, p. 26). However, at the Saint John campus of the University of New Brunswick, with a student enrolment of approximately 3,000, the ratio is 25:1, suggesting that it might be more manageable (and important) for smaller universities to have a lower ratio. The ACIT report notes that this issue will have to be addressed as part of each university's strategic plan.

On-campus resources dedicated to accessing scholarly materials off-campus will therefore need to be examined. For example, the new £8-million library being built at the University of Abertay Dundee in Scotland is intended to increase the storage of and access to electronic resources. All 700 study spaces will be connected to the university's computer network and will also have a 24-hour study area (Wojtas, 1995, p. 4). This can be seen as the library variant of the Acadia strategy, yet the option remains very costly. It also points to the challenge facing libraries in balancing traditional expectations of a well-stocked collection with investments associated with the just-in-time library. As the head librarian of Oxford Brookes Library said, it is important to invest in technological and electronic resources, "but we must be careful not to develop these at the expense of covering the increasing demand from students for books" (Tysome, 1994, p. vii).

For students, it is not simply a matter of rising debt loads. Paradoxically, student loan programs are becoming more restrictive and bursaries have been virtually eliminated. Government-sponsored computer loan and rebate programs, in collaboration with the university community, might be one alternative, but these would have to be designed carefully, paying attention to tuition rates and the composition of the student body of each university. As well, as opposed to the lease strategy of Acadia, students at least would have the tangible benefit of computer ownership.

Hiring

Much concern has been expressed with respect to the impact of the "academic reward system" on the crisis in scholarly communication. Stripped to its core, the basic argument is that there are tremendous pressures on faculty to publish in order to reap the benefits of the reward system. An unintended consequence of this is the great explosion in the body of published knowledge, which, as we know, is increasingly difficult for university libraries to acquire.

With respect to students and hiring, this trend is likely to continue. First, there is the matter of the shortage of academic jobs in Canadian universities versus the increasing pool of qualified candidates. For the universities, at one level, this is a positive development. They are able to hire relatively inexpensive, ambitious, and active researchers at the junior level in the face of funding constraints and aging (more expensive) faculty. In such a soft labour market, any reform of the academic reward system that limits the number of publications under consideration in the reward system (as recommended by the AUCC-CARL Task Force's final report) is unlikely to have any bearing on young scholars and graduate students seeking academic employment. An aggressive and diverse research agenda is one way to differentiate oneself from the competition. Thus the propensity to publish associated with early productive research and publication is likely to continue.

For example, at the June 1997 meetings of the Canadian Political Science Association (CPSA), the section on political theory (a field in which there are few tenure-stream jobs but a great many masters' and doctoral students) had 62 papers, 32 presented by graduate students. This demonstrates both the vitality of graduate research and the extent to which students wish to gain exposure and experience, not to mention publication, in the hopes of developing a curriculum vitae that will lead to an academic job.

Learned societies play a role in this socialization process. For example, the CPSA publishes *Careers for Political Scientists* (Pal, 1996). While geared to non-academic jobs, there is a section on academe, and here the guide offers conflicting advice. It paints a gloomy picture, conservatively estimating four to five applicants for every position in political science in Canada (not including overseas applicants). Wisely, the book recommends that only the top 5% to 10% of students should consider academic careers. It advises students to complete their doctorates as quickly as possible—the key to hiring—and suggests students avoid or be judicious in taking on any extracurricular activities such as teaching assistantships, conference participation, and job searches until they have nearly completed their dissertations. Further advice: given that the first job is likely to be a limited-term appointment, students should also develop a publishing strategy (including articles or a monograph based on the dissertation) and a new research agenda involving a book or several articles when they are hired.

Thus, this professional society in effect acknowledges and indeed socializes students into thinking that publication is the key to getting hired or tenured (even though the crisis of scholarly communication makes that less and less an option). The issue for the CPSA guide is not whether publishing and conference participation is key, but making sure the timing is right. For example, regarding conference participation, the book says: "Too many Ph.D. candidates present too many mediocre papers at the annual meetings in the hopes that their efforts will be noted for future job applications. Yet a single publication will garner more attention and respect than several CPSA paper presentations" (Pal, 1996, p. 19).

However, given the fierce competition for tenure-track positions, people never know when (or if) the next opening or interview will come. In such an environment, it is likely that the dramatic growth of published knowledge will continue as young scholars remain active and aggressive.

However, some forces might mitigate the impact of these factors. Pressures on young scholars produce the risk that there are too many unread first books (the dissertation) and compromised (by the pressures of teaching and research) second books (Brooks, 1996, p. A52). Indeed, there are growing doubts as to whether that first book will even get published. As Sanford Thatcher notes, surveys indicate that faculty cite author's reputation as a key factor in deciding to purchase monographs. Given the pressures on university presses to cope with the crisis of scholarly communication, including contemplating a reduction in the reliance on the monograph because of low sales and rising costs, they will be increasingly reluctant to publish that first book, making it more difficult for young scholars to become tenured (Thatcher, 1995, p. B1).

Brooks offers one possible coping strategy, namely, that the PhD (at least in the humanities) become more like a teaching and research apprenticeship. Fewer students should be admitted, they should take more time to complete (as opposed to the current belief in reducing completion time), and they should have better support and more post-doctoral opportunities to ease the transition, all in the name of addressing the academic job crisis. Brooks' strategy clashes with contemporary objectives and values such as the extension of mass education, the prestige associated with doctoral programs, and pressures to reduce and not increase the time required for completion of doctoral studies (Brooks, 1996, p. A52). In other words, the concept is counter-hegemonic, yet it might somewhat ease the contributions of graduate students to the crisis in scholarly communication.

Intellectual property

Restrictive copyright legislation for electronic publications would be damaging for students. Students would be less able to surf the Internet and the Web to find resources and scholarly material, an activity in part required to overcome the inadequacies of the just-in-case library. If students were required to pay directly (in some type of cash transaction) for simply browsing material found on the Internet or the Web, then many simply will not browse. On the other hand, if universities were to pay for students in an indirect manner, as in the current CanCopy arrangements, then this would place even greater strains on strapped university coffers (Advisory Committee on Information Technology, 1996, p. 18). In either case, fee-based browsing rights would further the crisis of scholarly communication insofar as they only accentuate the cash crisis and undermine the democratizing potential of electronic scholarly resources and the ability of university students, faculty, and the just-in-time library to access them.

Another area of concern, particularly for graduate students, that is not often discussed in the literature on scholarly communication pertains to the results of faculty research. The primary issue in the social sciences and humanities relates to publications emerging from student research paid for by a faculty member's research grant. Often, faculty members will extend co-authorship to these research assistants, which acknowledges their intellectual contributions as well as assists them in their careers (with a publication). In other cases, faculty, fully in accordance with granting council regulations, assume full authorship and responsibility. In the sciences, engineering, and computer sciences, concern is increasingly expressed about profits that result from academic research. Issues include allocation of profits; the relationship between a student's research and private contracts held by supervisors; delays for patent applications; and the desire of sponsors to keep results private. (See Saunders, 1995, for an overview of the issues.)

Overriding all of these are the traditional concerns: disputes over who came up with the original research ideas and faculty and students who abuse their positions and responsibilities (for example, professors who take ideas from the work or proposals of students and pass them off as their own, leaving the students in a delicate position). Given all that is at stake, particularly as the role of the university in the new economy is redefined, it is likely that students will continue to aggressively protect and promote their interests as universities establish or revise their policies on intellectual property.

Bringing students into the debate: Conclusion and policy recommendations

Failure to seriously address the interests and concerns of students in the scholarly communication debate will undermine efforts to implement reforms. An inability to provide students with adequate library and computing services is likely to contribute to further uncertainty in enrolment levels. Indeed, many students are questioning the value of a university degree, as evidenced by fluctuations in enrolment levels; students going to community colleges where they can obtain "practical" skills; concern about increasing debt burdens; and students' fears that they will not obtain jobs upon graduation. If universities do not offer what students perceive to be the tools and preparation required to participate fully and actively in the labour market, then they will seek alternatives.

In an era of restrictive budgets, with increased investments in computing and electronic infrastructure and the growing costs of published knowledge, the position of universities is not enviable. However, as one university examining these issues noted, universities must face these challenges and assume technological leadership, for if they do not, they will "... leave their students ill-prepared to meet the expectations of their workplaces, academic or otherwise" (Senate Library Committee, 1995, p. 20). In other words, there are identifiable computing and communication technology skills that students can take with them when they leave university and, in fact, are increasingly required in order to work in the new economy (Statistics Canada, 1996). These new skills therefore complement the traditional benefits of a university education, namely, research skills and critical thinking.

The university community will also need to examine how it is training and socializing future scholars. This is perhaps the greatest challenge in reforming our system of scholarly communication. While universities can attempt to reform their academic reward systems in the hope of reducing publications, they have far less control over the new scholars they are hiring, who, as I have suggested, are likely to be even more productive.

Still, we can build on recent initiatives and reports such as *The Changing World of Scholarly Communication* (AUCC-CARL/ABRC, 1996), *Beyond Gutenberg* (Advisory Committee on Information Technology, 1996), and *Scholarly Communication, Serials and Technology* (Senate Library Committee, 1995) to ensure that student issues are included in the debate and in the reform process. These reports demonstrate an understanding not only of the breadth of the scholarly communication issue, but, as importantly, reflect an awareness of the complexity of the university community itself (that is, that students matter in the scholarly communication debate) and the ways in which this complexity further muddles efforts to effectively promote change.

Universities, individually and collectively, must therefore re-evaluate their policies and practices with regard to the scholarly activities of graduate students. In a similar fashion, scholarly societies should continue to examine the employment prospects of graduate students as part of their examination of scholarly communication issues. Universities and scholarly societies, in reviewing the relationship between publishing and the academic reward system (as recommended by the AUCC-CARL/ABRC Task Force), must pay particular attention to hiring and employment issues. Failure to do so will only perpetuate the problems associated with the dramatic increase in published knowledge.

In their surveys of users and in their transition to the just-in-time model, university libraries should evaluate the diverse needs of their client community and how these clients use the library. Given the inability to maintain the just-in-case library, which appears to be useful for students, libraries must take action to educate students, particularly at the undergraduate level, to use the just-in-time library. As well, students must be better educated in the use of journals. These initiatives could involve, where practical, the offering of library courses for credit. Furthermore, librarians and academics need to work together to refine discipline-specific research methodology courses to ensure that search skills, particularly with respect to the Internet, the World Wide Web, and electronic databases, are adequately taught and developed.

Students must have adequate access to their universities' computing infrastructures. Universities should set targets for the number of public-access computers available to students at a level that reflects the size and composition of the student body, and they must ensure adequate off-campus access to the computing infrastructure. Universities and governments should also review student loan programs so that computer purchasing is made easier for students regardless of discipline.

Finally, copyright legislation must ensure that electronic browsing rights for all university members are preserved. As well, universities should review their intellectual property policies to ensure that the concerns of students about the communication of research results are addressed.

Notes

1. I would like to thank Joan Adams, David McCallum, John Teskey, and Rowly Lorimer for their comments on earlier drafts of this paper.
2. In 1994, AUCC estimated that there were 1,577 new appointments. However, the gap between PhDs granted and new appointments is not as large as it initially appears, in part because of international students who do not stay in Canada and because of graduates who are not interested in academic positions.

References

Adams, Mignon S., & Morris, Jacquelyn M. (1985). *Teaching library skills for academic credit*. Phoenix: Oryx Press.

Advisory Committee on Information Technology. (1996). *Beyond Gutenberg: Access to digital scholarly resources*. Vancouver: University of British Columbia.

Association of Research Libraries. (1996). *ARL Statistics 1994-95*. Washington: Author.

Association of Universities and Colleges of Canada. (1996). *Trends 1996: The Canadian university in profile*. Ottawa: Author.

AUCC-CARL/ABRC Task Force on Academic Libraries and Scholarly Communication. (1995). *Towards a new paradigm for scholarly communication*. Ottawa: Author.

AUCC-CARL/ABRC Task Force on Academic Libraries and Scholarly Communication. (1996). *The changing world of scholarly communication: Challenges and choices for Canada*. Ottawa: Author.

Birenbaum, Rhonda. (1995, August-September). Scholarly communication under siege. *University Affairs*, p. 7.

Boynton, G. R., & Creth, Sheila D. (1993). Introduction: Re-inventing learning. In G. R. Boynton & S. D. Creth (Eds.), *New technologies and new directions: Proceedings from the symposium on scholarly communication*. Westport: Meckler.

Brooks, Peter. (1996, December 20). Graduate learning as apprenticeship. *The Chronicle of Higher Education*, p. A52.

Canadian Association of Research Libraries. (1996). *Statistical profile of research libraries in Canada*. Ottawa: Author.

Frank Fox, Mary. (1985). The transition from dissertation student to publishing scholar and professional. In M. Frank Fox (Ed.), *Scholarly writing and publishing: Issues, problems and solutions* (pp. 6-16). Boulder, CO: Westview Press.

Greenberg, Douglas. (1993). You can't always get what you want: Technology, scholarship, and democracy. In G. R. Boynton & S. D. Creth (Eds.), *New technologies and new directions: Proceedings from the symposium on scholarly communication*. Westport: Meckler.

Heard, Andrew. (1997, January 6). Internet resource links. Message available in the Polcan Archives. URL: http://www.sfu.ca/igs.polcan.html

Hsieh-Yee, Ingrid. (1996). Student use of on-line catalogs and other information channels. *College and Research Libraries*, *57*(2), 161-175.

Joint Funding Councils' Libraries Review Group. (1993). *Report*. Bristol: Higher Education Funding Council for England. URL: http://ukoln.bath.ac.uk/follett/follett_report.html

Manoff, Marlene. (1996). Revolutionary or regressive? The politics of electronic collection development. In R. P. Peek & G. B. Newby (Eds.), *Scholarly publishing: The electronic frontier* (pp. 215-229). Cambridge, MA: MIT Press.

Marchionini, Gary, & Maurer, Hermann. (1995). The roles of digital libraries in teaching and learning. *Communications of the ACM*, *8*(4), 67-75.

Martin, Robert Sidney (Ed.) (1993). *Scholarly communication in an electronic environment: Issues for Research Libraries*. Chicago: American Library Association.

McCarthy, Cheryl Ann. (1995). Students' perceived effectiveness using the university library. *College and Research Libraries*, *56*(3), 221-234.

Pal, Leslie A. (1996). *Careers for political scientists* (2nd ed.). Ottawa: Canadian Political Science Association.

Porter, John. (1965). *The vertical mosaic*. Toronto: University of Toronto Press.

Saunders, Doug. (1995, December 4). Fruits of academe are golden for some. *The Globe and Mail* (Toronto), p. A1.

Senate Library Committee. (1995). *Scholarly communication, serials and technology: Problems and possibilities*. Vancouver: University of British Columbia.

Silverman, Robert J. (1996). The impact of electronic publishing on the academic community. In R. P. Peek & G. B. Newby (Eds.), *Scholarly publishing: The electronic frontier* (pp. 55-69). Cambridge, MA: MIT Press.

Statistics Canada. (1996). Computer literacy: A growing requirement. *Education Quarterly Review*, *3*(3), 9-29.

Thatcher, Sanford G. (1995, March 3). The crisis in scholarly communication. *The Chronicle of Higher Education*, p. B1.

TULIP. (1996). *Final report*. URL: www.elsevier.nl/locate/tulip/

Tysome, Tony. (1994, October 14). Life on borrowed time. *The Times Higher Education Supplement* (Multimedia section), p. vii.

University of California. (1996). *The University of California digital library: A framework for planning and strategic initiatives*. Berkeley CA: Author. URL: http://sunsite.berkeley.edu/UCDL/title.html

Williams, A. Paul. (1995). Conceptualizing academic library use: Results of a survey of continuing education students in a small Canadian undergraduate university. *The Canadian Journal of Higher Education*, *25*(3), 32-48.

Wojtas, Olga. (1995, December 15). High-tech library unveiled. *The Times Higher Education Supplement*, p. 4.

Cyberhope or Cyberhype? Computers and Scholarly Research

Marlene Manoff
MIT Libraries

Abstract: With the expansion of electronic products and services for libraries, two questions continue to demand our attention. What is the impact of new tools on scholarly research? And how is scholarship affected by libraries' decisions to remake or reorganize themselves so as to accommodate new technologies? This paper looks at the social and political implications of various electronic tools, especially in the humanities, and particularly in literary fields.

Résumé : La prolifération de produits et services électroniques disponibles dans les bibliothèques soulève deux questions qui ne cessent de requérir notre attention. Quel est l'impact de nouvelles technologies sur la recherche savante? Et quels sont les effects sur la recherche lorsque les bibliothèques décident de se refaçonner ou de se réorganiser pour mieux s'accommoder de nouveaux outils technologies? Cet article se propose de discuter des questions sociales et politiques soulevées par un certain nombre d'outils électroniques dans les humanités et surtout dans les domaines littéraires.

As we transform our libraries into postmodern institutions that offer an increasing number of electronic products and services, it is crucial that we understand the way these transformations will affect the disciplines we support. Computers do not simply increase access to scholarly material. They reshape the objects of study, alter research possibilities, and even begin to redefine what constitutes research. This paper is part of an ongoing exploration of what this means, especially for humanities fields. It is also an attempt to explore some of the social and political implications of electronic tools for scholarly research.

Marlene Manoff is Collections Manager, Humanities Library, MIT, Cambridge, MA 02139. E-mail: mmanoff@MIT.EDU

***Canadian Journal of Communication*, Vol. 22, No. 3/4 (1997) 197-212**

Not long ago, in pursuit of these goals, I singled out a special issue of *Computers in the Humanities* (Fortier, 1993) as illustrative of a misguided determination to harness the computer to literary research (Manoff, 1996). I cite it again as it offers an interesting example of the complexity of the problem. Titled *A New Direction for Literary Studies?* it is a collection of articles demonstrating and discussing possible uses of literary computation. There is a plaintive subtext: Why are there not more literary scholars doing this kind of work and why does so little of it appear in prestigious literary journals?

One participant proposes that humanists could benefit from the use of high-speed computers if only they would learn to address different kinds of issues. Instead of focusing on particular texts or particular authors, they should formulate new questions involving large corpora because this is where computation can be most productive (Olsen, 1993). My response was that it made no sense to redesign the field of literary studies to accommodate the abilities of high-speed computers. This is precisely how not to make use of a new technology. Four years after the publication of this proposal to jump-start literary computation, it "remains largely dominated by a narrow range of concerns and strategies and has . . . failed to be a serious presence in even the narrowest fields of literary studies, let alone a factor in the broader intellectual conversation" (Renear, 1995, p. 389). Our success in implementing new technologies will depend on our ability to think critically and learn to recognize the ways in which some computer applications may be fruitful and some may not.

Does the failure of literary computation mean that electronic technology has nothing to contribute to literary studies? Not at all. It has been a godsend to the creators of scholarly editions and has sparked a renewal of interest in textual editing. As Jerome McGann (1995) points out, "Scholarly editions comprise the most fundamental tools in literary studies." Nevertheless the print medium has not been hospitable to the creation or publication of such editions. A print edition of, for example, an early novel, has required editors to either choose one among many available versions or to compile a "best" version from numerous sources. As there are frequently multiple versions of important works of literature, selected pieces of alternate versions might be provided in footnotes, endnotes, or an appendix. But to include in full all extant variants of most literary works between two covers has simply not been an option. Even where there is sufficient space to include a few variants, the textual apparatus tends to be cumbersome and rarely allows for easy comparison of different versions of the same passage.

But electronic editions entail no such constraints. They can typically accommodate all versions of a particular text and can be made to offer split screens where one might be able to view and compare four variants of the same passage in four different windows. Such editions may also incorporate facsimiles of original editions, allowing scholars to study something as close to the original artifact as one might get without traveling to a special collection to view it. And though there can be no substitute for handling primary source materials, computer facsimiles allow for the magnification and manipulation of screen images for very close scrutiny of particular documents.

The ability to represent multiple variants of primary texts has come at a moment when theoretical concerns have focused on textual instability and multiplicity (Tanselle, 1996, p. 52). Just when literary theory has subverted the notion that it is either desirable or possible to create an "ideal" version of a text, the technology is allowing scholars to create editions where they are not forced to choose between variants or assemble best possible editions. According to Ronald Tetreault (1996), even the idea of a "base text for collation" is "a relic of print culture." This is an instance where the advantages of the electronic medium are incontrovertible.

Tetreault, who is editing a new electronic edition of Wordsworth to be published by Cambridge University Press on CD-ROM, argues that the print medium is inadequate to present the work of someone like Wordsworth who was an inveterate reviser. His poems were essentially works in progress. Print editions are merely a snapshot of a particular moment and cannot map the transformation of Wordsworth "from Romantic rebel to Victorian sage." Wordsworth scholarship has acknowledged that the 70-year-old poet still revising his early works bears little resemblance to the 20-year-old who first composed them. Tetreault claims that an electronic product "may be the most effective way yet to represent Wordsworth in development." Not only can it include numerous variants so as to represent change over time, but it can also provide linkages between versions for easy comparison. Whereas the print medium is more conducive to presenting a stable self, the electronic medium lends itself to representing an evolving and fragmented self, much more in sync with contemporary theories of identity.

But even as technology is providing faster and easier ways to navigate between texts and parts of texts, this activity demands a new kind of literacy. Users must develop a familiarity and level of comfort with reading and manipulating documents on a computer screen. They may find it easier to move between passages in an electronic edition, but they may also feel that the context of any particular passage may be much less immediately obvious than in a printed volume where one sees where any page is in relation to the whole. Many people do not have the ability to look at a computer screen and intuit all the possible options available at a given moment. Many find it difficult to follow a path through a series of computer documents without getting lost and without losing the ability to retrace their steps. Even those who have grown up with computers need to develop more advanced forms of computer literacy in order to make the best use of hypertext archives.

Electronic editions and software for the manipulation of humanities texts are still in the early stages of development. Although Tetreault has some good things to say about the DynaText software available from Electronic Book Technologies that is the basis of his forthcoming edition of Wordsworth, he nevertheless declares it "a blunt instrument when it comes to the presentation of poetry," unable to provide the kind of line-by-line navigation he would like. Current editors of these new editions are being forced to improvise in ways that will perhaps be less necessary as more software specifically tailored to literary applications becomes available. Work of this sort is being done at the Princeton/Rutgers Center for Electronic Text in the Humanities and at a number of similar institutions.

In order to distinguish between more or less productive applications of electronic technology, I propose that we attempt to discriminate what I will call technology-driven applications from content-driven applications. Of course, the distinction is one of emphasis or degree. Nevertheless, I think it might be useful to reflect on the difference between technology that meets a pre-existing need (for example, the ability to represent multiple versions of a text simultaneously) and technology in search of a need (for example, literary computation requiring projects seeking to analyze huge bodies of text). Douglas Greenberg, of the American Council of Learned Societies, has drawn a similar distinction. He claims that humanists must "continue striving to adapt technology to fit their values as scholars and teachers, rather than permitting technology to reshape their values" (1993, p. 6). Undoubtedly, scholars' needs will evolve with the growth of technology, but surely it makes more sense to focus our energies on providing tools for which a need already exists, rather than creating tools in search of both needs and users.

Nor can scholars make productive use of new tools just because we make them available. This fact is highlighted by a recent project conducted by the Getty Information Institute (formerly the Getty Art History Project). In order to study "how advanced humanities scholars operate as end users of on-line databases" (Siegfried, Bates, & Wilde, 1993, p. 273), a small group of such researchers was offered a few hours of Dialog training. (Established in 1972 and recently taken over by Knight-Ridder, Dialog is a leading provider of on-line searching and data retrieval, supplying access to several hundred databases.) They were then provided fully subsidized access to all humanities-related Dialog databases. Complete logs were kept of all searches and scholars were interviewed "in depth." Though not the ostensible purpose of the study, to me the most striking finding was that Dialog searching proved to be of limited interest or use to the humanities scholars involved. As Marcia Bates, one of the project's co-ordinators, has observed: "Though the Getty scholars had the better part of an academic year to search and could do all their searching for free, only eight of the 27 scholars searched more than two hours total during all that time (1994, p. 335). And, she further notes, "Five scholars did no searching on their own after training" (1996, p. 516).

The study raises several important questions, some perhaps unintended by its sponsors. What struck me as I read the six articles analyzing a massive accumulation of data was: why on earth was the decision made to concentrate so much time, money, and energy on examining Dialog searching by humanists? As the articles acknowledge, "It is difficult to master and retain Dialog searching well enough in a fairly short time to be really successful with it" (Bates & Wilde, 1995, p. 17). And, more importantly, Dialog databases are not strong in humanities resources:

> Available databases often proved not to be what the scholars wanted. They wanted access to more European literature, earlier literature, and primary research materials. Most databases cover only literature going back to the early 1970s, which is often just a small part of the range that a humanities scholar is interested in. (Bates, 1996, p. 518)

None of this should have been news to the people who selected Dialog as the basis of their project.

Certainly, some explanation of their choice of Dialog would be in order. How much ought one to generalize from the results of a study of a set of databases difficult to search and missing important material? This seems to be a case where the assumption was made that an electronic product would inevitably prove useful to scholars if only they could be taught to use it. But the response of many of the participants was, in effect, a polite "no thanks." Librarians who assume that Dialog or any other product is necessarily meeting the needs of their constituents might well look for concrete evidence.

In a recent article addressing the use of information technology by humanists, Stephen Wiberly & William Jones speculate that the limited use such scholars make of on-line databases may have to do with the high volume of citations found in their professional reading (1994, pp. 505-506). Humanities scholarship tends to include so many bibliographic references that they may feel no need to initiate systematic database searches. Humanities scholars may assume that in their specialized fields such as Renaissance drama or U.S. colonial history, they would inevitably come across a reference to any important book or article of interest. Wiberly & Jones also convincingly argue that "humanistic evidence is not easily categorized and entered into a relational database and not readily subjected to quantitative measure or statistical analysis." Furthermore, they claim that there are no generally accepted software packages for analyzing the kinds of evidence humanists collect (1994, p. 505). They conclude that we must not assume that information technology provides the same solutions for everyone.

In any case, the narrow coverage afforded humanities materials in Dialog databases should remind us how important it is to consider precisely what we are making available through our new electronic tools and, perhaps more importantly, what we are not making available. In 1995, I found it a cause for some concern that electronic databases in academic libraries were getting disproportionately heavy use at the expense of print indexes, despite their often limited coverage. We seemed to be devoting a considerable amount of our resources to providing electronic access to some fields rather than others. Moreover, the products we did offer contained little in the way of alternative perspectives. Our CD-ROMs were providing relatively little oppositional material, either of the Left or Right. The technology had the effect of reducing access to alternative or non-traditional periodical literature as students increasingly determined that consulting print indexes was too time-consuming (Manoff, 1996, pp. 220-221).

In some ways the situation has improved although the larger issues have yet to be resolved. Most major print indexes have been converted into CD-ROM products and new indexes have been created as well. Vendors are now searching out less mainstream indexes to create or digitize and hawk to the library market. Libraries therefore have many more options than they did in the recent past. The *Alternative Press Index* is now available on CD-ROM; so is the *Black Studies Database* (*The Kaiser Index to Black Periodicals* since 1948); and *Ethnic Newswatch* provides full-text access to scores of minority newspaper and magazines. Two years ago there were no electronic indexes specifically devoted to women's studies; now there are four (*Contemporary Women's Issues*, CD-ROM, Beachwood, OH: RDS, Inc.; *Women's Resources International*, CD-ROM, Baltimore, MD: NISC; *Women's Studies on Disc*, CD-ROM, New York: G. K. Hall & Co.; and *Women "R,"* CD-ROM, Stanford, CT: Softline Information, Inc.).

The boom in women's studies indexes has created its own problems. The CD-ROM market will not sustain four such indexes for long, even if they do cover different materials. Some of these may not survive long enough for libraries to sort out which of them are the best products and the most appropriate for their institutions. Will shoestring operations like the *Alternative Press Index* survive in the electronic age? We cannot be certain. What is clear is that many producers of less mainstream material exist pretty close to the edge. If they do not get library support they will probably not last.

But even if the more diverse resources survive in CD-ROM format, access may continue to be problematic unless their producers can keep up with the technology curve. Right now, academic libraries are most interested in offering electronic databases through their own campus networks so students and faculty can consult them on their own computers regardless of location. No doubt, this provides greatly expanded access. Most libraries prefer these databases to be Internet accessible because this means they do not have to mount tapes locally or provide much technical support.

Although some small producers of electronic databases have found it relatively easy to establish an Internet presence, others are struggling and have so far been unable to create Web versions of their CD-ROM products. As many libraries are not much interested in mounting additional CD-ROMs on crowded local area networks, producers of new CD-ROMs unable to quickly meet the demand for Internet access may not survive.

What is the responsibility of libraries in such cases? It is certainly in the interest of libraries to contribute to the sustainability of diverse resources. But libraries are also driven by technology-related requirements and increasingly choose not to buy products for reasons having less to do with their content than with their electronic format. Traditionally, libraries have been able to offer more marginal and diverse materials by acquiring small and alternative press titles. Many such presses depend on library dollars. But it has proved more difficult for libraries to collect alternative materials in electronic formats. They will therefore have to devise new strategies if they are to continue to maintain broad collections and access and not cede their role as a major outlet and support for independent publishers.

Libraries will also need to continue to apply pressure to the producers of mainstream electronic databases to broaden their coverage. All-purpose indexes available on campus networks are often the first and sometimes the only databases consulted by students. It is therefore critical that producers of databases like OCLC's *FirstSearch, Expanded Academic Index*, and *UnCover* (formerly *Carl UnCover*) be made aware of our concerns. We need to pay attention to what particular areas of study are better or less well served by these multidisciplinary indexes. Librarians can be effective in pressing for the inclusion of additional material. OCLC, for example, agreed in 1996 to add a number of women's studies journals to its *ArticleFirst* and *ContentsFirst* databases at the urging of the Association of College and Research Libraries (ACRL) Women's Studies Collection Development Committee. And several task forces of the American Library Association's (ALA) Social Responsibilities Round Table have effectively lobbied index publishers to broaden their coverage or have been successful in convincing vendors to include more independent presses in their approval plans.

The proliferation of electronic resources is slowly eroding the traditional library model where collection decisions are made by individual subject specialists. When large expensive electronic databases become available, especially multidisciplinary databases, collection decisions require input from a number of subject specialists and also staff with technical expertise as well as staff knowledgeable about licensing and copyright. Technical staff may simply declare certain products so difficult to mount as to eliminate them from the running. Many libraries are turning over the decision-making for large electronic databases to committees representing various kinds of expertise.

Broader input may lead to better decisions; but it also leads to the bureaucratization of the collections process, a dilution of the input of subject specialists and all the expeditiousness of committees divvying up scarce resources.

A further bureaucratic complication is that more libraries are participating in consortia as a way of achieving price breaks for expensive electronic products. As libraries enter into discussions with one another over which products to purchase as a group and as they work out the details of site-licenses, passwords, numbers of simultaneous users, etc., individual libraries are further drained of authority over decisions. In the brave new world of electronic resources, it is becoming less clear precisely where responsibility for choosing important new materials lies.

However, consortia may also provide a way for libraries to use their joint purchasing power to support progressive electronic products, to apply pressure to vendors to improve other products, and to write licensing agreements that represent their interests. If libraries can learn to make the most of their very substantial combined purchasing power, they may be able to create an environment more conducive to the building of effective collections and access.

We also need to be aware that the Internet is radically altering the kinds of material available to students and researchers. Regardless of the size of their libraries and whatever their intentions, institutions with network access are making available a great deal of progressive as well as reactionary and alternative material. In this way, the Web, in particular, has begun to compensate for some of the limits of the print environment by becoming a place to find material previously excluded from intellectual debate or material simply deemed unmarketable by commercial presses. Although many people are aware that there is a considerable amount of junk on the Internet, few are aware of the amazing breadth of material available. There are countless Web sites devoted to ethnic, minority, and religious groups; to every imaginable political perspective and ideology; to interest groups and disciplinary subspecialties of all sorts. Many of these sites do contain valuable and interesting information, although plenty do not. As our local and national collections shrink as a result of serial inflation and as we collect more narrowly because we cannot afford to do otherwise, we should recognize and make the most of the compensations offered by the Net.

Individual librarian subject specialists can cull the best Internet resources from their disciplines and assemble impressive collections of material. Library organizations like ALA's *ACRL Western European Specialists Section* (URL: http://www.lib.virginia.edu/wess) and its *Women's Studies Section* (URL: http://www.library.yale.edu/wss) have been putting together Web pages with important discipline-related material. Also the *WWW Virtual Library* (URL: http://vlib.stanford.edu/Overview.html) provides very large collections of discipline-specific Internet resources.

To cite a specific example of the value of Internet resources, at MIT I maintain a Web site with links to material we could not dream of offering in the print environment. For years the MIT libraries have been approached by students wanting us to subscribe to newspapers and magazines in their native languages from their cities and countries of origin. But, for the most part, all we could afford was material in the few languages taught at MIT, primarily in support of course work. In 1996 I took over from a departing faculty member in the department of Foreign Languages & Literature a Web page with over 600 links to newspapers and magazines in eight languages (Manoff, 1997). I cannot say I was enthusiastic about the prospect of maintaining it, but it was a perfect complement to our rather weak collection of foreign language magazines. Our statistics suggest that it is the most popular page on the MIT libraries Web site, and I get a good deal of e-mail from people telling me how much they appreciate the service. All it costs is my time and storage space on the libraries' Web server. (The conversion of the newspaper Web site from the format in which the faculty member had set it up into a clearer and more attractive site took about 10 hours. Upkeep requires about an hour per week. Creating a Web site like this from scratch with over 600 links could easily take about 60 hours. Many more hours than that have been devoted to the site thus far.)

We are just beginning to see the effects of the availability of a broader range of resources in particular disciplines. Looking again to literature, perhaps the most profound way in which the Internet is influencing this field is in the area of canon formation. Now that many more authors and works are being made available electronically than were available in print, critical attention is being focused on the ways in which this may be helping to redefine how a particular period or genre is studied.

At the December 1996 Modern Language Association (MLA) conference, a session was devoted to exploring these kinds of issues. Titled Reconfiguring Romanticism in the Information Age, the papers presented at the session addressed the convergence between the availability of on-line resources and canon revision. In the proposal for the session, Alan Liu (1996) describes how there is now a critical mass of electronic projects in Romanticism being provided by places like the University of Virginia, Oxford University, the University of Alberta, and the University of Pennsylvania. In the paper environment, faculty depend on textbook anthologies to define a period or genre. Anthologies constitute a statement about who are the central figures and which works are deserving of attention. In Romanticism, which has been undergoing canon revision for several years, there has been a move to include more women and other previously underrepresented authors in new anthologies. But the constraints of a print volume mean that there is just so much space; devoting more of it to previously excluded authors means devoting less of it to "major" figures. The results are often an unhappy compromise. But in electronic archives or "anthologies," no such compromise is necessary. Including the work of additional authors does not require eliminating the work of others. This has raised a number of intriguing questions that were addressed by the MLA session:

> . . . what will happen to the canon in a medium that at least in principal does away with space limitations, rethinks the logic of the "page" . . . diminishes the role of capitalized middlemen (editors and publishers), has no permanence, and resists hierarchical structure. For example, who will be canonically "marginal" on a Web that technically has no "center"? (Liu, 1996)

Having experienced the dilemma of the out-of-print status of material they would like to teach, many faculty members are not just sitting around waiting for publishers or librarians to solve their problems; they are taking matters into their own hands. So, for example, Elizabeth Fay at the University of Massachusetts, is putting together what she calls the *Bluestocking Archive* (URL: http://fay.english.umb.edu/archive/toc.html). She is mounting a collection of texts on the Web by or relating to eighteenth-century British women authors who were contemporaries of the better-known male Romantics. Fay claims she began her archive because the material "was no longer in print and not otherwise available for classroom purposes." She considers it to be "both a scholarly and a teaching tool" (Fay, 1996).

Like many others who are developing electronic resources, Fay sees their potential to transform or reconfigure the fields in which they are created. She describes her archive as providing a way to "rethink the bounds of the Romantic period" by making clearer the connections between the Bluestocking Circle and the work of High Romanticism. It allows for a consideration of how these women authors created a female version of Romanticism as well as the tools for reconsidering "basic beliefs about the autonomy, rebellion, and masculinity of Romantic texts." Electronic access to material not previously available is thus helping to rewrite the history of various literary periods.

Many other faculty and graduate students are assembling alternative collections on the Web. Paradoxically, it is this new technology that is allowing access to old and forgotten works of literature that can now be taught for the first time. However, the simple availability of more material is no panacea. Electronic archives may be broader than print anthologies, but a semester still has the same number of weeks. Faculty must still decide what to include on a syllabus. Nevertheless, they do have much more choice about which texts to assign and students have more choice about what to read.

One of the most well-known and systematic attempts to recover more marginal material is the *Women Writers Project* at Brown University (URL: http://www.wwp.brown.edu/wwp_home.html). Devoted to the work of authors from 1300 to 1850, this is a major undertaking. So far, they have digitized about 200 texts, most previously out of print. They are also pioneering the establishment of standards for textual encoding as well as contributing to research on literary databases and text management systems.

Oxford University Press has published 10 printed volumes from the Brown project and other volumes are planned for this year and next. All 200 titles are available in either electronic or paper format directly from the Brown project. Unfortunately, the textbase will not be available over the Internet for another three years. Nevertheless, the accessibility of this material for teaching and other scholarly purposes has had a significant impact on the discipline. According to Robert Hamm & Rebecca Wood (1996a), texts "are now being added to the Renaissance canon" that surfaced only as a result of the *Women Writers Project*.

Increasingly the Web is becoming a place to explore questions of marginality and canonicity, rather than just being a place to find alternative resources themselves. And again individual scholars or small groups of scholars are building Web sites devoted to addressing these issues. A few examples include *Electrifying the Renaissance* (Hamm & Wood, 1996b), *The Victorian Canon* (Jones & Raley, 1996), *The Romantic Chronology* (Mandell & Liu, 1997), and *Women of the Romantic Period* (1997). All of these sites are being used in support of teaching.

The Victorian Canon Web site, for example is devoted to exploring questions of taste and aesthetic value and is "concerned with the shifting categories of the 'high' and the 'low' or the 'canonical' and the 'noncanonical' " (Jones & Raley, 1996). It raises some interesting questions about the current popularity of Victoriana; it poses questions about the relation of the Victorian canon to Victorian kitsch and proposes syllabi to address these questions. In doing so, it demonstrates the connection between the presence on the Web of a great deal of alternative material and the presence of many sites addressing the implications of this proliferation. Over time, these new approaches to assembling texts and secondary material will inevitably reshape the way scholars conduct their research. Julia Flanders (1996), the text-base editor of the Brown project, makes a similar argument about the transformative effects of electronic technology: "The computer can no longer be regarded simply as a tool which assists in doing what we already do, but must be understood as a medium in the true sense: an integral part of our systems of communication, with the potential for profound influence on our habits of thought and work."

Recognizing this potential, a number of small groups of scholars are trying to harness electronic technology to create new models for both publishing and research. One of the newer and more ambitious of such projects is a Web site called *Romantic Circles* (URL: http://www.inform.umd.edu:8080/RC). Steven Jones (1996), one of the general editors, declares it to be nothing less than an attempt to "help transform the way Romanticists conduct their business, both in the classroom and in their work as critics and scholars." The Web site is devoted to the study of Byron, Mary Shelley, Percy Shelley, Keats, and their contemporaries. Its goal is to provide not only new scholarly electronic editions, but also a variety of other scholarly resources and space for critical exchange.

One striking aspect of the *Romantic Circles* Web site is the collaborative nature of the enterprise. The editors are determined to set a precedent in literary studies for the kind of collaborative and "radically distributed" work much more common in the sciences. In order to make this possible, they are attempting to create a way to offer traditionally accepted "means of vetting scholarly work—namely peer review and editorial control" (S. Jones, 1996) in the electronic environment. To this end they have assembled a distinguished group of editors and advisors:

> Especially given the slipshod quality of much do-it-yourself "publishing" on the Web, it seems absolutely essential that users know that all texts and research tools at our site have been produced under careful editorial control. Local Area Editors are responsible for guiding and vetting the production of texts and resources in their sections, and the General Editors have similar responsibility for the site as a whole. Area Editors, along with the General Editors and the long list of prominent Advisors, form the kind of Editorial Board that *is* recognized by the discipline. (S. Jones, 1996)

Not surprisingly, this project is raising questions not unlike those being addressed by many of us concerned with the future of electronic scholarship. Jones identifies four central issues confronting the project: (1) How are editorial control and common standards maintained while creating a large scholarly archive with many contributors? (2) What role can/should such a site play in the electronic marketplace? What kind of relationship might it have to university presses? (3) Will it be possible to remain a scholarly Web site in what is rapidly becoming a mass medium? and (4) How will a site like this affect the current canon and system of hierarchies in its field?

One particular advantage of the model being offered by the *Romantic Circles* project is a commitment to keeping scholarly production within the control of its producers. Though the editors anticipate that there may be some resources on their site for which there would be a fee, they do not envision anyone making excessive profits off their labours. This could also be said for all the humanities projects mentioned in this paper. Libraries should welcome and encourage this new recognition on the part of faculty that they bear some responsibility for the way their scholarly output is marketed and distributed.

So while administrators, publishers, and librarians debate the future of scholarly publishing, others are writing their own blueprints. Some institutional sites experimenting with new ways to provide authoritative resources include the *Institute for Advanced Technology in the Humanities* (URL: http:// jefferson.village.virginia.edu/) at the University of Virginia, *Labyrinth: Resources for Medieval Studies* (URL: http://www.georgetown.edu/ labyrinth/labyrinth-home.html) at Georgetown University, *Project Bartleby* (URL: http://www.columbia.edu/acis/bartleby/) at Columbia, the *American Memory* project (URL: http://cweb2.loc.gov/) at the Library of Congress, the *Victorian Women Writers Project* (URL: hhtp://www.indiana.edu/~letrs/ vwwp/index.html) at Indiana University, the *American Verse Project* (URL: http://www.hti.umich.edu/english/amverse) of the University of Michigan Press, and *Project Perseus* (URL: http:www.perseus.tufts.edu/) at Tufts University.

Two particularly salient features of many of the new humanities initiatives are the desire to experiment with new forms of collaboration and to pioneer new models of graduate training. *The Orlando Project* (URL: http://www. ualberta.ca/ORLANDO), at the University of Alberta, for example, is seeking to create new models for research. As described on their Web site, the final product will be a five-volume scholarly history of women's writing in the British Isles in both printed form and on CD-ROM. The project is an experiment in team research, with its co-investigators, research collaborators, and advisory panel drawn from universities in Canada, the United States, and the United Kingdom. Graduate students are participating in authoring, researching, and data entry, and they are gaining new kinds of experience in team research and advanced humanities computing. Similarly, the *Women Writers Project* (URL: http://www.wwp.brown.edu/wwp_home.html) at Brown, described above, is "exploring the educational advantages of integrating undergraduate and graduate students into a technology-intensive interdisciplinary research project" (*Overview of the Brown Women Writers Project*, 1996). Both of these are devising new apprenticing models for humanities scholarship as well as new forms of collaboration.

Although initiatives like these are clearly cause for interest and excitement, it is important that we maintain our perspective on what we can accomplish with technology. At the moment, major impediments to the use of electronic text are the limitations of the computer screen. For the foreseeable future, print will continue to be much easier to read. So despite the fact that electronic text provides many more options for interaction, print will remain a preferred means of reading for material of any length. For this reason, even projects like the forthcoming *Pennsylvania Electronic Edition of Frankenstein* on CD-ROM (due in 1998) will be accompanied by a "thoroughly traditional paperback of the 1818 text bundled with the computer disk." This electronic *Frankenstein* will perhaps be the most heavily annotated edition ever produced, running to the equivalent of about 20,000 pages in print without its multimedia material (Lynch, 1996). And yet its producers believe that users will require a paper volume for portability, extended reading, and the opportunity to write in it as they see fit.

New technology is posing new challenges for all of us. Librarians, in particular, will need to educate themselves so as to be less dependent on technical experts who would define the library of the future in the narrower terms available to them. Although many libraries have offered their staff training in particular applications of technology, they have not provided the kind of comprehensive information technology training that Michael Harris & Stan Hannah (1993) claim is more often available in the private sector. "The almost universal lack of an information technology program in libraries continues to be a major obstacle to the effective utilization of information technology" (1993, p. 31). I agree with Harris & Hannah that we need to develop better and broader information technology training programs for librarians, but I think that it is equally important to cultivate staff with an understanding of the information needs of all the disciplines we support. As libraries have come to place a premium on managerial and technical skills as a way to cope with the new electronic environment, it is essential that we also recognize the value of subject expertise and faculty input.

Librarians are constantly being exhorted to embrace change, to stop resisting technology, and to look to the future—specifically technology—as a solution to the complex problems facing libraries today. But this is simply not enough. More than technical skills and an appreciation of technology will be required to make informed decisions. Our success in implementing new technologies will depend on our abilities to discriminate between the potentially useful and the merely new. This will require a deep-enough understanding of the nature of our scholarly communities to gauge the potential value of all the electronic tools and products that vendors keep telling us we cannot do without. A healthy scepticism about particular products and services will serve us well. Our greatest libraries were built by scholars and librarians with a vision of what both present and future generations would require to conduct their research. This kind of vision will also be required to build even the most virtual of future libraries.

References

Bates, Marcia J. (1994). The design of databases and other information resources for humanities scholars: The Getty Online Searching Project Report No. 4. *Online & CDROM Review*, *18*(6), 331-340.

Bates, Marcia J. (1996). The Getty end-user online searching project in the humanities: Report No. 6—Overview and conclusions. *College & Research Libraries*, *57*(6), 514-523.

Bates, Marcia J., & Wilde, Deborah N. (1995). Research practices of humanities scholars in an online environment: The Getty Online Searching Project Report No. 3. *LISR*, *17*(5), 5-40.

Fay, Elizabeth. (1996). *MLA 96 session on the Web and the canon: The bluestocking archive*. URL: http://fay.english.umb.edu/archive/fayblue/talk.

Flanders, Julia. (1996). *Editorial method and the electronic text*. URL: http://www.wwp.brown.edu/NASSR/Argument.html

Fortier, Paul (Ed.). (1993). A new direction for literary studies? [Special issue]. *Computers and the Humanities*, *27*(5-6).

Greenberg, Douglas. (1993). Remarks. In *Technology, scholarship and the humanities: The implications of electronic information* (pp. 35-36). Summary of proceedings of conference, Technology, Scholarship, and the Humanities: The Implications of Electronic Information, September 30-October 2, 1992. Santa Monica: American Council of Learned Societies and the J. Paul Getty Trust.

Hamm, Robert, & Wood, Rebecca (Eds.) (1996a). *Canon revision and the Renaissance*. URL: http://humanitas.ucsb.edu/depts/english/coursework/rar/crandr.html

Hamm, Robert, & Wood, Rebecca (Eds.) (1996b). *Electrifying the Renaissance: Hypertext, literature, and the World Wide Web*. URL: http://humanitas.ucsb.edu/depts/english/coursework/rar/

Harris, Michael, & Hannah, Stan A. (1993). *Into the future: The foundations of library and information services in the post-industrial era*. Norwood, NJ: Ablex Publishing.

Jones, Jennifer, & Raley, Rita. (1996). *The Victorian canon*. URL: http://humanitas.ucsb.edu/depts/english/coursework/raley/canon/victoriana.html

Jones, Steven. (1996). *The Romantic Circles project and emergent forms of scholarly production on the Web*. URL: http://orion.it.luc.edu/~sjones1/nassr96.htm

Liu, Alan. (1996). *Reconfiguring Romanticism in the information age*. URL: http://humanitas.ucsb.edu/liu/mla96/descrip.html

Lynch, Jack. (1996). *Workshop of filthy creation, cyberspace division*. URL: http://www.english.upenn.edu/~jlynch/Frank/frank.html

Mandell, Laura, & Liu, Alan (Eds.). (1997). *Romantic Chronology*. University of California at Santa Barbara. URL: http://humanitas.uscb.edu/projects/pack/rom-chrono/chrono.htm

Manoff, Marlene. (1996). Revolutionary or regressive? The politics of electronic collection development. In R. Peek & G. Newby (Eds.). *Scholarly publishing: The electronic frontier* (pp. 215-229). Cambridge & London: MIT Press.

Manoff, Marlene. (1997). *Foreign language newspapers and magazines*. MIT. URL: http://libraries.mit.edu/humanities/flnews

McGann, Jerome. (1995). *The rationale of hypertext*. University of Virginia. URL: http://jefferson.village.virginia.edu/public/jjm2f/rationale.html

Olsen, Mark. (1993). Signs, symbols and discourses: A new direction for computer-aided literature studies. *Computers and the Humanities*, *27*(5-6), 309-314.

Overview of the Brown Women Writers Project. (1996). Brown University. URL: http://www.wwp.brown.edu/overview.html/

Renear, Allen. (1995). Understanding (hyper) media: Required readings [Review essay]. *Computers and the Humanities*, *29*(5), 389-407.

Siegfried, Susan, Bates, Marcia J., & Wilde, Deborah N. (1993). A profile of end-user searching behavior by humanities scholars: The Getty Online Searching Project Report No. 2. *Journal of the American Society for Information Science*, *44*(5), 273-291.

Tanselle, Thomas. (1996). Reflections on scholarly editing. *Raritan*, *16*(2), 52-64.

Tetreault, Ronald. (1996). *Electrifying Wordsworth*. URL: http://is.dal.ca/~tetro/nassr96/wordsworth.html

Wiberly, Stephen E., & Jones, William G. (1994). Humanists revisited: A longitudinal look at the adoption of information technology. *College & Research Libraries*, *55*(6), 499-509.

Women of the Romantic Period. (1997). URL: http://www.cwrl.utexas.edu/~worp

A Prognosis for Continued Disarray in Electronic Scholarly Communication

Gregory B. Newby
University of Illinois at Urbana–Champaign

Abstract: Activities scholars undertake to be viewed as productive and tenurable (publication in traditional media) are out of sync with the activities they must engage it to be well informed and well connected (participation in electronic communication forums). This work examines the challenges and provides a time line for the legitimization, codification, organization, and general maturation of electronic scholarly publishing. It is anticipated that the role of relatively unstructured, uncontrolled, and informal electronic scholarly communication will be of continued importance, yet will largely remain independent of efforts to create standards and protocols for electronic books, journals, and other transformed traditional media.

Résumé: Les activités propices à faire avancer la carrière de chercheurs (à savoir la publication dans les médias traditionnels) ne sont pas les mêmes que celles leur permettant d'être bien informés et apparentés (à savoir la participation aux forums de communication électronique). Cet article examine les défis que présentent la légitimation, la codification, l'organisation et le développement général de l'édition savante électronique, et propose un calendrier pour surmonter ces défis. Il prévoit qu'une communication électronique relativement non-structurée, non-contrôlée et informelle continuera à avoir un rôle important, tout en échappant en grande partie aux efforts d'établir des standards et des protocoles pour livres et journaux électroniques ainsi que pour d'autres médias traditionnels transformés.

Since delivering this paper, Gregory B. Newby has become an assistant professor in the School of Information and Library Science at the University of North Carolina in Chapel Hill, CB #3360 Manning Hall, Chapel Hill, NC 27599-3360. E-mail: gbnewby@ils.unc.edu. URL: http://www.ils.unc.edu/gbnewby/

***Canadian Journal of Communication,* Vol. 22, No. 3/4 (1997) 213-225**

Introduction

Scholarly electronic publishing of all types plays an extremely important role in the academic world. Access to the Internet is nearly ubiquitous for scholars in North America and Europe. The network's role is crucial for everything from announcing conferences, distributing calls for papers, and publicizing preliminary conference programs and tables of contents to researching, preprinting, and publishing scholarly works. Scholars frequently subscribe to electronic journals, mailing lists, or network news discussions, and make use of the World Wide Web to retrieve current literature, news, and research. The Internet is a big part of academic life.

Scholarly publishing is the primary means by which the outcome of academic work is shared (at least in modern times). Journal articles, books, conference proceedings, and the like have been the primary delivery vehicle for scholarly work. There is little doubt that the Internet will soon augment these print media as a means of delivery and is, indeed, already doing so.

Why is the transition to electronic media taking so long? Why are we not receiving our academic journals on the Web, by e-mail, or in some other electronic form instead of in print? Examples of electronic journals, conference proceedings, and books abound, yet these are in the minority (and are often of lesser quality) when compared with print publications.

There is no short answer to the question of "what is taking so long?" This paper will present parts of a longer answer and attempt to estimate when the various components of scholarly electronic publishing will come into place. It is assumed without question that scholarly publishing will, by early in the millennium, take place largely in electronic forms. Whether this is "good" or "bad" is subject to debate elsewhere—it is submitted here that such a debate is comparable to debating whether automobiles or microwave ovens are good or bad. Scholarly publishing *is*. In the near future, scholarly publishing *will be* largely in electronic form.

There are many questions left unanswered in the debate. For example, the Web is often viewed (especially by Internet neophytes) as synonymous with the Internet. In fact, they are different: The Web (short for World Wide Web) only refers to the content and the content servers that transmit data using the hypertext transport protocol (http). The Internet, on which the Web is based, includes such facilities as electronic mail, remote login, and file transfer using protocols other than http, especially the file transfer protocol (FTP). The Web as it exists today is evolving and will eventually be superseded. The nature of computing will change; new standards for data exchange and networking will be introduced; television and other media will merge with Internet media. It is very difficult to predict what scholarly publishing will look like in 20 years, but it is not nearly so difficult to look at scholarly publishing in the late 1990s to determine what needs to change, what is changing, and what needs to be overcome to allow change.

This section discusses the move towards electronification of scholarly publishing, examining four major categories of challenges. Later sections will introduce details on components of the four categories.

Standards

One major area of challenge is the relative lack of standards of all types for electronic publications. Web-based publications, electronic journals, mailing-list contents, and so forth are difficult to retrieve due to the lack of controlled vocabulary and fields, such as are found in bibliographic databases (for example, Library of Congress Subject Headings, Title/Author fields, etc.). Indexing and searching tools on the Internet—the Internet search engines—are not able to distinguish the relative scholarly value of, for example, a 12-year-old's page of favourite television shows and a media scholar's critique of the state of network broadcasts.

Similarly, the provisions for including basic information about a particular document (meta-information) are weak. Simply identifying the author and title is difficult to do automatically, as is getting information about the publication date and history. These characteristics are particularly evident on the Web, but are not made easier when publications are distributed by e-mail or other means. Standard general markup language (SGML) offers a method to include significant meta-information, but it is not yet widely used in public Internet forums. (In addition, the diversity of document-type definitions [DTD] makes standardized generalized markup language [SGML] problematic for standardization.)

Legitimacy

A second area of challenge for electronic publishing is perceived *legitimacy* for the purposes of promotion and tenure. One of the motivations behind a great portion of scholarly publishing is the need of the authors to demonstrate the quality of their ideas through acceptance of written work in peer-reviewed journals. For every field, there is a hierarchy of journals with the best reputations. Similarly, some conferences have much higher standards than others by which papers, topics, or speakers are selected for presentation. Even for those electronic publications with strict peer review and a complete editorial board, these electronic journals, conferences, and books do not have the perceived status that print publications do.

Quality

The *quality* of electronic scholarly publications is also a problem. Quality can include issues such as the presentation, page layout, design, and graphical quality of articles, the peer review and editorial process, or the credentials of authors whose work is published.

Perceptions

A final main area of challenge is *perceptions* or models that academia has of scholarly electronic publishing. Even if issues of quality, legitimacy, and standards are met, the role of electronic (versus print) publications in academic life is based on perceptions the academic community has of that role. If e-journals are not perceived to have the same value for tenure decisions as print journals, then they will not have the same value. If conferences that only have electronic proceedings, not print proceedings, are not perceived as being of as high quality with those with print, then the perception will apply.

Specific instances associated with standards, legitimacy, quality, and perceptions will be discussed in the following sections, along with the prognosis for overcoming them. Overall, we can anticipate a multi-year transition towards an increased role for electronic publishing. There are, today, hundreds of examples of electronic journals, books, conference proceedings, etc. and millions of examples of Internet resources that are useful or play some role in academic work. In the future, we can anticipate that the term "scholarly publishing" will refer to materials in electronic form, with print used for specific subsidiary purposes such as archiving or appearing opulent. However, there are still many steps to be taken to reach this future.

Informal communication

Network newsgroups, mailing lists, and Web pages are frequently used to share preliminary research results, discuss issues, and to keep in touch with other scholars. The importance of these types of forums varies somewhat in different academic disciplines, but there can be no doubt that many individual scholars are able get important benefits from informal electronic communication.

Although books may be published on the Web, and electronic journals may be distributed by e-mail, the largest current use of newsgroups, mailing lists, and Web pages is for content that is not yet ready to be published as a journal article, conference submission, or book. Such forums may be used for "sky-writing" (Harnad, 1996), for pre-publication of results, and many other purposes.

Today, it is easy for scholars to distinguish between, for example, e-mail discussion lists and print journals. Few scholars would be inclined to list the network newsgroups they read on their curriculum vitae, yet most would list every conference presentation or journal article. Although some grey areas exist, there is a fairly definite boundary between "communication" activities of scholars and their "publication" activities. (One notable grey area is that many e-journals publish materials such as short essays that might have also been suitable for distribution to public mailing lists.)

Several areas of change to informal scholarly communication are under way. The first is that archives of communication forums are frequently used as information stores. Archives of mailing lists, current newsgroup contents, and even (though less frequently) logs of Internet Relay Chat (IRC) sessions or other interactive network forums are available for search or retrieval. (IRC is an informal synchronous channel for text-based Internet communication similar in structure to Citizens' Band radio). This does not necessarily force a change in the communication that takes place in the forums, but it does change the means by which such forums might be accessed.

A second area of change to informal communication is somewhat less obvious, and has to do with gatekeeping and membership in the forums. Moderated newsgroups and mailing lists have been with us for some time, but private lists for scholars are seen less frequently. What we can anticipate is a more structured order for the ability to participate in or post to the most important informal communication forums. This stratification will be for purely pragmatic reasons: readers of the forums are frustrated when the level of discussion is limited by the frequent messages of newcomers or when commentary is more likely to come from graduate students than from well-known scholars. Private mailing lists already exist, but the model of these lists being for private discussion among eminent scholars but which may be observed by anyone interested is less frequently seen.

A final area of gradual change to informal scholarly communication is the means by which participation occurs. Currently, mailing lists have the feature of arriving in one's personal electronic mailbox. Network newsgroups, however, must be sought out by a separate news-reading program. Electronic journals might arrive by e-mail, be posted as Web pages, or made available in other formats. We can expect some shifting in how materials are distributed as search and retrieval techniques are refined. For example, we might anticipate that query-by-profile systems will identify and deliver materials of interest from mailing lists without a subscription to the lists. Another example is the use of unified front-ends for network news, e-mail, and Web pages that we see in 1997's Web browsers.

Informal scholarly communication is greatly facilitated by the Internet. The current generation of new scholars might find it difficult to imagine times when meetings, conferences, letters, and telephone calls were the primary method of discussing and sharing academic discussion. To the extent that "weak ties" among scholars are the truly important ones for getting their work done, there is a great promise that continued enhancements to how we use the Internet for informal scholarly communication will prove tremendously empowering for all scholars.

The organization of information

Electronic library card-catalogues, bibliographic databases, CD-ROMs, and other systems for information retrieval rely on fields for identifying different types of information, and on controlled vocabularies for subject indexing. The tools we use today for accessing the Web, e-mail, electronic journals, etc. do not usually have these capabilities. Even when the meta-information about a particular document is present, there is no guarantee that automatic search engines or browsers will be able to access it correctly.

Standards for the communication of meta-information do exist, however. SGML may be used to tag author, title, and subject fields. Z39.50 is a bibliographic interchange standard that can allow multiple interfaces to access a database, such as a library card-catalogue. (WAIS [Wide Area Information Server], a set of standard tools for networked information retrieval developed in the early 1990s, was based on an earlier implementation of Z39.50.) Even with HTML, the META tag allows for the communication of fielded data.

The problem is not so much in the ability to include meta-information as in the lack of an ability to use it effectively. Perhaps more important is the problem of people self-authoring their own materials on the Internet (for Web pages, e-mail discussion groups, or even scholarly papers or conference proceedings) without knowledge of how to apply such meta-information.

The solution to this problem will likely come in the near term, through the tools we already use to access electronic information. New hypertext markup language (HTML) tags are introduced frequently (the current META tag may be used to communicate author information), and TITLE already exists but is used more for a running heading than an actual document title. Other fields can be introduced, and search engines will be able to offer the capability to search on these fields. This will lead to problems of training people to use such fields effectively, but this is less of a problem for the academic community than the general public. Regardless, the fact that millions of computer users have overcome the difficulty in mastering such arcane skills as HTML, uniform resource locators (URLs), and e-mail addressing gives hope that the public can learn to use features such as fields, authority lists, and query expansion and truncation effectively.

Information retrieval (IR) tools for full text exist, but they do not usually perform very well except with trained searchers. While efforts are under way to develop more sophisticated means of dealing with full text (Harman, 1994), the greatest hope for the near term is to add capabilities to search network-based publications using existing types of IR systems.

Involvement of commercial publishers

Commercial publishers (for the purposes of this section we include academic presses in this category) are in the business of creating products for sale. It has been demonstrated that the actual physical publication—the journal or book—accounts for only a portion of the costs of the publication process (see Fisher, 1996). Editing, reviewing, proofreading, publicizing, and many other activities are involved. In the case of commercial publishers, a goal is to profit from the income generated from the publications. Even in the academic press world, there is a necessity to strive to break even, if not profit.

Solutions to the needs of publishers to profit from their work on electronic publications are forthcoming, but have not yet emerged. A variety of economic models exist (see Newby, 1996), none of which are exactly matched to the type of one-item-one-fee approach amenable to books and journals.

The forthcoming solutions involve stronger emphasis on copyright and the creation of forums for the distribution of published items on a per-use basis. Although subscriptions to book series and journals will still exist, we can anticipate a far greater role for pay-once-use-once schemes for accessing electronic publications. For example, a Web search might yield an abstract for a scholarly article. Someone seeking to read the article could provide payment, then get access to the article to read and perhaps print one copy. The publisher would thus expect to generate revenues for their products over a far longer period of time than they do currently. This is because current models for print publications involve getting a copy of a book, journal, etc., then using it in perpetuity. In the new model, the publisher would sacrifice the one-time payment for the book, but then reap profits from its perpetual use.

Many forces on the Internet are working to assure the security of network-based transactions, where information or goods are delivered immediately, based on interactive payment. Use of the Internet for commerce is already upon us, and the amount of commerce on the Internet will grow exponentially through at least the first years of the millennium. Publishers will be able to use the same mechanisms as any merchant.

A remaining problem of concern to publishers is the issue of copyright and piracy. Currently, there is little to prevent someone with a single electronic copy of, say, a journal article from distributing that article to her friends and colleagues without a charge. Publishers want to be able to insure they can get compensation for every copy, without fear of illegal duplication. Although past history with software, music, and even print publications demonstrates the difficulty of preventing piracy, every indication is that piracy will be getting far easier. For example, one impediment to my copying an entire electronic conference proceedings to my personal hard drive (and perhaps making copies for my friends) is the size of the files involved. But as the storage capacity on my home PC exceeds several gigabytes, and the ability to write

CD-ROM becomes commonplace, the size of the files involved (and even the network bandwidth needed to retrieve them) will become trivial.

Publishers must work in several areas to overcome the difficulties of avoiding piracy. First, an effort must be made for authoritative sources to be easily and cheaply obtainable. If a pirated copy is easier and cheaper to get than the original, this will create a problem for publishers. Second, publishers and others need to provide the public with better knowledge about copyright laws. Many individuals will prefer to do the "legal" thing, but today's Internet offers plenty of evidence that most people do not understand the copyright status of electronic documents. Third, publishers must make their materials non-trivial to copy. This point is in conflict with current easy standards such as hypertext markup language (HTML), but fits reasonably well with Adobe publication distribution format (PDF) files and SGML. An example from the software world is the case of Microsoft Office on the Macintosh, where files are stored in at least four different locations on the computer, making it impossible to simply copy one directory to another computer to steal the software. Finally, and most importantly, publishers should strive to give reason to end users to make use of their publications on an ongoing basis. This can be accomplished by embracing the dynamic capabilities of the electronic world: providing interactive forums for readers; updating publications on a frequent basis; being pro-active about developing publications based on interest in current publications; and so forth.

Editorial structure

Print journals and conference proceedings of the mid-1990s involve entire teams of people. Editorial boards, layout experts, graphic designers, a reviewing corps, and so forth. At the same time, most electronic journals and conference proceedings are the work of only a few people; sometimes only one person. The great empowerment that the Internet plus modern computing tools offer to authors enables such electronic publications, but at the cost of some quality from having other people, with their expertise, involved.

There are only a handful of electronic journals that have editorial quality comparable to that of print publications. Yet it is the editorial board, the editor, and the publisher that help to maintain the stature of leading print publications. In turn, this leads to increasingly high-quality submissions—which leads to an ability to attract higher profile editors, publishers, etc.

There is no quandary here, it seems: the definition of the "best" or "most important" publications is, and has been, based on the quality of the works they contain, the authors they attract, the editorial board they list, and the overall professional presentation of the publication. There is every reason to suspect this set of criteria applies regardless of whether the format of the publication is print or electronic. There is some doubt about whether publishers are a necessary component or not, but the print world has certainly demonstrated the value that publishers can add to scholarly publications.

The mission for creating "important" scholarly publications in electronic form is fairly clear, and some publications have already taken the necessary steps. Resolution of some of the other problems mentioned here will aid in progress towards the creation of electronic publications with the same editorial quality as print publications, but (as some key electronic journals demonstrate) there is no significant technical or social barrier to their creation today.

Longevity of electronic publications

The Internet has not yet been successful as an archival location for storage of publications (with few notable exceptions; see URL http://www.archive.org). On the Web, outdated material (such as announcements for last year's conference) can lead to the appearance that the site is not maintained properly—especially when, instead of leading to this year's conference, Internet search engines lead directly to last year's conference or the sponsoring organization's home page.

Only 50% or so of mailing lists and newsgroups are archived, and the archives are seldom perpetual. Rather, archives of last year's mailing list content might be deleted to make space for this year's archives. The cost of on-line storage is the culprit here—for even as disk drives get cheaper, the demands on system administrators for new mailing lists, more Web pages, and large disk quotas force continued diligence over allocation of resources.

In academic settings, there is typically an office for archives, or an archival library that is part of the main library. Modern archivists are well aware of the limitations of storage in electronic form, and only accept items such as floppy disks or magnetic tapes with the foreknowledge that these materials will be almost completely unreadable within just a few years. In the academic library setting, there is competition among budget items to acquire books and periodicals and develop computing facilities, in addition to general upkeep, salaries, etc. It does not seem likely that many libraries will be able to develop electronic archival capability (even for their own in-house materials) without significant changes in their budget allocations.

At a typical college or university, a computing services office maintains campus-wide facilities for computing, networking, Web-page storage, etc. Even in the universities that have appointed an "information czar"—a vice-chancellor or other highly placed individual with joint responsibility for the library and the computing environment—it is unlikely for the computing services office to engage in active archival activities.

What we can expect for the next few years is a tremendous and ongoing—and permanent—loss of electronic materials. As individual faculty move on, or as old computers are retired, or policies shift, or this semester's classes start, the old Web pages, mailing-list archives, newsgroup contents, and so forth will be removed. As a new version of an electronic book is authored, the old version will be purged. It will take years yet for the academic environment to adjust to the needs of identifying and permanently archiving electronic materials. This function seems destined for the library, yet the library is not yet ready. One important step to their readiness will begin shortly, when libraries start to acquire publications in electronic form. A few have taken steps in this direction by subscribing to and archiving mailing lists and electronic journals. The larger step will not occur until the library must pay the same large annual subscription fee for an electronic journal as it already does for a print journal, CD-ROM database, book, etc.

In the commercial world, we can forecast a brighter near-term future. Inasmuch as access to older materials is valuable, there will be database providers or other vendors who will maintain such access. Thus, we can imagine that issues of electronic journals that are commercially published will remain available. There is still cause for concern, however: we know that out-of-print books still retain their copyright (at least for 75 years or so, depending on the country). Yet obtaining legal permission to reprint these out-of-print books, perhaps for a college seminar, is difficult and costly. Can we expect the same difficulties occurring with out-of-print electronic publications, where unusually large fees are levied for access to materials?

Luckily the role of scholarly commercial publishers will still be tightly bound with the need of scholars to have their work published for the purpose of obtaining tenure. We can expect some level of responsibility, then, on the part of the publishers to maintain permanent access to such works, even if a different fee structure applies for older materials.

Libraries can be expected to play their part in maintaining permanent access to materials they acquire (at least to the extent they currently do for print materials). However, they may be limited by the copyright or licensing constraints of the publisher. For example, it is current practice for many CD-ROM database vendors to require that all old copies of the CD be returned when a revision comes out and that the library may not keep any copies after they cancel the subscription. In this case, the library is unable to retain access to materials except as provided by the vendor.

Legitimacy of electronic publications

As should be clear from the sections above, there are some good reasons why tenure review committees are not, largely, ready to accept electronic publications as having the same value as print publications. Apart from the editorial process and quality of the electronic publications, the main issue is simply that most current electronic publications do not have editorial boards with the same "big names" as leading journals do. Many are maintained by one or a few junior faculty, and many more encourage the publication of student papers or do not enforce peer review.

When, as is inevitable, the proportion and visibility of electronic scholarly publications shifts so that there is a far greater number of electronic journals, books, conference proceedings, etc. that have the same indicators of high quality and respectability as current print publications do, there will be no further need to convince tenure review committees of their worth. It appears unlikely, however, that this shift will be accompanied by a wholesale power shift away from commercial publishers and faculty with tenure.

While there is adequate room on the Internet for all types of scholarly publishing activities, there is also a continued role for commercial and academic publishers. Even as the fee system, copyright laws and expectations, and publication process evolve to encompass new electronic media, the basic role of scholarly publication as a means towards achieving tenure will remain. Indeed, even in many current academic environments where the role of tenure is changing, there still exists the need for scholars to self-legitimize through publications, in order to maintain or increase their academic status.

In 1997, there is a tremendous demand for quality control in electronic information. The level of interest in the Internet expressed by the corporations that already dominate Western media and communications makes clear that the obvious and easiest means of judging quality will be by source, not content. This is the same reason why public-access cable television is not popular, yet dreary situation comedies are—the glitter, the colour, and the snappy patter that media corporations produce cannot be matched by a single creative individual with a camcorder.

Similarly, we can expect that brilliant scholarly publications will have difficulty reaching their widest audience unless they are published by an important publisher or written by an already important author. There is still plenty of room to bypass the major players in the scholarly publishing field (whomever they turn out to be), just as independent films can win awards and independent music labels can get mass-market airplay. The 80/20 rule still applies: 80% of the material we see will come from 20% of the sources. Current television, newspaper, and radio ownership is closer to a 99/1 rule, as fewer than 20 companies control 99 percent of the mass media in the United States in 1996. See, for example, the June 3, 1996 special issue of *The Nation* (Miller, 1996). The democratic nature of the Internet, such that it is, combined with the specialized needs of the scholarly community, can give us hope that the ratio will be more favourable.

Good signs

In conclusion, the overall picture presented here is one of challenges, but also of considerable progress in meeting those challenges. Perhaps the largest single force is the desire of scholars to participate in the electronification of scholarly publishing. It is in scholars' best interest for publications to be widely and instantly available and to avoid at least some of the delays inherent in the print publication process. From the consumer end, what scholar or student has not found it more convenient or expedient to search the Internet for publications of interest, rather than the library's card catalogue?

There is no reason why scholars cannot list electronic publications on curriculum vitae, and, provided they are Internet users, no reason why members of tenure review committees cannot take them into account. Perhaps the names of the new electronic journals will not be familiar, but the sponsoring institutions, editors, reviewers, or other authors may be.

Academic and commercial scholarly publishers have been relatively slow to move wholesale to electronic format, but almost all are interested and have some active projects. The level of maturity found in transmission protocols such as http and the extent to which expectations for royalties and subscriptions are reasonable seem to indicate that there is indeed little reason to hurry, lest the hurrying lead to poor products or lost profits.

The Internet as a whole, and the means we use to communicate, store, and transmit information, is not yet in a nearly finished state. There is every reason to suspect that the desktop computer of the near future is today's supercomputer; that today's T-1 network connection is tomorrow's modem; that interactive graphics and displays of tomorrow will make today's VR games look like "pong." Even if problems of effective retrieval from full-text databases prove difficult, we will be able to engineer current means for searching to work more effectively with electronic publications.

This work has attempted to paint a realistic picture of ongoing activities and some important challenges in the move towards the electronification of scholarly publishing. It is accepted at the outset that scholarly publishing as we know it will take place largely in electronic formats. The exact timing of this change is difficult to predict, as is the timing for overcoming specific challenges discussed here. On the whole, though, there are no problems that appear intractable, and enough interest in solving them from outside the academic world (media outlets, microcomputer vendors, database providers, banks) that we can expect these problems to be solved fairly rapidly. New problems will arise, no doubt, and the road to scholarly publishing of 2010 or 2020 will be rocky. Even though the destination is unclear, the path for the upcoming few years is before us.

References

Fisher, Janet. (1996). Traditional publishers and electronic journals. In R. P. Peek & G. B. Newby (Eds.), *Scholarly publishing: The electronic frontier*. Cambridge, MA: MIT Press.

Harman, Donna. (1994). *TREC-4 Proceedings*. Gaithersburg, MD: National Institute of Science and Technology.

Harnad, Stevan. (1996). Implementing peer review on the Net: Scientific quality control in scholarly electronic journals. In R. P. Peek & G. B. Newby (Eds.), *Scholarly publishing: The electronic frontier*. Cambridge, MA: MIT Press.

Miller, Mark Crispin. (1996, June 3). Free the media [Special edition]. *The Nation*, p. 42.

Newby, Gregory B. 1996. Digital library models and prospects. In *Proceedings of the American Society for Information Science Mid-Year Meeting*. Medford, NJ: Learned Information.

Appendix 1

Scholarly Communication in the Next Millennium—Final Program

Wednesday, March 5

Public Forum

Opening addresses:

The Honourable Jon Gerrard, Secretary of State for Science, Research and Development and Western Diversification

Paul Ramsey, British Columbia Minister of Education, Skills and Training

David Gagan, Acting President, Vice-President Academic, SFU

John Gilbert, Co-ordinator of Health Sciences, UBC

Rowland Lorimer, Director, Canadian Centre for Studies in Publishing, SFU, and Conference Chair

Presenters:

Roberta Lamb, Computer and Information Science, University of California–Irvine—*After Scholarship: Making Information Actionable*

Ann Okerson, Associate Librarian, Yale University—*Ownership of Access? New Models for the Electronic Era*

Respondents:

Rowland Lorimer, Director, CCSP, Professor of Communication, SFU

Margot Montgomery, Director General, CISTI

Thursday, March 6

Usage Analysis of Scholarly Journals

Chair: Richard Nimijean, History and Politics, University of New Brunswick

Presenters:

Erwin Warkentin, Germanic and Slavic Languages and Literatures, University of Waterloo—*Consumer Issues and the Scholarly Journal*

Ruth Noble and Carol Coughlin, Associate Librarians, Concordia University—*Information-Seeking Practices of Canadian Academic Chemists: A Study of Information Needs and Resources in Chemistry*

Aldyth Holmes, Senior Editor, NRC Journals—*Electronic Publishing in Science: A Reality Check*

Margot Montgomery, Director General, CISTI—*Providing Links Among Government, Academia, and Industry: The Role of CISTI in Scholarly Communication*

Constancy and Change I

Chair: Carolynne Presser, President, CARL

Presenters:

Michael Jensen, Electronic Publisher, The Johns Hopkins University Press—*Here there Be Tygers: Profit, Non-profit, and Loss in the Age of Disintermediation*

Marlene Manoff, Collections Manager, MIT—*Cyberhope or Cyberhype? Computers and Scholarly Research*

David McCallum, Principal Consultant, Electronic Publishing Project, Industry Canada, and David Beattie, Director, Virtual Products, Industry Canada—*Promoting Electronic Scholarly Publishing in Canada: Initiatives at Industry Canada*

Policy and Legal Foundations

Chair: Aldyth Holmes, Senior Editor, NRC Journals

Presenters:

Elaine Isabelle, Director General, Programmes, SSHRCC—*A Funding Council Perspective on Scholarly Communication*

Tony Fogarassy, Legal Advisor, UBC, and Angus Livingstone, Office of Research Co-ordination, UBC—*Digital and Internet Issues: Scholarly Communications and Canadian Copyright Law*

Tom Delsey, Director General, Corporate Policy and Communications, National Library of Canada—*The National Library's Role in Facilitating Scholarly Communications*

Kenneth Field, Chair, Librarian's Committee, CAUT, and Professor, Trent University—*Faculty Perspectives on Intellectual Property*

Constancy and Change II

Chair: David McCallum, Principal Consultant, Electronic Publishing Project, Industry Canada

Presenters:

Don Nichol, English, Memorial University of Newfoundland—*Copyright in the Brave New World Wide Web: Scholarly Concerns*

Raymond Hudon, Chair, Aid to Scholarly Publishing Programme, Management Board, Université Laval, and Michael Carley, Aid to Scholarly Publishing Programme, HSSFC—*Keeping a Place for Traditional Scholarly Publishing*

John Tagler, Director, Corporate Communications, Elsevier Science—*The Scientific Journal in the Electronic Future: How Do We Get There from Here?*

Friday, March 7

Critical Components in Scholarly Publishing in an Age of Transition

Chair: Sally Brown, Senior Vice-President External Relations, AUCC

Presenters:

Fytton Rowland and Ian Bell, Information and Library Studies, Loughborough University, UK—*Human and Economic Factors Affecting the Acceptance of Electronic Journals by Readers*

Richard Nimijean, History and Politics, University of New Brunswick—*And What About the Students? The Forgotten Role of Students in the Scholarly Communication Debate*

James O'Donnell, Vice-Provost, Information Systems and Computing, University of Pennsylvania—*On Thinking Strategically without Closed Systems*

David Fenske, Head, William, and Gayle Cook, Music Library, Director of Information and Technology Services, University of Indiana School of Music, and speaker for IBM Canada—*The Digital Library and the VARIATIONS Project at Indiana University*

Electronic Journal Initiatives

Chair: Sandra Woolfrey, Director, Wilfrid Laurier University Press

Presenters:

Rod Parrish, Executive Director, Society of Environmental Toxicology and Chemistry—*Escaping the Giant: A Real Life Story About Becoming a Society Publisher*

Jonathan Borwein, Mathematics, SFU, and Richard Smith, Communication, SFU—*On-Line Journal Publication: Two Views from the Electronic Trenches*

Harry Whitaker, Université du Québec à Montreal, Editor, *Brain and Language*, and Joseph Schmuller, Université du Québec à Montréal, Editor, *PC Artificial Intelligence—Combining Paper and Electronic Publishing in Journals and Scholarly Reviews*

Transition Dynamics

Chair: Peter Milroy, Director, UBC Press

Presenters:

Michael Ridley, Chief Librarian, University of Guelph—*The Public-Access Computer Systems Review: Observations, Lessons, and Strategic Choices*

Brian Kahin, Director, Information Infrastructure Project, John F. Kennedy School of Government, Harvard University—*Communities and Markets: The Marriage of Volunteerism and Commercial Enterprise*

Gregory Newby, Library and Information Science, University of Illinois—*A Prognosis for Continued Disarray in Informal Scholarly Communication*

Robin Peek, Library and Information Science, Simmons College—*The Scholarly Journal Dissected: The Parts, the Whole, the Enterprise*

What the Future Holds

Chair: David Beattie, Director, Virtual Products, Industry Canada/SchoolNet

Presenters:

Sharon Cline McKay, Technical Sales Manager, Blackwell's Publishing—*Strategic Partnerships: Delivering Information from Multiple Sources*

Jean-Claude Guèdon, Comparative Literature, Université de Montréal—*Financing Electronic Scholarly Journals: New Ideas, New Alliances*

Gail Dykstra, Director, Publisher and Government Relations, Micromedia/SilverPlatter—*Moving from Linear to Dynamic: Technology Creates New Relationships in Scholarly Publishing*

Saturday, March 8

President's Address

David Strangway, President, University of British Columbia

Models

Chair: Margot Montgomery, Director General, CISTI

Presenters

Carolynne Presser, President, CARL—*View from a Librarian*

Alan Mackworth, Computer Science, UBC—*Beyond Gutenberg: Access to Digital Scholarly Resources*

John Gilbert, Co-ordinator of Health Sciences, UBC—*UBC ACIT Reports: One University's Response*

Closing Speech

Rowland Lorimer, Chair, SCNM Conference Steering Committee and Director, Canadian Centre for Studies in Publishing, SFU

Appendix 2

The Changing World of Scholarly Communication: Challenges and Choices for Canada

The Final Report of the Association of Universities and Colleges of Canada–Canadian Association of Research Libraries/ Association des bibliothèques de recherche du Canada Task Force on Academic Libraries and Scholarly Communication, November 1996

Conclusion and Recommendations[1]

Our system of scholarly communication, like our entire university system, is at a critical juncture. Advances in electronic communication are changing patterns of knowledge creation and communication among scholars so profoundly that it is impossible to predict the state of scholarly communication even in the medium term.

Nonetheless, the task force remains convinced that key players in the scholarly communication system—individual scholars, senior university administrators, librarians, directors of university presses, students, government policy makers, and members of learned societies—have the power to make choices that can have a positive effect on future patterns of scholarly communication. It is our system of scholarly communication, and we can and must make choices, individually and collectively, to ensure that Canadian scholarship flourishes in the global network of knowledge dissemination of the future.

Canadians are well positioned to make a significant contribution. We are world leaders in the development of telecommunications and electronic technology; we have a solid communications infrastructure; we have support for electronic publishing from government; and we have put in place a number of mechanisms to enhance our understanding of the complexities of the scholarly communication system and the influences to which it is subject.

It is from this perspective that we offer the recommendations contained in this report.

Raising Awareness

Local Action

Recommendation 1. The task force recommends that executive heads of Association of Universities and Colleges of Canada (AUCC) member institutions, in collaboration with their chief librarians and senate or other institutional library committees, put in place an internal process to undertake a comprehensive review of the issues and recommendations set forth in this report.

Recommendation 2. In order to raise awareness among faculty and administrators of the significant connection between library development and other planning issues, the task force recommends that executive heads of AUCC member institutions, in consultation with their chief librarians and Senate and other institutional library committees, identify the key committees and structures within their university that address issues relating to scholarly communication and ensure that the library is represented on them, where this is not already the case.

National Action

Recommendation 3. The task force recommends that AUCC make the evolution of scholarly communication the theme of an upcoming annual membership meeting, utilizing the recommendations contained in this report as a starting point, and that this forum also provide an opportunity for the executive heads of AUCC member institutions to report on their local initiatives and to share information on how they are dealing with these profound changes.

Recommendation 4. The task force recommends that other scholarly organizations, such as the Canadian Association of Graduate Studies, the Humanities and Social Sciences Federation of Canada, and the Canadian Society for the Study of Higher Education, focus on the future of scholarly communication as a central theme of upcoming meetings and that the three federal research granting councils organize a tri-council conference on the subject.

Recommendation 5. The task force recommends that the federal government consider hosting an international symposium in 1998, perhaps under the auspices of the G-7, to provide a forum for discussion of the international dimensions of the evolution of the scholarly communication system to increase Canadian awareness of the international dimensions of the issues involved and to ensure that Canadian needs and concerns are heard and accommodated.

Implementing Best Practices

Local Action

Recommendation 6. Academic libraries should continue to identify and implement "best practices" that assist in the evolution of the scholarly communication system.

National Action

Recommendation 7. The task force urges the Canadian Association of Research Libraries/l'Association des bibliothèques de recherche du Canada (CARL/ABRC) and the Canadian Association of Small University Libraries (CASUL) to find ways of promulgating "best practice" success stories of member libraries so that all Canadian research libraries can benefit from innovations in such areas as service delivery, cataloguing, access, digitization of holdings, and networking. The task force suggests that CARL/ABRC and CASUL consider means of publicly recognizing successfully implemented "best practices," perhaps through an annual award.

Developing Analytical Tools

Local Action

Recommendation 8. The task force recommends that universities and their libraries apply new statistical indicators to review their collections and document delivery operations on a regular basis to ensure that these match the academic strengths and priorities of the institution.

National Action

Recommendation 9. The task force recommends that, following the release of the final report of the CARL/ABRC committee on statistics and performance measurement, CARL/ABRC and CASUL work together to catalyse a debate within the academic library community on the issues raised in that report with a view to agreeing on standard statistics and indicators that reflect the emerging system of scholarly communication.

Establishing an Electronic Communications Infrastructure

Local Action

Recommendation 10. The task force urges universities to give high priority to establishing the electronic and computing infrastructure that scholars require to disseminate and access knowledge electronically.

Recommendation 11. The task force recommends that universities survey the state of their computing and telecommunications facilities and ensure that all their scholars have equitable access to them, regardless of discipline.

Recommendation 12. The task force encourages universities to support information literacy on campuses by facilitating student access to campus networks from student labs, from residences, and from home.

Recommendation 13. The task force recommends that Canadian universities develop training programs to enable faculty and students alike to become conversant with electronic scholarly communication. Specifically, the task force encourages university libraries to include some guidance on the efficient use of electronic and networked information resources in their library instruction programs.

National Action

Recommendation 14. The task force recommends that the federal and provincial governments develop programs to provide material assistance to universities to develop the technological infrastructure needed to network their campuses and make full use of the Internet. The proposed new shared-cost Infrastructure Works Program would be one avenue through which some of this support could be channelled.

Building a Distributed Digital Library

Local Action

Recommendation 15. University libraries are encouraged to identify what rare or unique holdings in their collections should be assigned the highest priority for digitization and to develop their own digitization projects as a means of becoming familiar with the process and its implications.

Recommendation 16. The task force urges university libraries to work cooperatively in building a distributed digital library and to develop the tools and standards needed to facilitate access to electronic and networked information resources, as well as to ensure long-term preservation and availability.

National Action

Recommendation 17. In order to ensure that common standards and practices for digitization are adopted and that the concerns of university libraries relating to digitization (such as document integrity, archiving, and retrospective access to documents) are taken into account, the task force recommends to Industry Canada that the digitization task force include representation of the chief librarians of Canadian universities.

Recommendation 18. The task force further recommends that the federal task force address the issue of the development of a national strategy for retroactive digitization, so that works of highest national priority are digitized first and duplication of effort is avoided.

Supporting Electronic Publishing

Local Action

Recommendation 19. The task force recommends that universities regard appropriately peer-reviewed electronic publications as comparable to print-based publications when considering such matters as grant applications, hiring, promotion, and tenure.

Recommendation 20. The task force recommends that Canadian scholars work within their learned societies, including international societies, to ensure that viable, high-quality systems of not-for-profit publications, both in print and electronic form, are developed.

National Action

Recommendation 21. The task force recommends that the Canadian scholarly community explore the feasibility of creating a university-controlled common site for the formatting and dissemination of Canadian scholarly information in electronic form (for example, journals, monographs, primary sources), possibly in conjunction with the appropriate organizations outside of Canada.

Recommendation 22. To ensure resources are not wasted on duplication of effort, the task force recommends that the federal government establish a clearinghouse of information on scholarly electronic publishing projects in Canadian universities within the Science Promotion and Academic Affairs Branch of Industry Canada.

Recommendation 23. The task force recommends that the learned societies and the federal research granting councils regard appropriately peer-reviewed publications as comparable to print-based publications and modify their relevant policies and practices so as to support the development of electronic publishing.

Creating an Appropriate Copyright Environment

Local Action

Recommendation 24. The task force recommends that each university work with its faculty to establish a mechanism to discuss and debate the role of copyright in the scholarly communication system.

National Action

Recommendation 25. The task force urges the federal government to ensure expeditious passage of Bill C-32 without further restrictions to the proposed educational and library exceptions and with an amendment to ensure that the proposed interlibrary loan (ILL) exception applies to current ILL practices. The federal government must then move forward quickly on the next phase of copyright law reform, which must address the question of fair dealing both in the print and in the electronic environment.

Recommendation 26. The task force recommends that AUCC and the Canadian Association of University Teachers jointly explore the implications of the current copyright model on scholarly publications and research workable alternatives for the Canadian academic community.

Renewing the Academic Reward System

Local Action

Recommendation 27. The task force recommends that universities debate the relationship between the academic reward structure and the publishing activities of scholars, and explore the possibility of implementing other reward models that focus on the quality rather than the quantity of publications.

National Action

Recommendation 28. The task force recommends that the federal granting councils review their policies on the eligibility of publications that grant applicants may cite to ensure that they adequately emphasize the quality of research publications, in both print and electronic format, rather than their quantity.

Note

1. AUCC-CARL/ABRC Task Force on Academic Libraries and Scholarly Communication. (1996). *The Changing World of Scholarly Communication: Challenges and Choices for Canada* (pp. 12-14). Ottawa: Author. Copyright 1996 by AUCC and CARL. Reprinted by permission.

Appendix 3

Scholarly Communication in the Next Millennium—Sponsors

The following organizations, institutions, and companies contributed funds towards operating, research, and dissemination costs.

Association of Canadian University Presses

Association of Universities and Colleges of Canada

British Columbia Ministry of Education Skills and Training

Canada Institute for Scientific and Technical Information, National Research Council of Canada

Canadian Association of Research Libraries

Canadian Association of University Teachers

Canadian Centre for Studies in Publishing, SFU

Centre for Experimental and Constructive Mathematics, SFU

Centre for Policy Research on Science and Technology, SFU

Elsevier Science

Humanities and Social Science Federation of Canada

IBM Canada

Industry Canada/SchoolNet

Medical Research Council of Canada

Pacific Institute for the Mathematical Sciences

Simon Fraser University

Social Sciences and Humanities Research Council of Canada

University of British Columbia

Biographies of Participants

David Beattie

David Beattie has been Director of Virtual Products for SchoolNet since January 1995. Prior to this assignment, he was responsible for the Canada Scholarships Program and the Prime Minister's Awards for Teaching Excellence. Mr. Beattie has served as a senior advisor to the Prime Minister's National Advisory Board on Science and Technology and as Departmental Advisor to several federal ministers of science and industry. He has also worked for the Treasury Board and the House of Commons. Mr. Beattie is a graduate in philosophy from Trent University.

Ian Bell

Ian Bell carried out research into e-journals at a pharmaceutical firm, Glaxo Wellcome, during the spring and summer of 1996. This involved the interviewing and study of information professionals and research-based staff. He now works at the British Tourist Authority in the Information Management Department, with particular responsibility for multimedia development.

Jonathan Borwein

Jonathan Borwein, FRSC, is Shrum Chair of Science at Simon Fraser University and Director of the Centre for Experimental and Constructive Mathematics. A Rhodes Scholar, he has co-authored two books on Pi and built two interactive CD/Web Mathematics Dictionaries. His research interests span pure (analysis), applied (optimization), and computational (complexity and numerical analysis) mathematics.

Tom Delsey

Tom Delsey is Director-General, Corporate Policy and Communications, at the National Library of Canada. He has been actively involved in committees of the Canadian Library Association (CLA), the American Library Association (ALA), the International Federation of Library Associations and Institutions (IFLA), and the International Organization for Standardization (ISO), and has published several articles, primarily in the area of bibliographic standards.

Catherine Falconer

Catherine Falconer is an assistant librarian at Brooklands College of Further and Higher Education in Weybridge, Surrey, UK.

Kenneth Field

Kenneth Field is Chair of the CAUT Librarian's Committee and currently Serials Librarian at Trent University. Born in Sydney, Nova Scotia, he received his MLS from UBC in 1985 and subsequently worked on both the British Columbia and Nova Scotia Newspaper projects.

John Gilbert

John Gilbert is Co-ordinator of Health Sciences at the University of British Columbia and has published widely on phonetic aspects of child language. His major research interests include articulatory and acoustic phonetics, particularly in language acquisition and linguistic aphasiology as they relate to linguistic theory. He chairs a number of key university committees, including UBC's Senate Library Committee and has played a leading role in the development of programs for information technology through his work with the Advisory Committee for Information Technology.

Aldyth Holmes

Aldyth Holmes is Director of NRC Research Press, which has been in existence for 66 years and publishes 14 scholarly journals, 8 of which are already in electronic format. She has a degree in chemistry and economics from the University of Keele.

Michael Jensen

Michael Jensen has been involved with electronic publishing since the days of Telnet sessions. He has been architect and producer of several scholarly CD-ROMs and on-line publications, including most recently the on-line reference works, *The Johns Hopkins Guide to Literary Theory and Criticism Online* and Walker's *Mammals of the World Online*. He directed the three Electronic Publishing Workshops put on by the Association of American University Presses, is a member of the AAUP's board of directors, and is a frequent speaker on electronic publishing issues.

Roberta Lamb

Roberta Lamb has recently joined the Weatherhead School of Management at Case Western Reserve University as an assistant professor of Management Information and Decision Systems. She conducts research on the organizational use of information resources, including digital libraries and scholarly communication systems. Dr. Lamb received her PhD in Information and Computer Science from the University of California–Irvine in 1997.

Rowland Lorimer

Rowland Lorimer is Editor of the *Canadian Journal of Communication*, Director of the Canadian Centre for Studies in Publishing and the Master of Publishing Program, and a professor of Communication at Simon Fraser University. Currently, he is president of the Canadian Association of Learned Journals. He is the author of a number of books including *The Nation in the Schools: Wanted a Canadian Education* (1984), *Mass Communication in Canada* (1987, 1991, 1996), and *Mass Communication: A Comparative Introduction* (1994). He has written some 20 articles on publishing.

Walter Ludwig

Walter Ludwig is Managing Partner of The Prospect Group, a Washington, DC, consultancy specializing in assisting non-profit organizations to professionalize their publishing operations and better exploit their publishing properties. This paper has become a *cause célèbre*, first when presented at the 1994 Council of Biology Editors annual meeting and in 1997 at the Vancouver International Association of Scholarly Publishers Conference.

Marlene Manoff

Marlene Manoff is Collection Manager in the MIT Humanities Library. She has taught literature and women's studies at MIT and collection development at the Graduate School of Library and Information Science at Simmons College. She has published a number of articles on electronic journals and on the social and political implications of building electronic library collections.

David L. McCallum

David L. McCallum is President of David L. McCallum Consulting Services, specializing in group facilitation, information management, and strategic planning. Originally a professional librarian (MLS, University of Toronto, 1978), Mr. McCallum has worked for Statistics Canada, the Library of Parliament, Bell Canada, and the National Library of Canada. He served as Executive Director of CARL/ABRC from 1986 to 1997 and is currently on contract to Industry Canada, a federal government department, promoting electronic scholarly publishing within the Canadian academic community.

Margot Montgomery

Margot Montgomery was the Director General for the Canada Institute for Scientific and Technical Information (CISTI), a part of the National Research Council of Canada (NRC), from 1991 to 1997. She was recently appointed the Director General of NRC's Industrial Research Assistance Program. Prior to her appointment to CISTI, Ms. Montgomery was with the Library of Parliament. She has extensive experience in the academic environment, as a reference librarian and manager of various services in a community college library. Ms. Montgomery is fluent in English and French.

Gregory B. Newby

Gregory B. Newby has written on information retrieval, human-computer interaction, electronic publishing, uses and norms for the Internet, and new technologies for business use. His research interests are focused on information retrieval, information space, human-computer interaction, and new electronic media. His courses include "Data Communication Networks" and "Distributed Systems and Administration." Professor Newby obtained his master's in communication from State University of New York at Albany and his doctorate from Syracuse University.

Richard Nimijean

Richard Nimijean is a doctoral candidate in the Department of Political Science, Carleton University. His dissertation examines industrial policy in Ontario and Quebec. In 1996-97, he was a lecturer in Politics at the University of New Brunswick. From 1994 to 1996, he was a Senior Policy Analyst at AUCC, where he was a resource person for the AUCC-CARL/ABRC Task Force on Academic Libraries and Scholarly Communication.

Ruth Noble and **Carol Coughlin**

Ruth Noble and Carol Coughlin are Associate Librarians at Concordia University in Montreal, Quebec. As information services librarians they provide reference services at the Webster Library and have specialized subject responsibilities for collection development and other services to faculty and students. Ms. Noble is librarian for chemistry and physics, while Ms. Coughlin is librarian for computer science and electrical engineering.

Ruth J. Patrick

Ruth J. Patrick is on administrative leave (1997-98) from the University of British Columbia, where she has just completed a seven-year term as University Librarian. She has a PhD from the University of California–Berkeley, where she majored in Library Systems Analysis and Automation at the School of Library and Information Studies.

Fytton Rowland

Fytton Rowland, originally a biochemist, worked first on the *Biochemical Journal* and later for many years on the staff of the Royal Society of Chemistry, ultimately as Publications Production Manager. In 1989, he joined Loughborough University, where he is now Programme Tutor for the BA Information and Publishing Studies programme.

Richard Smith

Richard Smith is an assistant professor in the School of Communication in the Faculty of Applied Science and Associate Director, Management of Technology, in the Centre for Policy Research on Science and Technology (CPROST) at Simon Fraser University. His research investigates the innovation process for new services, especially in telecommunications and financial services industries; new applications for information technology equipment and services in support of teamwork, distance education, training, and competitive intelligence gathering; and innovation and collaborative R&D management in a cross-cultural setting.

Erwin Warkentin

Erwin Warkentin has taught at Memorial University in Newfoundland and currently teaches at the University of Waterloo. Since 1990 he has developed a number of computer programs designed to aid in the learning of foreign languages. His most recent publication is a book on the unpublished plays and poems of the German author Wolfgang Borchert and their reflection of National Socialist ideology.